I0083805

Stephen Humphreys Villiers Gurteen

The Arthurian Epic

A Comparative Study of the Cambrian, Breton and Anglo-Norman Version of the Story

Stephen Humphreys Villiers Gurteen

The Arthurian Epic
A Comparative Study of the Cambrian, Breton and Anglo-Norman Version of the Story

ISBN/EAN: 9783743397552

Manufactured in Europe, USA, Canada, Australia, Japa

Cover: Foto ©Thomas Meinert / pixelio.de

Manufactured and distributed by brebook publishing software (www.brebook.com)

Stephen Humphreys Villiers Gurteen

The Arthurian Epic

THE ARTHURIAN EPIC

A COMPARATIVE STUDY OF THE CAMBRIAN, BRETON, AND ANGLO-NORMAN VERSIONS OF THE STORY ✿ ✿ AND TENNYSON'S IDYLLS OF THE KING

BY

S. HUMPHREYS GURTEEN, M.A., LL.B.

GRADUATE OF THE UNIVERSITY OF CAMBRIDGE

✻

NEW YORK AND LONDON ✿ G. P. PUTNAM'S SONS ✿ 1895 ✿ ✿

The Knickerbocker Press, New York

PREFACE.

IN writing the following work on the Arthurian Epic, my chief object has been to aid lovers of our old English literature, in their investigations of this most interesting corner of romantic fiction.

This cyclus of romances, which has now commanded the attention and won the admiration of seven centuries of readers, has been to me an ever-fascinating field of study and research; and when, a few years ago, I was asked to deliver a course of lectures, in aid of a charitable object connected with the parish of which I was then rector, I could think of no subject that would be likely to interest a highly intelligent audience, to a greater degree, than this, the noblest religious prose-poem of which England can boast.

These lectures have served as the basis of the

iii

present work, but while the substance of the lectures has been retained, the subject-matter has been entirely recast, rewritten in book form, and greatly enlarged by important additions.

The true character and aim of the Arthurian cyclus of romances has been so thoroughly misunderstood, not only by the popular mind, but by many who, otherwise, are well informed, that I shall consider my time and labour well expended, if I can aid in dispelling the popular misconception and, in even the slightest degree, help in restoring this national epic to its rightful place in the esteem of intelligent men.

In the composition of this work, I have made free use of the materials that already existed; although, in every case, where it has been necessary to do so, I have verified statements of fact, and have, at times, departed widely from the conclusions adopted by others.

I acknowledge, with great pleasure, my indebtedness to the writings of the following gentlemen:

M. Paulin Paris, membre de l'Institut and editor of *Les Romans de la Table Ronde*, etc., etc.

Sir Frederic Madden, editor of *Layamon*, *Syr Gawayne*, etc., etc.

M. le Vicomte de la Villemarqué, membre de l'Institut and author of *Les Bardes Bretons*, etc., etc.

Mr. Thomas Stephens, author of *The Literature of the Kymry.*

Mr. F. J. Furnivall, M.A., editor of *Le Roman du Saint Graal, La Queste del Saint Graal, The Morte Arthur,* etc., etc.

Mr. D. W. Nash, editor of *Taliéssin* and author of the Introduction to *Merlin* in the edition of the Early English Text Society, etc., etc.

Mr. Thomas Wright, author of the *Biographia Britannica Literaria,* etc., etc.

Prof. David Masson, LL.D., author of *Life of Milton, British Novelists and their Styles, Chatterton,* etc., etc.

I am also indebted to various articles in the *Dublin University Magazine, The Saturday Review, The Englishman's Magazine, The Athenæum,* and perhaps one or two other periodical publications.

If, in any instance, the indebtedness which I am under, is not formally acknowledged, it is simply because, at this late day, I am unable to recall the source of the obligation, and, in advance, stand ready to apologise for any such unintentional oversight.

In the comparative studies, Chapters VII., VIII., and IX. I have taken the prose extracts from Mr. Wright's reprint of Malory's *Mort Darthur,* edition of 1634.

In the case of *Merlin and Vivienne* (Chapter VI.)

I have translated from the French of De Borron, as Malory all but ignores this episode.

In the case of *Geraint and Enid* (Chapter X.) I have adopted Lady Guest's admirable translation, as this episode is entirely omitted by Malory.

S. H. G.

New York, *February 14, 1895.*

CONTENTS.

———

Contents

THE ARTHURIAN EPIC CYCLUS

ACCORDING TO THE NARRATIVE OF

THE ANGLO-NORMAN TROUVÈRES

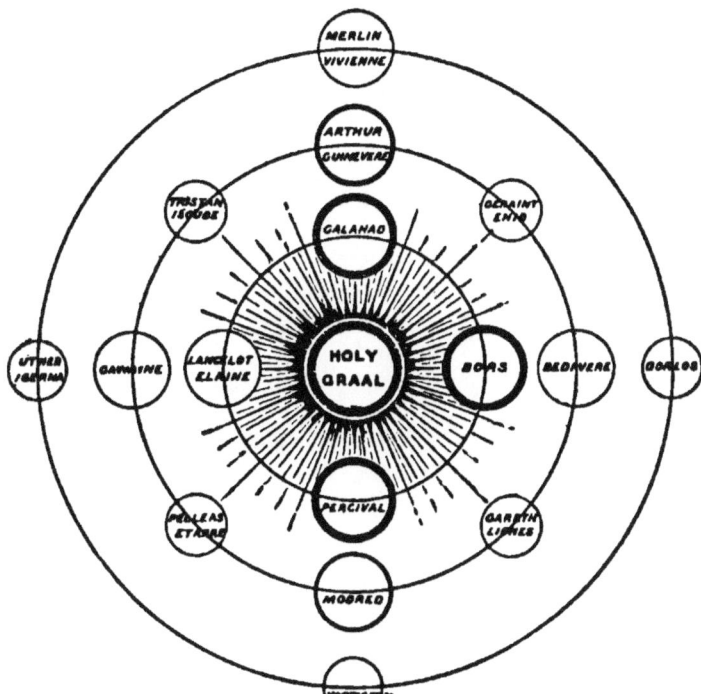

THE ARTHURIAN EPIC

1

*Marginal notes point up authors' dismal
ignorance and resulting errors which
are numerous*

THE ARTHURIAN EPIC.

CHAPTER I.

Historical Sketch.

THERE is scarcely any subject in the whole range of English literature which presents so tempting a field for research, or one which so well repays careful investigation, as the cycle of Anglo-Norman romances relating to King Arthur and the Knights of the Round Table.

Strangely enough the impression seems to exist, even among those who are otherwise well informed on literary questions, that these romances are the crude outgrowth of an illiterate age, based on legendary tales and fantastic mediæval conceits which render them unworthy of serious study except, perhaps, as they reappear in modern setting and adorned with the polished verse of the late Poet Laureate.

As we advance, however, in our survey of the

Arthurian Epic, the true character of the work will be brought out in bold relief, and we shall see that instead of its being an inartistic collection of " monastic " legends it is, on the contrary, a grand religious prose-poem of marvellous power and beauty, the production of some of the most learned and gifted trouvères of the Plantagenet era.

This cyclus of romances, built up as it was on a tiny germ of history, on the bardic poems of Wales and Brittany, on local traditions, Church legends and Latin chronicles, was nevertheless, in its fully developed form, the outgrowth of the political, ecclesiastical, and social conditions of the court of Henry II. of England.

Walter Map, who may be considered as the originator and author of nearly all that is imperishable in these tales, was a man of consummate genius, vast learning, and of high repute at court. His object in writing these tales of chivalry, as we shall subsequently see, was not only to amuse and entertain his readers, but to instruct them in the recognised theology of the day ; and so skilfully and successfully did he accomplish his object that his works obtained an instantaneous popularity and were read or recited (for it was the listening age) in castle, town, and hamlet.

Nor was his influence confined to England alone.

The chord which Map struck, vibrated throughout the whole of Europe. In France, North and South, Normandy and Provence, in Germany, in Spain, in Italy, in Flanders and even in Greece, the brilliant creations of the English writer seized upon the imagination of the Continental trouvères who reproduced, in whole or in part, the chaste fantasies of the English narrator; or, enchanted with so successful a form of writing, invented additional romances based on episodes which Map had omitted. Indeed, the whole of Europe was seized, at this time, with an intense passion for narrative or romance literature, and the tales of Map and his *confrères* supplied and satisfied the cravings of the popular imagination.

In England, these romances retained their place in the heart of the nation for many a long year. Even when the "listening age" had passed away and the "reading age" had taken its place, among the first works printed by William Caxton in the Abbey of Westminster, was Sir Thomas Malory's *La Mort Darthur*, a stately folio, though of no artistic merit. This compilation of earlier romances, however, with all its defects of arrangement and sins of omission, was doubtless regarded as a literary treat by the lords and ladies of the court of Edward IV., as they lounged in the bowers of their ancestral castles and dreamed of the heroic past.

Even as late as the reign of Queen Elizabeth, some of the more censorial of the clergy deplored the still existing popular taste for these " vain deceits "; and Roger Ascham, tutor to the Queen, loudly complains (1570) that " In this booke, [*La Mort Darthur*] those be counted noblest knightes, that do kill most men without any quarell, and commit fowlest aduoulteres by sutlest shiftes. . . . This is good stuffe for wise men to laughe at, or honest men to take pleasure at. Yet I know when Gods Bible was banished the Court and Morte Arthure received into the Princes chamber. What toyes the dayly readyng of such a booke may worke in the will of a yong jentleman or a yong mayde, that liveth welthelie and idelie, wise men can judge, and honest men do pitie."

Still, the wonderful popularity which these romances had enjoyed for five centuries was then on the wane, and in 1634 the last black-letter edition of *La Mort Darthur* was issued from the press.

It was not until the time of the Reformation that the Arthurian Epic so much as began to lose its hold upon popular favour; nor does it seem to have sunk into total oblivion until England had entered upon the prosaic era of the Commonwealth. The smoke of theological strife, which darkened so many years of the Tudor period, blinded the eyes of the

masses to the high artistic merits of England's old
masters in letters. The exciting character of the
times gave rise to a class of theological writers whose
works were full of hard, earnest thought, though at
times marred by a spirit of subtle, time-serving
hypocrisy. Men felt that an opinion too hastily
expressed or too tenaciously held might lead to
the stake ; that the battle being waged was a battle
to the death. The libraries, public and private, of
England were ransacked for books, ancient or modern, which might be pressed into their service and
furnish arguments in support or confutation of current dogmas. In this way, only the more noted
theological writings of the early Anglican Church
were taken down from the dusty shelves to which
they had been consigned as *vetusti et inutiles*—old
and worthless—to support the views of one or other
of the contending parties. Had the theological writers of that day been acquainted with the original
romances of Walter Map instead of Sir Thomas
Malory's inartistic compilation, they might, per-
chance, have relieved the acrimony of their discus-
sions by quotations from a lighter style of literature.
As it was, these romances passed for the time being
into comparative oblivion.

No sooner had the clashing of contending creeds
partially abated, than the literary splendour of the

Elizabethan age arose upon England; a dazzling outburst of genius such as no one age and no one country had ever before witnessed. The Pastoral romance, the Allegorical romance, the Drama of real life, and even the Lyrics produced during this period, reached a degree of perfection never before attained, and one which in modern times has rarely been equalled and seldom, if ever, surpassed. The works of Sir Philip Sidney, Spenser, Shakespeare, Ben Jonson and others too numerous to mention, supplanted in popular esteem the previous writers of England. The Arthurian romances shared the general neglect of all pre-Tudor literature; the subtle allegory of the *Faerie Queene* eclipsing the mysticism of the Holy Graal, while its subdued chivalry was amply sufficient to gratify sixteenth century ideas of gallantry and adventure.

Fifty years passed, and again civil and religious discord cast their darkening shadows over the country. It was an age of scepticism and of the first fruits of uncompromising Dissent, when false ideals filled the shrines of truth. The Church was regarded as the embodiment of an ecclesiastical myth, and piety consisted in steering a middle course between excessive sin and excessive sanctity. Art was divorced from religion; painting, architecture, and music were banished from the sanctuaries of the land,

and the Cross itself was veiled from the eyes of the people and melted into a faint line of beauty.

Then followed the Restoration and a new school of writers eager to show their loyalty by pandering to the French tastes of King and courtiers; and finally, came the *Annus Mirabilis*, as it has been styled, of Queen Anne's reign, a period unmarked by men of pre-eminent genius yet abounding in clever, pleasant writers.

During the whole of this period, as might readily be inferred, the older literature was either forgotten, or read only by the few who had the taste and the leisure for antiquarian research. But a change came at last. With the passing away of the " poor " eighteenth century, rich in prose but poor indeed in ideality, a new era in the history of English literature was ushered in, one of the chief features of which was the revival of the national interest in these tales of chivalry. True antiquaries arose who, not content with a knowledge, however intimate, of the works of the Elizabethan and subsequent writers, had the ambition to go back and drink deeply at the very springs of England's national life. The celebrated *dictum* of Bishop Warburton, that " antiquarianism is to true letters what specious funguses are to the oak, which never shoot out and flourish till all the vigour and virtue of the grove are nearly exhausted," was doubtless the all but universal opinion of the literary pundits of his day.   But this *ipse dixit* of the learned prelate, uttered on the first appearance of Percy's *Reliques of Ancient Poetry*, was based on a false estimate of the aims and objects of literary antiquarianism.   The writings of a by-gone age are of interest to the true antiquary not so much on the score of their age as for their intrinsic merit and the light which they throw on the problems of to-day. The modern antiquary passes by that which is dead and seizes upon the living thought.   He can discern the true metal amid the alloy of old verse-systems and obsolete forms of language.   He can point out the true gems though incrusted with moral impurities.   He can detect genuine literature under whatever form it is presented, and antiquarianism, *malgré* Warburton, not only unfolds and irradiates many of the beauties of modern literature, but is the only true basis of the critical study of the literature of the present day.   "We, who from our youth up," writes Sir Walter Scott, " were accustomed to admire classical models, became acquainted, for the first time, with a race of poets who had the lofty ambition to spurn the flaming boundaries of the universe and to investigate the realms of Chaos and Old Night." Scott himself took a plunge into Chaos and his revival of chivalric legends was the result.   Southey dashed

into the realms of Old Night and brought back the
most potent weapon which he could have seized
upon to shatter the remaining vestiges of literary
prejudice and thraldom; viz.: Caxton's text of *La
Mort Darthur* which was published in 1817.

From the time of Southey down to the present
day the cyclus of Arthurian romances has been investigated in all its wealth of national, ecclesiastical, and social lore by some of the ablest scholars
and most profound critics of Europe; while in England, this study has naturally attracted especial
attention among *littérateurs* from the fact that the
Epic is national property, and is the starting-point
of English romantic fiction.

Great, however, as has been the value of the labours of the antiquary and historian of English
literature during the past fifty years, in reclaiming
from oblivion these chaste productions of the Norman trouvère, it is doubtful if the Arthurian romances would once again have become familiar
household stories had not nineteenth century trouvères reproduced some of Map's finest creations
and clothed them with the subtle charm of their
poetic genius.

It is a significant fact that the most popular poets
of every age have turned to this fountain head of
European romance. Even Dante chooses a British

love tale as the subtlest charm for the ear of Francesca da Rimini,* a fact significant of the power of these earliest romances on the hearts and actions of Christendom.

A poet may go to them for hints and fancies already made to his hands. The body of legend here locked up has served as a magazine of ideal subjects to some of our greatest poets from Spenser, Shakespeare, and Milton to Swinburne, Lytton, and Tennyson, the last of whom has clothed the grand creations of crusade romance with the beauty of his most polished art. In his *Idylls* the antique figures of Lancelot and Arthur wander through English landscape; Guinevere apparelled in the " freshest manner " rides by her lover over fields of hyacinth that seem like the heavens upbreaking through the earth; knights converse in strains that combine the simplicity of primal art with the polish of latest culture, and yet even his pictures are beautiful only in proportion as he copies faithfully the exquisite, pathetic touches of the mediæval trouvère.

From the brief summary of facts here presented, it will at once be seen what a long and powerful hold these tales of chivalry have had upon the imagination of Europe; and when it is remembered that they are as attractive to-day as they were in the

* *Vide* Note A.

twelfth and thirteenth centuries, one is naturally led
to enquire into the secret of their unparalleled popularity.

One point in the history of this cyclus seems to
have been very generally overlooked. It is to the
clergy of the Anglican Church that we are indebted
for nearly all that is of lasting merit in these romances. The Latin Chronicler, Geoffrey of Monmouth, or Geoffrey " Arturus," as he was styled by
his critics, who wrote (or translated) the story which
formed the groundwork of all subsequent romances,
was a priest residentiary in the famous Abbey of
Monmouth and afterwards, Bishop of St. Asaph.
Layamon, who translated and amplified the Arthurian tale as it then existed, as part of his *Brut*, or
History of Britain, making use of that form of the
English language which has been called Semi-Saxon,
was a parish priest of the Church, living at Ernley,
or Lower Arley, on the banks of the Severn.
Robert of Gloucester, who incorporated in his
Chronicle the story of Arthur in the current Early
English of his day, was an Archdeacon of the Church,
familiar with University life at Oxford, and was one
of the most noted ecclesiastics of the age. And
finally, Walter Map, poet, theologian, wit, and courtier, whose genius transformed pre-existing traditions
and legends into a spiritualised romance in Anglo-

Norman French, was Archdeacon of Oxford, and
Chaplain to Henry II.

It is true that Norman trouvères like Robert Wace,
Robert de Borron, Luces de Gast, and Hélie de Borron, who were not ecclesiastics, added to the perfection of the Arthurian cyclus ; but granting all that can
be said on this score, the fact remains that this finest
of Christian prose epics owes its existence, virtually,
to the Anglican Church, since it is to the glowing
imagination of Map that we are indebted for the
greater part of all that is artistic and imperishable in
Arthurian Romance.

The fact that the writers of these tales were, for
the most part, trained theologians, and that Map
especially was, besides this, a man of commanding
genius, is highly important in its bearing on the present enquiry. Apart from a knowledge of this fact
it would be impossible to account for the unique
character of what we may call the aim, the idea, the
total meaning of this cyclus as a whole.

Judged merely by the standard of what the world
or society holds dear, these romances are true to the
highest and purest aspirations of every loyal member of the human commonwealth.

Viewed from the standpoint of the Church, the
idea or aim of the story is the inculcation of that
spotless spirituality and ideal perfection which

Christianity crowns with a beatitude and which saints battle to attain. In every romance, though pre-eminently in *La Queste del Saint Graal*, we find, clothed in richest imagery, the explication of some of the deepest and most sublime mysteries of the Faith, or the delineation of the forced marches, the ambuscades, and the fierce encounters which the Christian knight must surmount if he would attain ideal purity here and the Beatific Vision hereafter.

The theme is noble, grand, and imperishable, and one which, in the twelfth century, could have suggested itself only to a priest of the Church.

If now, we examine the plan or structure of these Arthurian tales, we shall detect at once the skilled hand of a master in letters. Not only is each one of Map's romances, considered separately and by itself, a masterpiece, but taken collectively they form, as we shall subsequently see, a cyclus of romances. They do not merely constitute a series of detached tales like the Waverley Novels, but an intimately connected narrative; and if, as Bunsen maintains, the novel at its highest, is a prose epic, Map's romances may lay claim to this dignity in more respects than one. They do not, it is true, so far as their *form* is considered, rise to the dignity of an epic in the classic sense of the word, as the narrative is not continuous; but they conform to the standard of the classic epic in one at least of its strictest and most essential canons of structure, in that there exists, most unmistakably, a central point of unity, viz.: the Holy Graal, around which the whole story revolves and which gives it, in this respect, the stamp of an epic—a spiritualised or religious epic—and which renders it, from an artistic point of view, immeasurably superior to any similar prose production of later times.

Doubtless, to the reader who knows these romances only as they have been reproduced in modern setting, they must seem little more than detached and oftentimes fantastic tales of the age of chivalry, and wanting in any well marked, underlying, moral, or spiritual idea of sufficient power to bind all the parts of the narrative together in one harmonious whole. A perusal of the original romances will dispel, once and for all, any such illusion and will help to explain the remarkable fascination which these works have ever exercised over the minds of both clergy and laity.

But there is a still more important point to be considered than the mere structure of these romances in forming a true estimate of their artistic excellence. These prose-poems, when critically examined, rank in every respect, with the best specimens of the truest literature of England. Professor Masson, in one of his essays, maintains that to the essence of true literature, especially the literature of the imagination, there is needed a broad, world-wide sympathy with human nature on the part of the writer. What he invents, if it is to live, must touch chords in the universal heart. It must be capable of arousing the nobler feelings not only of one country or of one age; but must be equally powerful in all countries and all ages. It must deal with man as *man*, and not as belonging to any particular nation, place, or time. It must appeal to that which is eternally true, eternally beautiful, and eternally right. A careful analysis of any one of the great writers whose works interest us at the present day, will show the correctness of this criterion. The secret of the hold which Shakespeare has upon the present age is not simply owing to his powers of imagination, though they are of the highest order; it is not merely that his language is highly figurative; it is not only that his style is pure, chaste, and perspicuous; it is not any one nor all of these perfections combined that gives the Poet of Stratford a hold upon the minds, and a place in the affections of mankind. He lives, and he will live, because he has shown human nature as it is all the world over; its deepest sorrows, its highest aspirations, its noblest sentiments, its most exalted characteristics. He sympathises with human

2

goodness, and reserves his scorn only for what is insincere and hypocritical, and the leading charm of his works depends on the imperishable character of his materials, and the security with which he has laid his foundation deep in the true hearts of true men.

These, which are the essential characteristics of genuine literature, are as distinctly present in the Arthurian romances as they are in the works of Shakespeare. Here all is ideal, all purely imaginative, and yet all rests on a basis of what is eternal and general in human nature, and in man's spiritual and social experience. There are no sensational effects; no vices painted as virtues; no escape from just doom for the villain, and yet a human sympathy breathes forth from every page and pervades every romance. It is idealised literature, the result of true poetic inspiration, in which, deep down beneath the chastened fantasy there lie hidden great spiritual truths which awaken responsive echoes in the heart of every reader. It is no wonder, therefore, that a work so noble in aim, so artistic in structure, so warm in its humanity, and so perfect in its finish, should have secured for itself a lasting place in the affections of mankind, or that so great a poet as Milton* should at one time have entertained the

* *Vide* Note B.

idea of taking this subject as the theme of his most
ambitious epic.

So far, we have been considering exclusively the
unique and fully developed romances of Walter Map,
since they come to us as the most perfect version
of the Arthurian Epic which we possess ; and we
have purposely passed by, with only a casual allusion, the writings of those who preceded him in this
department of fiction.

It is unquestionable that Map's version is virtually an original production, not only in its idea or
aim but also in the general invention of the story;
and yet a careful search among the older Arthurian
writers discloses the fact that Map was indebted to
others for the rough ground-work of one of his romances at least, and for the crude outlines of many
incidents and characters which he reproduced in
more polished and courtly form.

Nor was Map alone in thus making tributary the
writings of his predecessors.   The Arthurian *epopoiia*
was a thing of slow growth, the production of different ages and of many minds.   At each stage in its
history it received additions or embellishments which
stamped it with the characteristics of the individual
mind of the narrator, and of the times in which he
lived, each successive romancer taking from his predecessors just as much or as little as he pleased and

enlarging or adorning the result to suit his own caprice or that of the public.

If, therefore, we would obtain, in the simplest and
most natural order, a concise history of the gradual
unfolding of the Arthurian tale, we must follow it
in its chronological development, tracing the narrative step by step from its earliest, shadowy incep-
tion to its full and final completion. And this
course we propose to pursue in the present work.
We shall glance at the ancient bardic poetry of
Wales, Cornwall, and Armorica, so as to discover,
if possible, the birth-place of this famous cyclus.
We shall wander through the mazes of the later
Welsh and Breton minstrelsy and watch the subsequent history of the story as unfolded by the bards
of the Middle Ages. We shall visit the cells of imaginative monks who incorporated the story of Arthur as part and parcel of their Chronicles or Histories
of Britain; and finally, we shall pore over the scrolls
of the Norman trouvères of England whose exquisite
narratives show the Arthurian cyclus in its luxuriant
after-growth when as knightly tale or idyllic fantasy
it entwined itself around the imagination and en-
grafted itself into the heart of the whole of Christendom.

And when we have passed this, the golden age
of Arthurian Romance, and have arrived at the poets

of the nineteenth century, we shall take Tennyson
as the best modern exponent of the Norman epic
and shall compare, side by side, the old romances
and the poet's *Idylls of the King.*

The Arthurian tales of the late Poet Laureate are
in some respects the most highly finished of all the
versions of this celebrated cyclus.   Thousands have
read these, the most celebrated of Tennyson's poems,
and the time thus spent has passed like a dream.
At times the music of the verse rises in power as
the poet's imagination depicts the grand festivities
of Court, the brilliant tournament or the deadly
battle.   At times it sinks into the softest, tenderest
strains as Enid, gentle in her nature, bears without
a murmur the harsh commands of her suspecting
husband ; or when Guinevere receives in deep passionful repentance her King's withering rebuke.
And who is there that has not been fascinated
with the chaste and touching descriptions of the
late Poet Laureate?   Yet how few of these readers
know anything of the original romances from which
the poet borrowed the scenes which, in many instances, he has so faithfully reproduced.   No one,
doubtless, at the present day, imagines that the
Idylls of the King are the invention of the poet's
own brain ; still comparatively few, perhaps, could
give an intelligent opinion upon the faithfulness of

Tennyson's pictures, or point out the sources from which he drew his inspiration.

In this, as in every department of literature, the most interesting and effective plan of research consists in what may be called the *comparative* method. But let us explain what is meant by this term.

It is impossible to examine critically the early national literatures of Europe, without being struck by the fact that a great deal which is commonly regarded as original and peculiar to a given country, is in reality only a reproduction, in different form, of the creations of other countries and of an earlier age.

It was part of the duty of the minstrels—the first poets of Europe—to tell the mythic history of the past, and to have their memory well stored with the folk-lore of their time so that they might be ready on all occasions to recite whatever the caprice of their hearers might call for. The clever minstrel, whether attached to the court of some powerful prince or leading a more wandering life and practising his art from place to place, had to catch the widely different humours of different audiences and by a slight change or happy hit, to ensure the ready welcome which procured him his daily bread. These tales, whether in prose or verse, made as they often were, out of true literature and moulded artistically, were transmitted orally from minstrel to minstrel and receiving additions at the hands of successive men of genius, formed in course of time, popular cycles of national poetry. These cycles found their way into many different countries altered, rearranged, and enlarged to suit the tastes of those before whom they were to be recited. Passing from one country to another, they had to be translated into the language of their adopted home; national or local customs had to be changed ; names of men and places had to be naturalised ; and, in fine, the colouring of the whole romance or poem had to be retouched. In this way it might, and actually did happen that the very birthplace or original home of a cyclus eventually became forgotten, and exotic productions which had been adopted or borrowed in the first instance, and subsequently embellished or transformed, came at length to be regarded as native tales and national property.

The Arthurian romances present, perhaps, the best illustration of this literary assimilation. During the Middle Ages they were the common property of European minstrels at large. They were carried from country to country. They formed by far the most attractive part of the popular literature of the period, and hence they afford to-day in the national development of the story, one of the most interesting studies that comparative European literature presents.

It is not necessary, however, to travel beyond the
literature of England to find striking instances of
literary parallelism.   A thousand years before Milton
had dictated one word of *Paradise Lost*, the theme
had been attempted by the Anglo-Saxon poet Cædmon as part of his *Scripture Paraphrase*.   The early
poet sings, as Milton does, of the rebellion in Heaven,
of the traitorous archangel, of the expulsion of the
Satanic hosts, of the place of banishment, of the
council in Hell, and of the creation and fall of Man.

This poem, it is true, will not bear comparison in
point of structural perfection and scholarly finish
with that of the blind bard of the seventeeth century,
and yet throughout the entire work, there are many
and striking points of similarity between the two
poems.   Every line, indeed, of Cædmon's narrative
brings to mind some more elaborate and highly polished scene of the classic Milton, and although the
palm for superior genius, learning, and artistic merit
rests with the later poet, yet there is many a passage
in the Saxon poem that far excels in purity of thought
and expression the corresponding lines in *Paradise
Lost*.   Who, for example, can bear to read without
displeasure, Milton's coarse and repulsive description
of the scene immediately subsequent to the Fall;
and who that has read the corresponding passage in
Cædmon does not prefer the chaste simplicity of

the monk of Whitby ? It would well repay the lover of true literature to compare the " Angel of Presumption " of the old poem with Milton's colossal conception of Lucifer, or to contrast the archangelic *pride*, which is the motive of rebellion in the heart of Cædmon's hero, with the more ignoble motive of *jealousy* which Milton attributes to the hero of his epic. To gain a full appreciation of the grandeur of the narrative which flows, torrent like, from the glowing imagination of Milton it is necessary to have read the earlier poem with its less artificial arrangement and simple beauty of thought, since the *Paradise Lost* of the Saxon poet was the first strain of sacred song in England which was to receive its latest and most perfect expression in the epic of the neglected Secretary of the Commonwealth.

Even so unique a writer as Bunyan had been forestalled by Guillaume de Guileville, a French monk of the Cistercian Order, of the fourteenth century, in *Le Pélerinage de l'homme*, or as it was known in England, *The Pylgremage of the Sowle ;* and the two works have many points in common. How far the *Pilgrim's Progress* is original it is difficult to determine. Macaulay asserts that Bunyan had never read but one work of popular literature, viz.: *Sir Bevis of Southampton ;* but Bunyan's own words disprove this statement. " When I was in the world," he writes,

"the Scriptures, thought I then, what are they? . . .
a little ink and paper . . . give me a ballad, a news
book, George on horseback or Bevis of Southampton. Give me some book that . . . tells old Fables." The very mention of ballads and chap-books
proves how familiar this class of literature was to him
as well as to his readers. Anyone, moreover, who is
at home with the romances of chivalry can see in the
portrayal of Greatheart and in the introduction of
adventures with giants, lions, and demons, how well
acquainted Bunyan was with the traditional literature
of an earlier day. The popularity in England of De
Guileville's romance is proved by numerous facts.
The "venerable monk Dan John Lydgate" made a
metrical translation into English of the French work
by command of the Earl of Salisbury in 1426 under
the title of *Pilgrimage of the World.* In 1483 William Caxton printed *The Pylgremage of the Sowle*
"translated oute of Frenshe in to Englyshe." The
libraries of England contained numerous translations
of De Guileville's allegory both in prose and verse,
and these translations continued in popular favour
and influenced our literature down to the time of the
Great Rebellion, which formed as it were a chasm
between ancient and modern English writings.
Whether or not Bunyan had ever read the *Dreame
of the Pylgremage of the Sowle* translated out of the

French may be a matter of question and yet it is impossible to read the *Pilgrim's Progress* in the light of these translations without arriving at a moral certainty that Bunyan's inimitable allegory was suggested by De Guileville's romance and was largely indebted to it and to the romances of chivalry for much that has contributed to the popularity of his work.

In the French allegory the Pilgrim is inflamed with a desire of travelling to the heavenly Jerusalem. In a mirror he has a vision of the Holy City. The gate that bars the road is guarded by angels who defend it against the unworthy. Grace-de-Dieu, a lady of exquisite beauty, guides the Pilgrim to her house where she instructs him, baptises him, and confirms him. He receives the Holy Eucharist and is presented with the scarf and the staff. He is invested with the girdle of Justice and receives, as a guide, a book of the profession of the Faith. He is then armed with cuirass, helmet, buckler, sword and spear, but finding himself cumbered with all these accoutrements, he begs leave to put them off and arms himself instead with David's sling and the five pebbles that David used against Goliath. He then starts on his pilgrimage. Great dangers meet him. The Passions, in personified form, attack and at times vanquish him, but Reason and Grace-de-Dieu constantly come to his rescue. Tribulation overpowers him. He is assailed by Avarice, Heresy, and Satan. He is led astray by Fortune and takes refuge in a convent where he finds Discipline, Abstinence, Poverty, Charity, and Obedience. The convent being badly guarded is assailed by enemies and captured ; but the Pilgrim makes good his escape. At last he meets Infirmity who seizes him and Death who strikes him down.

The leading ideas (though not the doctrine) are very similar to those in Bunyan's great allegory. Death, however, comes at last not as Bunyan's higher fancy painted it in the shape of a cold river which must be passed, but in the more common image of an armed figure with a scythe. Still, the whole romance is under the semblance of a dream, and if Bunyan awakes when the phantoms of his brain have crossed the stream to the realisation of his prison, so does De Guileville when the cold scythe of Death cuts his Pilgrim down. "I scarcely knew," concludes the French allegory, "when I awoke whether I was dead or alive until I heard the clock strike the hour to rise and then also the crowing of the cocks."

> . . . Je ne me povoie
> Se j'a mort ou en vie jestoie
> Jusqua tant que jouy sonner

Lorologe de nuyt pour lever
Et aussi lors chantoient les cocqs

Now, Tennyson's *Idylls of the King* are the latest, and, in some respects, the most highly finished version of the Arthurian tales that we possess; they are moreover, avowedly based on romances already in existence and hence afford a wide field for critical comparison. The late Poet Laureate added but little that is positively new to the mass of incident that already existed. On the contrary he omitted large portions of the original cycle and presented only detached fragments of that which the old trouvères had left as a grand epic whole. He added, it is true, innumerable pre-Raphaelite touches; he elaborated the minor details, and he gave a more delicate colouring to passages which otherwise might have grated on modern ears. But, as this work proceeds, it will be seen that the fragments which Tennyson selected and rewrote, in so far as they are beautiful in incident, owe their beauty to the mediæval romancer; in so far as they are wanting in beauty, they owe it to Tennyson alone. *i. e. Tennyson was a back*

In one respect, perhaps, the results of the present work will be disappointing. Everyone would rather retain fancies which long possession has endeared, even though they may not be true, than have his little gods ruthlessly torn down from their accustomed niches in the Pantheon of his mind. The lady who had been in the habit of thinking that she saw in the shadows of the moon two fond lovers bowing gracefully to each other after the most approved fashion of modern society, was happy in the thought, and it was cruel in the Bishop to destroy the illusion by telling her that they were the spires of a lunar cathedral.

We do not like to entertain the idea that Homer, whom we have been accustomed to clothe with the halo of a blind bard, was nought but a fictitious name given to a cycle of old Grecian romances; nor can we bear to think that Shakespeare, our model of genius, was indebted to any previous writer for so much as the conception of creations which we have been used to regard as essentially his. And so, those who have gained their knowledge of Arthur and of his knights of the Round Table from Tennyson alone, are likely to have their poetic sensitiveness rudely shocked by many a discovery which the older authors will reveal. Sir Lancelot, for example, may prove to be a purely poetic creation of the Norman trouvère without the slightest historical foundation; still, can we not cherish his name and admire his noble nature as we do those of other creations in the realm of pure romance? Can we not admire the ideals of poetry, Æneas or Achilles, Beatrice or

Häide, Lucifer or Mephistopheles without believing in their actual existence? The early history even of Greece and Rome has fallen to pieces like a palace of cards at the touch of the disenchanting wand of the modern critic; and in the Arthurian romances, that which constitutes their chief charm, the adventures of heroes who surround King Arthur's Court and enhance the lustre of his reign, can scarcely be regarded, at the present day, as much more than a beautiful romance, an exquisite tale of ideal chivalry, a subtle allegory, a grand picture of life in England during the heroic age.

The very charm of these tales lies in the fact that they are works of fiction in which we are led over a vague land of plain and hill, lake and forest, which contains towns and fair castles; and that over this dreamland we pursue valiant knights riding in quest of adventures, jousting with each other whenever they meet, rescuing distressed maidens, and combating strange shapes and horrors; but these are pictures which have only to be read once, to remain in the mind as a vision forever; the flash of some incident conceived in the deepest spirit of poetry—the whole a noble epic.

"And even now," to quote the words of a distinguished living writer, "to recline on a summer's day under the shelter of a rock on the coast of the

Isle of Avalon, and with the solitary grandeurs of
the isle behind one and with the sea rippling at one's
feet and stretching in haze towards the opposite mainland, to pore over Map's pages till in the mood of
poetic listlessness the mainland over the haze seems
again the very region where Arthur ruled and the
knights journeyed and jousted, this is reading such
as is possible now but once or twice in a lifetime."

CHAPTER II.

The Arthurian Epic—Its Place in Literature.

TO those who have not bestowed much thought upon the subject, it may seem like an attempt at paradox to say that poetry may be found under the form of both prose and verse. And yet the statement is strictly true. So accustomed have we become, in our every-day speech, to treat the terms Poetry and Verse as identical in thought, that to speak of prose-poetry seems like a contradiction in terms. Nevertheless, the lover of literature can point out whole fields of genuine poetry, as sensuous and ethereal as the poetry of verse, lying scattered, up and down, in the works of many of our great prose writers.

It is scarcely possible, perhaps, to conceive of anything more chaste and beautiful than the description of the three Ladies of Sorrow in De Quincey's *Suspiria de Profundis.** It is a masterpiece of prose-poetry.

Indeed, the moment the force of the apparent

* *Vide* Note C.

3

paradox is recognised, its truth becomes self evident, and we see that even the most artistic versification does not necessarily constitute poetry, nor does the absence of versification necessarily constitute prose. In other words, poetry is altogether independent of the form in which it is expressed. This point will stand out in the strongest possible light as we proceed, since all of the Anglo-Norman romances are in the form of prose though rankling with the noblest poetry in our language.

In what then does poetry consist? Can it be logically defined?

Poets and philosophers, in both ancient and modern times, have tried to fathom the secret and formulate a definition, but have failed. Sir Philip Sidney styles it "The sweet food of sweetly uttered knowledge lifting the mind from the dungeon of the body to the enjoying of its own divine essence." Shakespeare in his well-known lines tells us:

> As imagination bodies forth
> The forms of things unknown, the Poet's pen
> Turns them to shapes and gives to airy nothing
> A local habitation and a name.

According to Milton, poetry is "The simple, sensuous, and passionate utterance of feeling and thought." Sir J. Stephens, who comes nearer to the true definition than any other, describes it as "The meet utterance of the deepest thoughts and purest feelings of our nature." Wordsworth characteristically speaks of it as " The utterance of emotions remembered in tranquillity." Shelley styles it " The record of the best and happiest moments of the best and happiest minds"; and Macaulay defines poetry to be " The art of doing by means of words what the painter does by means of colour."

The very nature of poetry is so ethereal, its life so sensuous, its expression so passionful, its very being so spiritual that even as we try to analyse it, it eludes our grasp and vanishes. To appreciate it is intuitive. As the scarcely visible, aerial form of the nymph in the Sclavonic tale takes the bodily shape of an earthly maiden beneath the yearning gaze of love, so poetry reveals itself in all the fulness of its charms only to those who have a soul in sympathy with it. As well might one try, by logical definition, to give a blind man an idea of the splendour of a dying autumn sun as to endeavour to supply poetic deficiency by a verbal definition of poetry.

The fact that poetry presents itself under the garb both of prose and verse will appear in a still stronger light if the ancient and generally accepted classification of Poetry, or the Literature of Imagination, be kept in view. According to this classification, Poetry compromises Lyric, Dramatic, and Epic or Narrative

literature. Lyric verse, as the name indicates, in-
cludes those exquisite Odes, Ballads, and shorter
pieces of sentiment which, in every age, have been
sung to the lyre or other instrument. Dramatic
verse, which is intended to be acted, comprises life-
scenes, real or imaginary, with plot, incident, dialogue,
and chorus, arranged for representation on the stage.
And, finally, Epic verse, which was originally intended to be simply narrated, comprises tales and
histories of grotesque adventures or heroic deeds to
be recited (or read) for the entertainment of the
castle, the market place, or the homes of the humbler
classes.

And each of these three classes of verse-literature
has its corresponding prose counterpart. In those
grand outbursts of feeling which now and again
sparkle in the oratory of the ancients or in the impassioned utterances of more modern times, we have
prose Odes rising in sublimity to the very highest
range of poetry. There are prose Dramas which, in
poetic power of creation and expression, can stand
side by side with the greatest masterpieces in verse.
And so with Narrative poetry. The Epic is not re-
stricted to verse. Its prose counterpart is the romance or novel. The Epic is a metrical romance;
the Novel is a prose romance. It may seem, perhaps, to the severely sensitive mind, to be degrading

the classic epic by thus placing it on a level with
the modern novel, or to mention modern writers of
romance in the same breath with Homer, Virgil,
Dante, or Milton. We do not refer, however, so
much to what the novel is, as to what the novel
should be. If, in the majority of instances, the romance of to-day has not fulfilled its high destiny,
it is because there have been and still are deadening
influences at work in the world of letters which
have dragged it down and chained it to the earth.
It has been said by one competent to judge in such
matters, that every novel should be a prose *Iliad*
or a prose *Odyssey*. The difference between the
classic Epic and the classic Novel is far from being
so great as many may imagine. But few countries,
throughout their entire history, have produced more
than one, or at most two, grand heroic poems, made
of such imperishable material as to stand their
ground in spite of adverse criticism and the ravages of time, and which have taken deeper and
firmer root in the hearts of men as the centuries
have rolled by. And this is equally true of the
prose literature of Imagination. In any one country there are but few red-lettered names on the entire roll of its novelists; but few prose romances
which will live and take their place side by side
with their metrical counterparts. Those, however,

which have lived and have attracted the attention of successive generations of men will be found, if closely examined, to approach very nearly to the epic standard; and the conclusion will be forced upon the mind that what the Epic is in unity of design, in grandeur of plot, in invention of incident, in delineation of character, in description of scenery, and in depth of human sympathy, that must the Novel be if it is to live and be worthy of comparison with the metrical epic.

Confining our attention, then, to Romantic or Narrative literature (the only subject with which we have any concern at present), it must be borne in mind, that *English* romantic literature has come down to us in three totally distinct and independent channels. In other words, there are three clearly marked kinds of Romance in English literature. There is the Romance of Real Life, which can be traced back to its origin in the French *Contes* and *Fabliaux*, many of which reappear in Chaucer's *Canterbury Tales*, as for example the story of *Griselda*. Subsequently, this class of romances formed the staple of the chap-books* of the sixteenth century, and can be traced onwards in an unbroken series, in home-made stories of English life, such as the *History of Thomas-a-Reading*, or the Six Worthy

* *Vide* Note D.

Yeomen of the West; the story of *Friar Bacon* and his famous deeds as a magician ; the legend of *Robert the Devyle;* the story of *Friar Rush*, who gained admittance to a monastery in the disguise of a servant and played the part of a merry devil; the *History of Tom-a-Lincolne*, and others which Mr. Thoms republished in 1828 in his *Early Prose Romances* and which he aptly styles the Waverley Novels of our forefathers. And finally, we can follow this class of stories down to the time of Mrs. Aphra Behn, the first English novelist in the modern sense of the term, whose novels were read by Charles II., by Dryden, Rochester, and Etherege, and so through Swift and Defoe, Richardson and Fielding, Smollett and Sterne, to the thousand novel-writers of our own day.

The next class of romantic literature is the Allegorical Romance which took its rise in the *Roman de la Rose*, that storehouse of quaint conceits, the work of two French writers of the fourteenth century, Guillaume de Lorris and Jean de Meung. This romance was the parent of an immense stream of allegorical verse. It fired the imagination of Guillaume de Guileville to write *Le Pelerinage de l' Homme*, and some of our greatest writers have studied it, copied it, and drawn inspiration from it. Even Chaucer was deeply indebted to it for more than one of his poems, and the taste engendered by its personifications lasted till the seventeenth century. In Spenser's *Faerie Queene* this allegorical style of writing is seen decked with the trappings of chivalry, shrouded with the weird, the fabulous, and the supernatural, and plaintive with the moans of distressed damsels. Subsequently, appeared Sir Thomas More's *Utopia*, a political allegory, and Sir Philip Sidney's *Arcadia*, a pastoral allegory, the legitimate and natural outcome of the popular taste of the day; and finally, the last wave of the movement, started by the *Roman de la Rose*, broke on English ears when Bunyan published his celebrated religious allegories, the *Pilgrim's Progress* and the *Holy War*.

The third class of English Romantic literature is the Romance of Chivalry. This, which in Norman times was extensively popular in England, consisted of four grand epic cycles that were sung or recited, to a greater or less extent, in every castle and hamlet, for many a long year, before either the Allegorical Romance or the Romance of Real Life had an existence, and no one desired anything different, anything new.

The first of these cycles of Chivalric Romance related to the Emperor Charlemagne, and included tales, histories, and songs, not only of the Emperor himself, but also of Clovis and Charles the Bald.

To this cycle belong the *Chanson de Roland*, the *Chronique de Turpin*, the *Roman des Loherains*, and stories of other august personages.

This series, which was French in origin, French in subject matter, and French in mode of treatment, was naturally the production of France, a native invention of the French mind, and although based on solid history, underwent an extensive course of home and foreign development. A skirmish in which Charles the Great suffered a comparatively insignificant loss in a pass of the Pyrenees, became, in the legends of later times, the great battle

> When Charlemain with all his peerage fell
> By Fontarabbia.

Next to the Arthurian cycle, this was perhaps more widely spread over Christendom than any of those which we are about to name. In England, however, it never took a firm hold of the popular imagination, the exploits of Arthur and his knights eclipsing, to a very great extent, those of Charlemagne and his peers. In fine, Arthur being a native British King became the hero of the English national epic; while Charlemagne being a native Emperor of France became the hero of the French national epic.

Scarcely inferior in point of importance to this

Carlovingian cycle was that of King Alexander,
or as it was sometimes styled the *Lyfe of Alisaun-
dre*. Four years after the battle of Hastings, Si-
meon Seth, a high functionary in the palace of
Antiochus at Constantinople (he is styled "magis-
ter" and "protovestiary," or chief of the wardrobe,)
wrote a Greek romance in which he collected, arranged, and translated from the Persian and Ara-
bian, legends of Alexander the Great, which had
floated down to his own times like the reverbera-
tions of distant thunder. This Greek romance
formed the foundation of succeeding tales. It was
translated into Latin, German, Spanish, Italian,
and even into Hebrew; but it was on the Latin
version that all subsequent developments were
founded. From this source the French legends
started, and from the French version the English
romance was developed.

Unlike the romances of Charlemagne, this cycle
became naturalised in England, and there is extant
a spirited metrical version of the romance of Alexander which dates back to the thirteenth century.*
We may note, in passing, that in the descriptions
of the battles which end in the overthrow of Darius,
and still more in the Indian campaign of Alexander,

* *Vide Metrical Romances of the Thirteenth, Fourteenth, and Fifteenth Centuries*, by Henry Weber, Edinburgh, 1810.

it is quaint, even to the verge of the ludicrous, to
see this hero of the Old World painted as a mediæval knight, called Syr Alesaundre, and surrounded
by all the most fantastic pomp and circumstance of
Norman chivalry.

We now come to the third cycle of the Romance
of Chivalry.

Long before England had passed into the possession of the Dukes of Normandy, there existed, in
the country, a Dano-Saxon cycle which, at one
time, formed, like that of Charlemagne and Alexander, an extensive epic series. This the Norman
trouvères made tributary. They translated it into
French, remodelled and embellished to suit Norman
tastes, but nevertheless showing the old Danish
groundwork in the colouring of the stories and
other details which no amount of French dressing
could hide.

The only specimens of this once famous cycle
which have come down to us, either in French or
English, are the romance of *Havelok the Dane* and
the romance of *King Horn*. Still, they form together an interesting study, filling up, as they do,
one corner in the shrine of early English wit and
fancy.

The fourth cycle is the Arthurian, that which we
are about to examine in the present work. These

four cycles, the Carlovingian, the Alexandrine, the Dano-Saxon, and the Arthurian, comprise collectively the body of Chivalric Romance with which the Norman trouvère helped to while away the leisure hours of those whose lives were spent on the battle-field or in the tournament ; or with which the *Jongleurs* and *Gestours** amused their less lordly patrons.

It will thus be seen that of the three classes of English Romantic literature, the Romance of Real Life, the Allegorical Romance, and the Romance of Chivalry, we shall touch only upon the last, viz., the Chivalric Romance ; and that of the four grand cycles of the Romance of Chivalry, the Carlovingian, the Alexandrine, the Dano-Saxon, and the Arthurian, we shall examine only the Arthurian.

At this point, standing as we do on the very threshold of the subject, it may help us to appreciate the perfection of beauty of the Arthurian Romance, if, for a moment, we view from a distance its vast proportions and its rich blending of mediæval effects.

Some of the writers on Romantic Fiction take it for granted that the Arthurian Epic has undergone a lengthened and gradual course of development. They see in Tennyson the latest and most artistically

* *Vide* Note E.

perfect reflection of pre-existing poems, histories, and
romances.   They regard the Anglo-Norman romances
in turn, as the outgrowth of pre-existing Breton traditions ; and these Breton traditions again, they view
as an embellished version of Welsh poems and folk-
lore.   According to this theory, the Welsh drew the
grand, rough outline on the canvas ; the Bretons
enlarged the original Cambrian design and put in
the ground tints ; the Norman trouvères added the
grouping and gave the colouring to the picture ; the
continental workers filled in the figures in the background ; and Tennyson supplied the finishing touches
and the massive gilt frame.

With all due respect for the opinion of these writers, it is impossible to take this view of the subject,
except in a very vague and general way.   The Welsh
bards give us at the most but a dim reflection of a
great historic fact, viz.: the death struggle between
the Kelt and the Saxon ; and even this reflection
becomes distorted almost beyond recognition as seen
through the haze of myth and fable which afterwards
grew up among the Welsh.   The Breton traditions
starting, like the Welsh, with a tiny germ of history,
transformed it into an idealised memory of a loved
chieftain, whom eventually they surrounded with a
halo of chivalric glory and canonised as a demi-god.
The Norman trouvère, throwing history altogether

out of the question, and taking from Welshman or Breton only such material as suited his purpose, reared an imperishable structure of spiritualised romance upon a poetic legend or tradition of the early Church; and Tennyson, though ostensibly reproducing mediæval romance, has simply painted a unique set of Arthurian pictures in which King Arthur becomes an idealised Prince Albert, a selfless gentleman.

These three versions (omitting Tennyson's for the present) differ from each other, not in minor details only, but in essential points. The Arthur of the Bards is a *lyric* character, the subject of a song. The Arthur of the Chroniclers is professedly a *historic* character, the central figure of an epoch. The Arthur of the Romancers is an *epic* character, one of the personages in a novel, a knight among other knights, and not in any sense the true hero of the plot.

Moreover, each of these three versions had an independent development of its own. By the bards, Arthur is eventually transplanted into the realms of myth; he is translated to the skies and the constellation Ursa Major became "Arthur's Chariot." By the chroniclers, on the other hand, he becomes an earthly emperor whose power and courtly splendour eclipse even that of Charlemagne. With the Anglo-

Norman and continental romancers he becomes the
regal figurehead of a spiritualised era in which Galahad shines forth like another St. Michael on a field
of celestial blue studded with golden stars—an era
when the Holy Graal sheds its pale light and the
Round Table its lustre over the scene only to render
more appalling the terrible darkness of a tragic
ending.

The truer view of the subject seems to be that, at
the present day, there exist at least *three* totally distinct and well-defined versions of the Arthurian
Epic, the Cambrian, or bardic; the Breton or historic; and the Anglo-Norman or romantic; the
study of each of these three co-ordinate versions
being essential to the unfolding of the others, and
of vital interest to one who desires to obtain a full
and complete view of the Romance as an artistic
whole.

Such are the proportions of this grand cycle which
a momentary glance discloses.

If now we approach still nearer and examine the
many-coloured cross-lights which fall upon the glowing picture we shall meet with some very interesting
and, perhaps, unexpected results.

As we gaze at the pageant before us, we see, here
and there, a ray of the pale, clear light of *History;*
the reflection, so to speak, of the lurid glare of war,

lighting up the dark background of the scene. Among the noblest, genuine poems of the Welsh bards of the sixth century, (for then History was in the form of song,) there is a poem upon the death of Geraint, the hero whom Tennyson celebrates as the husband of Enid. The author of this elegy was Geraint's bard, who was attached to his court, and paid to sing his noble deeds; and so when Geraint fell in the famous battle of Longport the poet celebrates the valour of his young patron during the fight :

Before Geraint, the terror of the foe,
I saw steeds fall in the toil of battle :—
And after the shout of war, a dreadful onset.

Before Geraint, the scourge of the enemy,
I saw steeds white with foam :—
And after the shout of battle a furious torrent (of
    blood).

.   .   .   .

At Longport I saw the raging of slaughter
And myriads of the dead ;
Warriors blood stained from the assault of Geraint.

This is a ray of historic light which, falling upon the person of Geraint, forms contemporary and unexceptional testimony to the fact that Geraint actually lived and fought during the sixth century.

Here and there a golden haze of *Mythology* hangs over the scene, blending with the genuine historic light, and needing the spectroscope of the critic to distinguish between the two elements.

It was a passion with chroniclers during the Middle Ages to trace the origin of their respective nations to Troy, after the true Roman model. A French chronicler derived the name and origin of his race from a noble fugitive of Troy, Francio, son of Hector. The English, not to be outdone, seized eagerly upon Brutus, the son of Ascanius, as an eponymous hero at least as respectable as Francio.

Geoffrey of Monmouth, one of the most distinguished of the Latin chroniclers, has left us a singularly beautiful elegiac poem in which this myth is clearly set forth as part of his History of Britain.

Brutus, after the fall of Troy, wandering through the Mediterranean and uncertain whither to go, arrived at a dispeopled island called Leogecia, where he found, in a ruined city, a temple and oracle of Diana, and addresses the goddess in the following incantation which he repeats nine times and then offers the " vase of sacrifice ' full of wine and blood :

Goddess of Shades, and Huntress who at will
Walk'st on the rolling sphere, and through the deep,
On thy third reign, the Earth, look now, and tell
4

What land, what seat of rest thou bidd'st me seek,
What certain seat, where I may worship thee
For aye, with temples vowed, and virgin quires.*

Having encircled the altar four times and having poured the wine into the sacred altar-fire, he lies down to sleep. At the third hour of the night the goddess herself stands before him, tells him of an island in the Western sea, and predicts that there he shall raise a second Troy, found an empire, and establish a royal line:

Brutus, far to the West in the ocean wide,
Beyond the realm of Gaul, a land there lies,
Sea-girt it lies, where giants dwelt of old ;
Now void, it fits thy people.   Thither bend
Thy course ; there shalt thou find a lasting seat ;
There to thy sons another Troy shall rise,
And Kings be born of thee, whose dreaded might
Shall awe the world, and conquer nations bold.†

Awaking from his slumber Brutus sets sail, reaches Britain, and there founds the ancient British empire.

Arthur, among other British sovereigns, was made a lineal descendant from this fictitious hero of Troy, and, as a consequence, even the companions of Arthur shared the same historical notoriety. Indeed some of the romances relating to Arthur are styled *The Romance of Brutus,* and such a firm hold did

* *Vide* Milton's *Works* Masson's edition, vol. iii., p. 32.
† *Ibid.*

these so-called "histories" take upon the minds of the people that Archbishop Peckham in his "Injunctions to the diocese of St. Asaph 1284" desired his clergy to warn their parishioners the Welsh "not to think too much of the idle dreams of their forefathers concerning Brutus and his arrival in Britain."

Now and again there are quaint *Ecclesiastical* tints cast over this knightly assemblage in the introduction of apocryphal legends and Church traditions. The Round Table legend, for example, shines forth in this dim ecclesiastical light. This famous table is represented as that at which our Saviour usually sat with his Apostles, and as that which was used at the Last Supper. Afterwards it was bequeathed, together with the Holy Graal, (so says the romance) to Bishop Joseph, a descendant of Joseph of Arimathea, who thus became the founder of the order of Round Table knights. Accordingly, the earliest knights were apostolic knights, who at their feasts sat around the Table with the Sangraal placed in the midst. By a similar transformation the "siege perillous" was that which our Lord himself had occupied when on earth, and hence was to be left vacant until the "virgin knight" appeared who alone was worthy to fill it.

Other lights which fall upon this scene we must pass by more rapidly.

Now and again, there is the reflection of a *Bible*
narrative, as for example that of the slaughter of
the Innocents.   Arthur is told by Merlin, when the
seer is in one of his prophetic moods, that " he that
should destroy him should be borne on May day,"
referring of course to Modred.   Thereupon the King
" let send for all the children that were borne on May
day, begotten of lords and borne of ladies   .   .   .
upon paine of death.   And so there were found many
lords sons, and all were sent unto the king, and so
was Modred sent by king Lots wife, and all were
put in a shippe to the sea, and some were foure weekes
olde, and some lesse.   And so by fortune the shippe
drove unto a castle, and was al to-riven, and de-
stroied the most part, save that Modred was cast up,
and a good man found him and nourished him til
he was fourteene yeeres old, and then brought him to
the court."

At times we meet with a *Classical* colouring, the
reflexion of the mythology, poems, and tragedies of
Greece and Rome.   In this connection we may
instance the fact that the most telling incident
in one of the plays of Euripides, the *Medea*, has
been transferred to the pages of the Romance
and forms a very striking episode in the legend.
" So on the morrow there came a damosell from
Morgan le Fay to the king, and shee brought

with her the richest mantell that ever was seene in the court, for it was set as ful of precious stones as might stand one by another, and there were the richest stones that ever the king saw. And the damosell said, 'Your sister sendeth you this mantell, and desireth you that yee will take this gift of her, and in what thing shee hath offended you, she will amend it at your owne pleasure.' When the king beheld this mantell, it pleased him much, but he said but little. And with that came the damosel of the lake unto the king, and said, 'Sir, I must speake with you in private.' 'Say on,' said the king, 'what ye will.' 'Sir,' said the lady, 'put not on you this mantell till ye have seene more, and in no wise let it not come upon you nor on no knight of yours till ye commaund the bringer thereof to put it upon *her*.' 'Well,' said king Arthur, 'it shall be done as ye counsaile me.' And then he said unto the damosell that came from his sister, 'Damosell, this mantell that ye have brought me, I will see it upon you.' 'Sir,' said she, 'it will not beseeme me to weare a knights garment.' 'By my head,' said king Arthur, 'ye shall weare it or it come on my backe, or on any man that heere is'; and so the king made it to be put upon her; and foorthwith she fell downe dead, and never more spake word after, and was brent to coles."

But apart from these and many other single rays of light which give colouring and beauty to the brilliant assemblage gathered together within this Epic, there hangs over all, as it were, a luminous atmosphere, the spirit of twelfth century chivalry and knight-errantry, and to crown this, the spirit of a healthy Christianity, which casts a mellow and irradiating glamour over the antique scenes and figures of the tale.

Parables lie hidden in every page of the Romance. As we read, the thought continually arises in the mind that there are grand and generalised ideas underlying the simple story. Arthur seems to be a representative of the human or physical force of the world ; Merlin, a representative of its intellect ; Galahad, of ideal purity ; Lancelot, of man's spiritual warfare ; the Round Table, an image of universal brotherhood ; and the Graal, an image of ideal perfection, to which only ideal purity can attain.

Throughout these romances, moreover, there is visibly the working out of an Æschylean Ate, the embodiment of the axiom that, sooner or latter, sin will find the sinner out ; for, from the first terrible fall of Arthur down to the final battle in which this " flos regum," this flower of knighthood, is carried from the field mortally wounded, the mills of the gods grind slowly but surely ; the clouds darken and gather until at length the storm bursts over the Court, and in its fury sweeps away

> The goodliest fellowship of noble knights
> Of whom this world hath record.

And is there not something very significant in the tenacity with which bard, chronicler, and romancer hold to the belief that " Arthur will come again, he cannot die " ?   The Bretons, even at a late date, used to cry aloud at their feasts, " Non le roi Arthur n'est pas mort."   In old Hellas, the great Achilles is not dead, but in the " Islands of the Blest."   In Switzerland, the three Tells sleep quietly in a cavern near Lake Lucerne until the time has need of them. Surely a cry so deep, so universal is more than a mere poetic utterance.

CHAPTER III.

Writers of the Arthurian Epic.

THE Arthurian Romance, in its dawn, carries us back to the dim twilight of British literature; to the time when the deadly struggle between the Kelt and the Saxon was being waged; when the daring deeds and heroic valour of the Welsh gave rise to the first faint beginnings of Welsh song, and when the bards attached to the Court of this or that powerful chieftain, sang of the deeds of their patrons in the din of battle or in the quiet munificence of home.

To show, however, to what an extent the outside world,—the civilised world of that day,—was ignorant of the far-off island of Brittia, and how its very existence was subject of myth and wild fantastic legend, we have only to open the pages of one of the most noted historians of the time, the illustrious Procopius, Secretary to the great Belisarius, who writing in the sixth century, *i.e.*, during the Arthurian epoch, presents us with a strange picture of the island.

"They say," he writes, "that the souls of men departed are always conducted to this place, but in what manner I will explain immediately, having frequently heard it from men of that region relating it most seriously. On the coast of the land over against this island, Brittia, are many villages, inhabited by men employed in fishing and agriculture, and who, for the sake of merchandise, pass over to this island. In other respects they are subject to the Franks, but they never render them tribute; this burden, as they relate, having been of old remitted to them for a certain service which I shall now describe. The inhabitants declare that the conducting of 'souls departed' devolves upon them in turn. Such of them, therefore, as on the ensuing night are to go on this occupation in their turn of service, retiring to their dwellings as soon as it grows dark, compose themselves to sleep, awaiting the conductor of the expedition. All at once, at night, they perceive that their doors are shaken, and they hear a certain indistinct voice summoning them to their work. Without delay, arising from their beds they proceed to the shore, not understanding the necessity which thus constrains them, yet nevertheless compelled by its influence. And here they perceive vessels in readiness, wholly void of men, not however their own, but certain strange vessels, in which embarking, they lay hold on the oars, and feel their burden made heavier by a multitude of passengers, the boats being sunk to the gunwale and rowlock, and floating scarce a finger above the water. They see not a single person, but having rowed for one hour only, they arrive at Brittia; whereas when they navigate their own vessels, not making use of sails but rowing, they arrive there with difficulty even in a night and a day. Having reached the island, and been released from their burden they depart immediately, the boats quickly becoming light, suddenly emerging from the stream, and sinking in the water no deeper than the keel. These people see no human being either while navigating with them or when released from the ship. But they say that they hear a certain voice there, which seems to announce to such as receive them the names of all who have crossed over with them, and describing the dignities which they formerly possessed, and calling them over by their hereditary titles."

But while such dense ignorance obtained among the scholars of Constantinople respecting Britain in the sixth century, the Welsh were fighting an unequal battle with their Saxon foes, and Arthur was laying the foundation of a fame which was destined to eclipse even that of Belisarius himself. Indeed, the story of his heroic deeds was destined to live and be made the subject of popular song when the folios of Procopius were mouldering on the shelves of University libraries.

Standing, as we do, in the very van of antiquarian research, when every field of literature has been scoured by earnest and hard-working students; when the oldest Welsh literature has been investigated in its inmost recesses by the leading scholars of Wales, England, and Brittany, we are apt to forget that this great achievement is of very recent date. It is only of late years that the literary wealth of Wales has been brought to light. For six hundred years, from the twelfth to the eighteenth century, its treasures were allowed to lie buried in oblivion, and few, during this period, cared to question the pretentions of Arthur or the valiant deeds of his knights ; on the contrary, the fictions of the poet or the chronicler were accepted as actual fact, were incorporated into popular handbooks, and for centuries were taught as part and parcel of English authentic history.

With the dawn of the present century, however, the spirit of criticism awoke into activity. Antiquarians rubbed their eyes, aroused themselves from their torpor, read, compared and weighed evidence, and with the reappearance of the Norman romances in Southey and Scott, came the critical study of the earliest Arthurian legends.

As we cast our eyes over the field of Arthurian romance and Arthurian poetry, and view its present luxuriant growth, the important question arises, Who were the writers of this grand cyclus and what did they severally accomplish? Or, to put the question in other words : What was there, already in existence, of the Arthurian tales, when Tennyson took the subject in hand?

The writers of Arthurian Romance we shall classify as the Bards, the Chroniclers, and the Romancers; or the men who sang; the men who historified ; and the men who invented. The first two classes need not detain us long, but the third class, since it is both highly important and highly interesting, we shall examine more at length.

One of the most distinguished of the pioneers in the revival of Welsh learning was Owen Jones, born about the middle of the last century (1741). While still a boy, tending cattle in his native Welsh fields, he was wont to indulge in reveries on the ancient literary and warlike glories of his country. He was accustomed to attend the various musical and poetical contests of the bards of his day, the Eisteddvods or Is-teth-vdds, and being a bright, clever lad he was initiated into the mysteries of music and poetry. He had heard from these bards accounts of the different castles, in which were preserved, among other

treasures, the ancient and valuable manuscripts which
contained the cherished poetry of his native land,
and to more than one of these he made a pilgrimage in the hope of getting access to the precious
documents. But it was all in vain. What could a
poor, country boy have to do with ancient poetry?
They thought him mad, and neither tears nor entreaties could gain him so much as a glimpse of the
well-guarded parchments. Repulsed and derided,
this inspired boy bent his steps homeward, time
and again, with a heavy heart and sick at soul.
But he was not to be foiled. Coming to the conclusion that money alone would forge a key to open
these dungeons of his loved literature, he travelled
up to London, entered in the year 1760, as a shop-
boy, a furrier's on Thames Street, and amid all the
drudgery of a menial office, lived in fancy among
bards, and warriors, and princes. From shop-boy he
rose to be clerk; from clerk, to partner; from partner, to head of the firm. The prize was now, after forty years of toil, within his reach. A man of
one idea, he devoted his riches to the attainment
of his life-dream. Copyists were employed; the
castle doors were thrown open; the priceless manuscripts were placed at his service; and by the beginning of the present century, he had collected
transcripts of a greater number of celebrated manu-

scripts of Welsh literature than he had ever dreamed to exist. By the year 1807, these were published at his own expense under the title of *The Myvyrian Archaiology of Wales.* Naturally enough, this collection was the most perfect of its kind,—indeed the only one worthy to be called a collection of Welsh poetry which existed for many years ; and even at the present day, notwithstanding the later achievements of Welsh scholars in this direction, the *Myvyrian Archaiology* continues to hold its place as the foremost work of its kind.

In this collection are the poetical remains of the three celebrated Welsh bards, Llywarch Hên, Aneurin, and Taliéssin, who lived just before or during the sixth century and were contemporary, or nearly so, with the historic Arthur.

If we try to peer into the darkness of these prehistoric times, we can catch here and there a glimmer of fact, a little bit of solid history regarding these oldest Kymric bards ; but the tissue of fable which grew up and surrounded them in after times, obscures or distorts nearly all besides. Two facts, however, stand prominently out and deserve especial notice. Llywarch Hên, when a youth, served together with Geraint in the army under Arthur and was present at the battle of Longport, A.D. 501, of which mention was made in the last chapter.

Aneurin, the second of this triad of bards, was the grandson of Geraint, the hero celebrated by Tennyson as the husband of Enid, and hence, these two bards might be supposed to know something of Arthur and of his renowned companions.

In addition to the genuine poems of these three bards, the *Myvyrian Archaiology* presents us with the remains of Welsh poetry from the sixth to the tenth century, a comparatively barren spot in Cambrian literature. Still, they contain valuable matter, since in the writings of this period we can trace a growing tendency to translate the Arthur of history into the world of mythology and fable.

This bardic literature, however, had always been produced for an exclusive class ; it was not the literature of the people ; it was the literature of the bards and of the initiated. Indeed, throughout their entire history, the Kymry have had two totally distinct forms of literature : the bardic and the popular. For hundreds of years there had been traditions floating among the people which formed the popular literature, and which, in course of time, were collected together, artistically arranged, and committed to writing under the title of *Mabinogion* or *Stories*. These Welsh tales were intended to while away the idle hours of the chieftains, or to be recited at the fireside of the humbler classes, and formed the in-

tellectual recreation of the bulk of the people; and
one of these collections, the *Red Book of Hergest*,
is extant and preserved in the library of Jesus College, Oxford. Some fifty years ago, Lady Charlotte Guest procured a copy of this manuscript and
translated it into English in order that she might
enact the part of a *Mabinog*, or Welsh minstrel to
her own children.* So excellent was her translation
of these Mabinogion, so vividly did it mirror forth
the spirit of these antique stories, and so remarkable
was it for both beauty and fidelity, that Lady Guest
was finally induced to permit its publication, and
has thus conferred a lasting obligation on the English student. Among these Welsh novels (for such
they are in their present form,) are three of the Arthurian romances, and hence the work is highly
interesting in its bearing on the present enquiry.

To sum up, then, what we have already said : the
earlier bards of Wales supply us with poems contemporary, or nearly so, with the historic Arthur ;
the later bards, inaugurating an age of fable, trans-
form whatever they touch into strange fictions ;
plain facts become in their hands myths, and the
natural assumes the form of the supernatural ; while
in the Mabinogion, oral traditions are developed into
stately prose romance.

* *Vide* Note F.

If now, we turn to the map of France, we shall find, just across the Channel from Cornwall, a section of the country still called Bretagne, sometimes Armorica, sometimes Brittany, and sometimes Little Britain. It is, to all intents and purposes, a Welsh settlement, and the literature of the people is found to be as full of Arthurian legends as that of the Welsh in England. How are we to account for this?

It is historically certain, that during the long struggle between the Kymry and the Saxons, great numbers of the oppressed British fled to the continent as an asylum. Those who thus left their native land poor and exiled, would naturally carry with them the poems, histories, tales, and all in fact that went to make up the literature of their former home. Moreover, they would naturally carry as a treasure, the remembrance of those chieftains who had defended their native land; and the most popular of these was Arthur. His image, idealised by sad thought and rendered real by a cruel and unwilling exile, kept in their hearts the high place which he, long before, had occupied at the head of their army. Thus, they sang his noble deeds, his death, and his hoped-for return. And some of these poems are still extant. A celebrated Frenchman of our time, the Vicomte de la Villemarqué, a native of Breton, spent a large amount of money and the greater part

s

of his life in collecting Breton ballads and romances of the olden time, and, in order to make his collection more valuable, he mingled freely with the Armorican peasantry so as to glean the many ancient traditions which were known to be floating among the people, and to reflect still more ancient tales. The result of his labors is comprised chiefly in the four following works: *Barzaz Breiz, Chants populaires de la Bretagne; Les Romans de la Table Ronde et les Contes des Anciens Bretons; Les Bardes Bretons Poëmes du VIme Siècle;* and *La Légende Celtique, en Irlande, en Cambrie et en Bretagne,* works, which throw all the light that we shall need on the Armorican phase of this famous cyclus.

From the close of the golden era of Welsh poetry to the dawn of the brilliant era of the Chroniclers, or from the sixth to the twelfth century, there was but little literature in any of the modern European tongues. The grand outburst of modern vernacular literature simultaneously, or nearly so, in the twelfth and thirteenth centuries, in the various European nations, it is needless to say, was metrical. All over feudal Europe during this period the passion for narrative was something unprecedented. Lords and ladies in their castles, burghers in their households, and peasants in their cottages, were all possessed of an intense passion for stories. The minstrel, whose

duty it was to satisfy this demand, invented, borrowed, and translated, now rehearsing known facts;
now collecting and shaping legends in which the
feats and personages of mediæval history were
worked into romances of chivalry; now remodelling
classic stories of the ancient world, and reproducing
Alexander as a French knight, and Virgil as a great
magician; now taking a subject out of ecclesiastical
lore, or adapting some Oriental tale which had been
brought Westward by the Crusades, or now telling
simply comic tales of everyday life.

In no country was the impulse to the narrative
form of literature earlier or stronger than in Britain.
The Norman conquest interrupting, as it did, the native tendencies of the Saxon mind, handed over the
conduct of literature in England to those who were
pre-eminently the trouvères of Europe, viz.; the
Anglo-Norman minstrels, (for we must remember
that a greater number of distinguished Norman
trouvères of the twelfth and thirteenth centuries
were born on the English, than on the French side
of the Channel), and so powerful was the infusion
into England of the Trouvère or Narrative as distinct from the Troubadour or Lyric spirit, that
throughout the whole course of English literature
since, we can see the Narrative impulse ruling and
the Lyric subordinate.

For nearly a hundred years after the battle of Hastings, the trouvères amused their patrons with narratives from the stock which they had brought with them from the continent, or with Dano-Saxon tales which they found already popular in England. But about the middle of the twelfth century, a strong impetus was given to writers of romance, the effects of which are felt even at this distance of time.

It was during the early part of the twelfth century that Walter Calenius,* a member of the University of Oxford, and Archdeacon, during one of his vacations, made a tour in Brittany. While there, he met a friend who showed him an antiquarian treasure, which he stated that he had found in some out of the way corner of his monastery and had preserved until he should find some one who could appreciate it. This treasure was an ancient manuscript, entitled in Welsh *Brut-y-Brenhined* or History of the Kings, *i. e.*, the Welsh Kings of Britain, which he entrusted to his English guest as a most valuable relic. Upon his return to England, the Archdeacon committed this precious manuscript to the care of the accomplished Geoffrey of

* Walter Calenius or Walter of Wallingford in Berkshire, the place of his birth. Wallingford=Lat. Caleva or Calena and hence Calenius. Leland, *Itinerary*, ix., 50.

Monmouth, a priest of the Anglican Church, who
tells us that he was agreeably surprised by a request
from Walter Calenius, Archdeacon of Oxford, to
translate a book from the British tongue, which he
(Walter) had brought from Brittany. He accordingly made a Latin translation of the work, probably
incorporating Welsh legends, and tales from other
sources, or from his own fund of native traditions.
This work was brought out in the autumn of 1147
under the patronage of Robert, Earl of Gloucester,
a man celebrated for his encouragement of learning,
and to whom the work was dedicated.

This *History* of Geoffrey's is a very quaint production. Weird Kymric legends, scraps of authentic
history, and fully developed romance are mingled
together and clothed in the grave style of a monastic
historian; the old groundwork being strangely em-
broidered with classical terms and crossed here and
there with threads of mediæval thought. But nevertheless, it was the most popular book of the day.
The sensation it created was beyond all parallel.
It turned the heads of young knights and young
monks and sentimentally inclined damoiselles and
made its author at once the best known and best
abused man of the time.

William of Newburgh, another priest of the Anglican Church, (perhaps through jealousy,) abused the

learned Geoffrey as vigorously, if not as politely, as a modern reviewer might have done.* Gerald of Wales said he knew a man who had seen legions of devils swarming about the book ; and many others regarded Geoffrey as a *splendide mendax*, a brilliant liar. But the work was a grand success ; and Geoffrey, who was henceforth known under the *sobriquet* of Arturus, could afford to laugh at their harmless rage. If this work was bad history it was nevertheless marvellously good romance, and is rightfully regarded as the starting-point of English Romantic Fiction. It is the spring at which all subsequent writers drank and drank deep, full draughts, and hence Geoffrey of Monmouth's name holds a deservedly high place in the annals of Fiction.

As we before stated, the Norman trouvères had hitherto been compelled to allay the insatiable desire for narrative, evinced by the nobility and lower classes, from the supply, (such as it was,) which they had brought with them from their native land. But now, they were in possession of an inexhaustible mine of treasure. We can fancy the delight of a minstrel with this *History* in hand framing therefrom a delightful series of romantic and magic stories, any one of which, versified and embellished with a few additional touches of fancy, would be sure to

Vide Note G.

fascinate the most fastidious assembly that could be collected in court or castle.   Indeed, we actually find them ignoring Norse or Norman traditions and occupying their talents with those of Wales and Brittany, *i. e.*, with the Arthurian Romance.

In the year 1155, or eight years after the appearance of Geoffrey's work, Maistre Robert (?) Wace, in order to please that unedifying woman Eleanor of Provence, translated into Norman French verse, the Latin prose of Geoffrey, under the title of *Li Roman de Brut*.   This production, however, is not a simple versification of the original, for Wace expands it considerably, adding, here and there, an incident taken from his own imagination or from popular tradition which he found existing in his native Brittany.   At the risk of anticipating, we may mention the fact that it is in this romance that we hear for the first time of the Round Table.

Fifty years later, at the close of the twelfth century, we come to the last of the Chroniclers with whom we have any concern.   At that time, there was a Welsh priest living in Worcestershire, on the banks of the Severn, known to us as Layamon.   He claims our attention as being the first writer of Arthurian Romance who made use of his mother-tongue, the English of his age and district, in other words, the Semi-Saxon.   We have said that Wace's

French *romance* was an enlarged translation of Geoffrey's Latin *History*, embellished with additional touches of fancy and with an occasional poetic addition to the story. In like manner, Layamon's English *History* is an expanded translation of Wace's French *romance* with some most important additions to the tale as for example, Arthur's romantic voyage with the fairies to the Isle of Avalon. But nevertheless, whatever developments or changes the story receives in after times, the main points as narrated by Geoffrey remain essentially unaltered in all subsequent romances. Henceforward, we invariably find in Arthur's company, his beautiful queen Guinevere, his traitorous nephew Modred, Sir Kay his seneschal, Sir Bedivere his butler, and Sir Gawaine his counsellor and ambassador.

It is worthy of notice, that all of these three works, whether called History or Romance, were really and truly professed *Histories;* and were regarded as such at the time of their publication. But at the present day they cannot be viewed in any other light than as works of fiction pure and simple.

The Arthurian Romance, then, up to and including the time of Geoffrey, was little more than a mediæval condensation of pre-existing poems, legends, and tales.

As we come to the twelfth century Romancers, a

marvellous transformation takes place, and the modern fully developed romances of Arthur begin to assume definite shape.

One of the most remarkable of the literary men at the Court of Henry II. was Walter Map, poet, wit, and theologian. Like Geoffrey and Layamon, he had lived on the marches of Wales, and within hearing of Welsh song. He calls the Welsh "our countrymen," and England "our Mother." He had studied at the University of Paris where he saw, and perhaps had taken part in, town and gown riots. He was afterwards on familiar terms with Thomas à Becket, and repeats conversations which he had had with that noted man. He was also a courtier about the palace of the King, with whom he was in high favour ; and such was his standing that he was appointed one of the Justices Itinerant of England, and was sent on more than one occasion to foreign courts on affairs of state ; so that, as he wittily says, he had scarcely leisure to live, (*vix vaco vivere*). Finally, we find him Canon of St. Paul's Cathedral ; subsequently Archdeacon of Oxford ; and then we hear but little further concerning him. We know, from authentic documents, that he was alive in the ninth year of the reign of King John (1207) and we also know, from a statement of Giraldus Cambrensis, that he died before the end of that reign (1216).

As a writer in Latin, he was highly distinguished ;
as a writer in Norman French he was equally distinguished.   But the point of chief importance to us, is
the fact that to him we are indebted for a large portion of the cycle of Arthurian romances, in the most
perfect form in which they are known to us. Indeed,
of all the writers of this cycle, Walter Map stands out
facile princeps.   It was he who put a subtle, spiritual
meaning into them, and made of detached and frag-
mentary tales a grand epic cyclus.   He it doubtless
was, who wrote the Latin originals of *Le Roman du
Saint Graal* and *Le Roman de Merlin.**   It is unquestionable that he was the author of *La Queste del
Saint Graal, Le Roman de Lancelot du Lac,* and *Le
Roman de La Mort Artus,* or the Passing of Arthur.
It is to him we are indebted for the creation of that
ideally pure knight Sir Galahad ; in a word, for
nearly all that is beautiful, chaste, and imperishable
in these romances.

If we look simply at the number and extent of
Map's works, it is immediately apparent, even from
so superficial a view, what an important advance
had been wrought in the perfection of the Arthurian cyclus by this learned cleric and novelist.   But
this is only one item, and that a very small one, in
the sum total of his services.   Previous to the time

* *Vide* Note H.

of Geoffrey of Monmouth, there existed in Wales, both North-Wales and Corn-Wales, little else than straggling tales, mythological poems, and scraps of authentic history; in Armorica, a mass of ballad poetry and traditions innumerable. Even Geoffrey and his followers simply arranged and amplified materials which had been collected in Brittany, as one chapter of a continuous narrative; as part and parcel of a professed *History*. Walter Map, on the contrary, coming close upon the heels of these writers, and while they were in the very noontide of their popularity as historians, stood boldly forth, not as a recorder of sober facts, but as a writer of *romances*, and thus laid the foundation for a species of fictional writings, destined for two long centuries to form the only popular literature of England, and to overshadow more pretentious works so late as the days of Queen Elizabeth.

But the fact of chief importance with respect to Map's writings yet remains to be noted. In every narrative poem which aspires to the distinction of an Epic, there must be (in addition to other perfections) a *central point of unity*, a point around which the whole story revolves, and towards which every thought gravitates and every incident points. There must be, so to speak, a soul, a vital principle, which animates every part, and throws life into its most remote ramifications. There must be an indwelling force which sets the whole machinery of the poem in motion; which controls every part, which makes the whole, work harmoniously together and finally brings about an appropriate ending.

Now, the *tradition of the Holy Graal*, constitutes this point of unity in the Arthurian Epic.

There was a Church tradition, or rather, perhaps, an apocryphal legend, current in the Middle Ages, which accounted for the miracles attending the early years of Christianity, by the mystic, unearthly powers attributed to a Cup or Graal which had belonged to Joseph of Arimathea; and as Church tradition regarded Joseph as one of the first Apostles of Britain, this Graal story could very easily be made the central point, or point of unity, in this Norman *epopoiia;* and this Map seized upon. According to the romance, the Holy Graal is represented as the cup or dish ordinarily used by our Saviour when he offered sacrifice, and from which he administered the Last Supper to the Apostolic band. Afterwards, when our Saviour was seized by the Jewish soldiers, one of their number carried off the Holy Graal and delivered it to Pilate; but the Governor, fearing to retain anything which had belonged to Jesus, gave it to Joseph of Arimathea, whom he knew to be one of our Lord's most devoted friends.

Accordingly, it was used as the receptacle for the sacred blood which flowed from the wounds of our Saviour both while hanging upon the Cross, and, also, when he was taken down by the loving hands of Joseph. Subsequently, when the Jews cast Joseph into prison, on charge of complicity in asserting that Christ was truly risen from the dead, the Graal was placed miraculously in his hands and kept him insensible to the pangs of hunger and the horrors of his dungeon during the forty and two years of his imprisonment. At length, released by Vespasian, he quitted Jerusalem, and taking with him the miraculous Vessel made his way through France into Britain, where it was carefully preserved in the treasury of a king of the island called the Fisherman King.

In this romance, which is evidently the introductory one to the whole cycle, none of the knights of the Round Table are mentioned; the Graal itself, and the legendary history of Joseph and his descendants, forming the sole subject of the romance.

In after times, the Holy Graal was supposed to be lost; its very existence was known only as a dim, traditional remembrance; only as a shadowy dream of a something mystic and holy; a treasure once possessed but now mysteriously gone.

Here then, was theme enough to fire the imagina-

tion of a less poetic mind than that of Walter Map.
What a grand subject for a romance of chivalry!
Why could not the national traditions of Merlin and
Arthur and the knights of his Court, who had appeared hitherto, only in connection with earthly
achievements, why could not these traditions be incorporated in an epic—a spiritualised epic? What
knightly adventure could compare with the Quest and
Achievement of the Sangraal? And so Map wrote
Le Roman du Saint Graal to give unity and completeness to the series, and *La Queste del Saint Graal* as
the adventure *par excellence* of the noble knights.

But the vessel was lost;

> The times,
> Grew to such evil that the holy cup
> Was caught away to Heaven and disappeared,

and the very memory of it had almost faded out of
the minds of men. How were these apocryphal legends to be fitted (so to speak) to the tales of chivalry? The task was not difficult. As the knights
of the Round Table sat at a royal banquet there
was heard "crying of thunder," and "in the midst
of the blast entred a sunne-beame more clear by
seaven times than ever they saw day, and all they
were alighted of the grace of the holy Ghost," and
"so they looked every man on other as they had
beene dombe. Then entred into the hall the holy

grale covered with white samite," and when it had vanished from sight all the knights present vowed to go in quest of the holy Vessel.

Such is the connecting link which Map's grand genius supplied to set in motion all the heroic deeds of the Round Table knights.

We are, therefore, brought face to face with a most startling fact, namely, that the whole current of Arthurian tale was now abruptly changed and turned from its ancient channel.

This sudden turn in the aim, purpose, or *morale* of the narrative; this entire remodelling of existing stories; this unprecedented departure from all extant originals, can only be explained on the ground that Map had resolved to recast the whole narrative; to introduce a new element, and that the work of spiritualisation had commenced.

Can we fathom Map's motive in all this? can we bring his object to light? Perhaps we can. At that day, no one knew whence Arthur came, what the Round Table meant, how Merlin was able to predict so much, how Lancelot and Tristan grew to be so strong. So Map, who was a poet-priest, resolved that where there were so many miracles, Religion ought to be concerned. One of the Apocryphal gospels spoke of a sacred cup. This might be made to give occasion to the institution of the Round Table; and the presence in Britain of the Holy Graal might serve as the mainspring to set all the romantic deeds of the noble knights in motion.   Merlin was a great prophet, but at best a weird, pagan prophet.   This could not be permitted, there must be no prophet disassociated from the Church.   He was modified, therefore, into the son of a Spirit-fiend, with his nature akin to that of a bad angel, but transformed by Baptism.   As for the superhuman valour of the knights of the romances, the only pious way of reconciling that with the faith of the Church was to make them all descend in direct line from Joseph of Arimathea ; and this Map does.   In this way, legends believed by the people were not contradicted ;   they were accepted as they stood, carefully arranged, sifted, purified, hallowed, and surrounded with a subtle atmosphere of piety.   In this way Map gained his object.   He satisfied the clergy, he amused and instructed barons and burghers alike, he pleased the scholar, and he filled the chasms in the popular tales by writing these introductory romances of the Saint Graal.

Taking Map's productions as a whole, they form a grand epic cyclus.   There is not, it is true, the steady marshalling of events in continuity, or the uninterruptedly sustained narrative which is essential to the epic : but there does exist, and that most unmistakably, a central point of unity which holds all the romances together, and for this reason we call these romances, as they came from the pen of Walter Map, an epic cyclus or series.

Three lesser lights in the galaxy of Romance writers of this time we must not entirely pass over. Robert de Borron is to be remembered as the reputed author, and actual translator into French, of the *Roman du Saint Graal* and of the *Roman de Merlin*, which appeared during the period when Map was busy with the Graal romances. Luces de Gast and Hélie de Borron, contemporaries of Walter Map, are also noteworthy as the authors of the first and second parts respectively, of *Le Roman de Tristan*, doubtless the most perfect of all the episodes which the early romancers introduced into the series in order to give completeness and symmetry to the epic. Even Matthew Arnold could find attractions in this romance sufficient to draw his attention, for a time, from the study of classical models. Still it is simply an episode, and in no sense essential to the unity of the narrative.

It will be remarked, that the writers of these romances, with only one exception, namely Layamon, were Norman trouvères, and their language the Norman French. The reason of this is obvious to those who are acquainted with the history of the English language. For two centuries after the Norman conquest, French was the language of the ruling classes. A French speaking royal family was on the throne, surrounded by ministers, vassals, courtiers, ecclesiastics, lawyers, soldiers, and minstrels, all speaking French, and eschewing the language of the conquered race, as too barbarous to express the chivalric ideas of those of gentle birth. During this period the good old Saxon was treated by Norman pharisees as a leper. It was outcast, it was insulted, it was oppressed. Whatever was intended for the perusal of the literate appeared in a Latin garb; whatever was written for the diversion of the noble appeared in courtly French. Yet, underlying the polished surface, the rough, powerful Saxon flowed an impetuous current. It broke, volcanic like, through the crust of French in Layamon, and then disappeared ; it was in revolt, but even then gave signs of the power which it was hourly acquiring and which was destined ere long to overthrow its oppressor. But, for the time being, its oppressor triumphed. Romance after romance appeared and the language was French ; but at last the crisis arrived. Though all the romances of Map and his compeers and followers had, with one or two exceptions, shown a preference for the Norman French of the trouvères, yet the great compilation, *La Mort Darthur* of Sir Thomas Maleore or Malory, published in 1485, was

translated " oute of certeyn bookes of Frensshe " into
Middle English : " After that I had accomplysshed
and fynysshed dyvers hystoryes," says Caxton in the
Prologue . . . " many noble and dyvers gentylmen of thys royame of Englond camen and de-
maunded me many and ofttymes wherfore that I
have not do make and enprynte the noble hystorye
of the saynt greal and of the moost renomed crys-
ten kyng fyrst and chyef . . . kyng Arthur. "
He accordingly complied with the request of these
" dyvers gentylmen," and then proceeds in this fashion : " For to passe the tyme, this book shal be ples-
aunte to rede in, but for to gyve fayth and byleve
that al is trewe that is contayned herin, ye be at
your lyberte ; but al is wryton for our doctryne and
for to beware that we falle not to vyce ne synne, but
texercyse and folowe vertu, by whyche we may come
and atteyne to good fame and renomme in thys lyf,
and after thys shorte and transytorye lyf to come
unto everlastyng blysse in heven."

Equally curious and interesting is the colophon
of this edition : " Thus endeth," writes Caxton, " this
noble and joyous booke, entytled *La Mort Darthur*.
Notwythstanding it treateth of the byrth, lyf and
actes of the sayd kynge Arthur, and of his noble
knyghtes of the rounde table, theyr marveyllous
enquestes and adventures, thachyevyng of the sang

real, and in the ende la Morte Darthur, with the dolorous deth and departyng out of this worlde of them al. Whiche booke was reduced into Englysshe by syr Thomas Malory, knight, as afore is sayd, and by me devyded into XXI bookes, chaptyred, and emprynted, and fynysshed in thabbey Westmestre the last day of July, the yere of our Lord MCCCCLXXXV Caxton me fieri fecit."

Sir Thomas Malory can scarcely be regarded as one of the Romancers except by way of courtesy, since this cyclus must be considered to have received its finishing touches when Walter Map published his *Roman de la Mort Artus.* Still, keeping this fact in mind, we may very justly accord Malory a niche in this old Poets' corner, as the last, for many a long year, indeed for over three hundred years, who did anything to revive an interest in England's oldest romances or legends, which are as famous, as brilliant, and as suggestive as those of early Greece or Rome. We must not forget, however, that it is not an original work but simply a compilation. That Malory's work is not an artistic or perfect production is evident to every critical reader. It contains no well-conceived plot, or rather no plot at all. Adventures, battles, tournaments, and festivities are commingled in such inextricable confusion, and with such a persistent disregard of the unities, that one might almost suppose the author to have been suffering from an intellectual *nihtmara* while performing his task.⟮ At one time we read of some famous battle in which Arthur is engaged, but before the issue is finally decided we are snatched away to witness a passage of love between Lancelot and Guinevere ; and scarcely is this satisfactorily concluded, when we are plunged into a *mêlée*, where spears are broken and swords clash together, to watch the prowess of Tristan.⟯ In addition to this want of system, the compiler has been guilty of so many sins of omission that anyone who has read the originals from which Malory transcribed, must regret a hundred times in so many pages that the execution of the work was not performed by more skilful hands.

Still, the *Mort Darthur*, with all its imperfections, has a subtle, magnetic charm which is irresistible. Even the conspicuous absence of artificial finish only tends to heighten the effect upon the mind, and to one who is accustomed to the close drawing-room atmosphere of the modern fashionable novel to turn to Malory, is to exchange the crowded city for the free air, the green fields, and the utter listlessness of an ideal landscape.

To digress for one moment. Malory's name suggests one of the many curious and unanswered problems of literature. Who was Sir Thomas Malory?

Strange as it may appear, we know more respecting the life of Llywarch Hên than we do of this knight of Edward IV.'s time. We know his name ; we know that he compiled this work; but that is all ; and naturally enough we do not rest satisfied with such meagre details. We like to become better acquainted with the men to whom we are indebted for our intellectual pleasure. We like to visit the Tudor Court and hear England's Queen call Sidney lovingly " my Philip." We like to go to Swift's apartments in London, on his return from a dinner at Lord Harley's, and watch him jotting down scraps of Court gossip, in a babbling way, to amuse his " little witch " Stella. We like to form one of the party when impecunious Goldsmith who " wrote like an angel but talked like poor Poll " is to read his Retaliation ; and so we should like to picture to ourselves this unknown knight as living in some quaint castle in the country or in some old city dwelling, with the French scrolls and folios about him, resetting the Arthurian Romance in connected English for Caxton to print. As it is, he is a *vox et præterea nihil.*

From the middle of the seventeenth century, when the last of the black-letter editions of Malory was issued from the press as a protest against Cervantes and Quixotism, we hear nothing of these romances till the beginning of the present century. That they should once again have seized upon the popular imagination, and at such a time, is a fact of surpassing significance.   It was then that Napoleonic ambition scared men, whether clerics or laics, from the torpor into which they had fallen, and gave the *quietus* to the masses who had grown sceptical of heroes.   The campaigns of the Iron Duke showed that heroism was not dead nor great deeds impossible.   Once more it was seen that the love of God and of one's country was not a poetic fiction : that self-denial and self-sacrifice in the pursuit of great ends were still attainable.   Nineteenth century trouvères instantly arose ; the old ideality of England revived, and with it, the Arthurian romances reasserted their ancient supremacy over the English mind.   Side by side with gazettes of battles —the reports of brilliant victories or crushing defeats — appeared Scott's chivalric legends ; then, two years after the battle of Waterloo, two editions of Malory's long-forgotten work, and a year later Southey's folio of the same.

We have thus sketched, as fully as will be necessary for our purpose, the Bards who sang or fabled, the Chroniclers who historified, and the Romancers who invented and have thus brought our subject down to the present day.

Had the fifteenth century produced a Homer,
a Virgil, a Dante, or a Milton, instead of a Mal.
ory, we might now be in possession of an epic of the
age of chivalry comparable with any which the world
has ever known. The grand and chaste creations
of Walter Map, the comprehensiveness and unity
of his inventions, formed a groundwork which had
only to be symmetrically developed and thrown
into the form of an epic poem to have gained for
its author an immortality of fame. As it is, the work
is still undone. Even Tennyson failed to produce
an epic of chivalry, and the theme awaits the fash-
ioning touch of some future poet.

Perhaps, after such an admission, it may be thought
superfluous to enter upon a consideration of the merits and demerits of Tennyson's Arthurian poems.
But this does not necessarily follow. In order to
form a correct opinion of any poetical work, we ought,
at the very outset, to discover, if possible, the class
of poetical compositions which the author pro-
poses to write and to judge him accordingly. Tennyson himself, classified his Arthurian poems under
the heading of *Idylls*. He does not, therefore, in
this direction, lay claim to the dignity of an epic
poet, and as this is all that we maintain, we cannot
possibly be doing any injustice to his memory.

It is, moreover, universally admitted that Tenny-

son's fame rests more especially on his ability as a
lyric poet, and that he was wanting in the comprehensiveness of grasp, the power of sustained thought,
and that high development of the dramatic faculty
which are the invariable characteristics of a great
epic poet. Were any proof wanting to show Tennyson's unfitness for the task which he undertook, the
chronological order in which he produced his *Idylls*
would show that he had never grasped the Arthurian tales as a whole, as an epic production.*

Judging Tennyson, therefore, in accordance with
the title which he himself prefixed to his tales of
chivalry, we are bound to regard them as so many
short, detached poems, forming collectively a series
similar to that of Map, and while superior to Map's
in point of pre-Raphaelite touch, yet strangely inferior to his in breadth of grasp, in grandeur of simplicity, and in powers of artistic construction.

* The *Morte d'Arthur*, or the Passing of Arthur, was the *first*
published poem of Tennyson's Arthurian series ; while the *Coming of
Arthur*, was among the later, if not the *latest* published of the *Idylls
of the King.*

CHAPTER IV.

Analysis of the Arthurian Epic—The Bards and the Chroniclers.

IN this and the following chapter, we shall endeavour to give a concise summary of the Arthurian Cyclus or Epic, tracing it through the three distinctly marked versions of the story, the Anglo-Kymric or Cambrian; the Franco-Kymric or Breton, and the Anglo-Norman or English; and when we arrive at the twelfth and thirteenth century romances of the trouvères, we shall endeavour to throw these detached tales into the form of a connected narrative so as to present a clear-cut outline of the cyclus as a whole, from the birth of King Arthur to the time when the shades of death close around the broken spirit of Sir Lancelot and utter darkness covers the entire scene.

In doing this, we shall have to bring into bold relief the history of the King, who, to a certain extent, is the central figure of the Round Table knights; yet we shall not, by so doing, in any respect lessen the interest which naturally gathers around the subject

of our ninth chapter, viz., the person and character
of the King; but shall be better prepared for a thor-
ough appreciation of his portrait as it is drawn by
later writers.

The first, most startling fact that meets us upon
the very threshold of this inquiry is the all but total
silence of the oldest Welsh bards and of early Welsh
and Saxon historians upon the subject of Arthur.

Llywarch Hên, or Llywarch the Aged, one of the
finest of Kymric poets, began his career as soldier-
bard in the army of Cornwall, and sings of the death
of his patron and friend Geraint in a deadly encounter with the Saxons.   In this Elegy upon the " Death
of Geraint," which is acknowledged by the ablest
critics of Welsh literature to be genuine, occurs a
stanza in which Arthur's name is mentioned for the
first time in Welsh song.   This, which we may call
the Arthurian stanza, is the concluding one of the
first part of the poem and is evidently introduced
as an effective ending to the line of thought which
the poet had been following out in the previous
stanzas.

The Elegy opens with a characteristic eulogy of
the warrior-chief of Devon :

When Geraint was born the portals of heaven opened ;
The Christ granted the prayers of men,
Prosperity and glory to Britain.

The poet then proceeds to describe the battle of Longport and depicts the scene most vividly; the thick mist hanging over the battle-field; the horses up to their knees in blood and covered with a gory foam; the dead, massed in heaps on the green sward; the warriors red with blood; the cries of carnage and flames of burning ruins—these, and other horrors of the struggle the aged bard pictures with the weird imagination of an eye-witness; and as a climax to the scene of blood, he tells of the death of Geraint:

> At Longport was Geraint slain,
> The valiant chief of the woodlands of Devon,
> Slaying the enemy in his fall.

Then, as though the intense sorrow of the bard for the taking off of his lord could be assuaged only by the thought of swift retribution, he adds:

> Yn Llongborth llas i Arthur
> Gwyr dewr cymmynynt a dur
> Ammherawdyrr llyiadyr llavur.

At Longport were slain by Arthur,
Valiant warriors, who smote with the steel;
(Arthur) the commander of armies, the director of the
      works (of war).

In another poem on the death of his own sons, who were killed on the field of battle, we hear the sorrowing of the aged Llywarch for heroes who were adorned with the golden chain, the mark of high military command.

In the opening stanza the poet mourns his favourite child Gwenn and pictures him as having watched the foe, from the banks of the Leven, the night before he was killed; and then bursts forth as though his valiant son reminded him of a still greater warrior :

Gwenn watched . . . there, on the spot whence
      Arthur ne'er withdrew ;

referring doubtless to the site of the desperate battle in which Arthur (according to Nennius) fought and vanquished his Saxon foes.

If there is one thing clearly established, by the poems of Llywarch Hên, it is that during the sixth century Arthur was at the head of the petty, independent sovereignties in the South of Britain and was commander-in-chief in their wars with the Saxons, and that Geraint, son of Erbin, was his subordinate in arms and subject to his orders.

It is also beyond dispute that Llywarch bestows greater praise upon warriors who served under Arthur's command, than upon the commander-in-chief himself. In the battle of Longport which Arthur directed, it was the valour of Geraint that

arrested the bard's notice. Arthur is simply mentioned as the commander and conductor of the war,
while Geraint is celebrated with " dignified peri-
phrase."

That Arthur was a courageous warrior is unquestionable ; but that he was the irresistible warrior of
the later histories and romances, a hero from whom
kings and nations sank back in panic, is disproved
by the meagre encomiums of contemporary bards.*

If we look to the oldest Cambrian poems, we find
that they have, for their central figure, not Arthur,
but a famous warrior named Urien, the patriot chief
who led the Kymry of the North of Britain in their
struggle against the forces of Ida the Angle. It is
Urien rather than Arthur whose praises the old bards
delight to celebrate.

> May I never smile if I praise not Urien.

And again :

> I should have ceased to be merry if Urien had per-
ished.

So sings Taliéssin, and the strain is repeated, in
various forms, in many of his poems.

This comparative silence of the bards of the sixth
century with regard to the historic Arthur becomes
complete as we approach the dawn of prose history.

*Vide Note I.

The Welsh Gildas, author of the *De Excidio Britanniæ*, the first Latin historian of Britain, does not
even mention Arthur's name.

The Venerable Bede, the great Saxon historian of
the eight century, whose *Historia Ecclesiastica* is the
chief source from which we derive our information
respecting the early history of the Anglican Church
and of England, makes no allusion whatsoever to
Arthur.

Now, simply because no early bard relates the
story of Arthur's great exploits, and because early
historians are silent on this subject, this, in itself, is
no insuperable argument against his actual existence
at the time when he is reported to have lived ; nor is
it a reason for discrediting his renown as a military
chieftain.

It must be remembered that the earliest recorders
of historic facts have, in every country, been the
bards, or men holding a similar position though
called by a different name.   Historians proper, belong to a later age.   These bards or minstrels, who
were men of genius and whose productions have
lived, were invariably attached to the court of some
powerful chieftain whose praises, whether or not deserved, they were paid to sing ; and the natural consequence of this, was the celebration of the deeds of
those who maintained a bard and the silence of the

poet with respect to those who were not sufficiently wealthy to do so.   At the risk of anticipating what we may subsequently say, we may mention the fact, that all the earliest accounts of Arthur agree in stating that he was a "petty prince," and that there were in Britain "many more noble."   Hence it is not surprising, but, on the contrary, simply what we might expect *à priori* that the heroic deeds of Arthur should never have been sung by the older bards, who were intent on acquiring rich gifts in return for their panegyrics on the more powerful chiefs by whom they were maintained.

Llywarch Hên was attached to the court of Geraint; Taliéssin to the court of Urien ; while Arthur, so far as we know, had no one of the bards in his retinue to sing his valiant deeds.

Moreover, the silence of professed historians need not astonish us.   Of Gildas, we know next to nothing, and can speak with certainty neither as to his parentage, his native land, nor even his name.   The period when he lived has been called in question, and even the works of which he is the reputed author. He quotes no book but the Bible, and in the preface to his history he candidly confesses, " it is my present purpose to relate the deeds of an indolent and slothful race rather than the exploits of those who have been valiant in the field."   It is no wonder therefore that the very name of Arthur is omitted by such a writer of history. But with Bede the case is somewhat different. Gildas wrote at the latest, only one hundred and fifty years after the Arthurian era, and might be expected to know something of the valiant deeds of his countrymen, at least from tradition. But Bede did not live until three hundred years after this epoch, and does not profess to relate what had happened before his own time except upon the authority of older writers; hence, his silence upon this matter is not surprising.

To disbelieve in the historic existence of such a personage as Arthur simply shows an unhealthy scepticism. If merciless critics, after having scoured the whole field of Welsh and Saxon literature prior to the ninth century, and finding little more than the bare mention of the name of Arthur, undertake to deny that such a being ever existed, we must call upon them to explain some very stubborn facts. We must ask the critic to explain how it comes to pass that the figure of a real, historic Arthur first found its way into Welsh literature; for were we to admit (which we do not) that the stanzas relating to Arthur, in Llywarch Hên's accredited writings, are interpolations, still the form of character of the language proves beyond dispute, that they must have been inserted at a very early day, and one not

far removed from the period when the Arthur of
Llywarch's poems was commonly believed to have
been fighting in the South of Britain.   But this is
not all.   We must ask the critic, if he denies the
existence of a historic Arthur, to account for the
mention of our hero in later Welsh tales, where he
looms forth, shrouded in the mists of an earlier age,
and indistinct in outline, but, nevertheless, too grand
a shadow not to have had some reality behind it.

We must ask the critic, moreover, to account for
the very presence of those Breton ballads which
exist among the peasantry of Little Britain, just
over the Channel from Cornwall; to explain the
meaning of many names of places which we find
there, like Lyonnesse, doubtless named by Cornish
refugees in memory of the place where

> King Arthur's Table, man by man,
> Had fall'n .   .   .   about their lord,
> King Arthur.

We must call upon him to explain what the Breton
peasants meant, not two centuries ago, when at
their feasts they used to cry out passionately:

No ! King Arthur is not dead, he will come again.

The burden of proof is on the side of the sceptic.
Critics may deny Arthur's existence if they will;
they may translate him to the land of myth or fable;

they may take whatever course they prefer, only they
must explain, if they can, on any other hypothesis
than that of an actual, historic Arthur, the living
testimony to his existence which is engraved deep
in the hearts, the literature, and even the pastimes
of the Kymry of Britain and of·France.

That he actually lived, no one can reasonably
doubt who has read the literature of Wales, Cornwall, and Brittany; and the only question that need
detain us is, what was his real character when stripped
of those romantic tales which have made him a world-
renowned hero.

The cumulative evidence of Welsh and Armorican
traditions, poems, and romances, forces the conclusion upon the mind that, while the Kymry in Britain
were fighting a deadly battle for the possession of
their ancestral lands, Arthur, by his heroic bravery,
stamped his image upon the unwritten records of his
country, and, dying, left behind him a memory dear
to the national heart, though unsung by the bards
of his own day.*

It is not until the ninth century that Arthur is
mentioned in any historical work, and then he appears in the *Historia Britonum*, or History of the
Britons, commonly attributed to a Welshman named
Nennius. "The magnanimous Arthur," writes this

* *Vide* Note J.

historian, (" with all the kings and military force of Britain, fought against the Saxons, and *although there were many more noble than himself*, yet he was twelve times chosen their commander, and was as often conqueror.) In the eighth battle . . . Arthur bore the image of the Holy Virgin, mother of God, upon his shoulders, and through the power of Our Lord Jesus Christ and the Holy Mary, put the Saxons to flight, and pursued them the whole day with great slaughter. In the twelfth battle . . . Arthur penetrated to the hill of Badon, and in this engagement nine hundred and forty fell by his hand alone, no one but the Lord affording him assistance. In all these engagements (the (Britons) He were successful, for no strength can avail against the will of the Almighty."

In this account, we have the first extant historic mention in prose of Arthur, and naturally enough as it was written by an ecclesiastic we have a religious element introduced into that which was a plain historical fact. Granted that the Arthurian stanzas above quoted are genuine, still the bard speaks of Arthur as a warrior only, while Nennius clothes him with an air of sanctity; states him to have borne the image of the Virgin on his shield; in fact, draws upon an ecclesiastical imagination rather than upon authentic history.

As we approach the remains of Cambrian poetry from the sixth to the tenth century, preserved in the *Myvyrian Archaiology*, we seem to be entering a luminous cloud of myth, fable, and poetic fancy: a mythological haze hangs over every person and scene, till even the outlines of the historic characters of former days can scarcely be discerned in this thick, poetic mist.

Among these remains, we find a poem attributed to Taliéssin, in which Arthur is represented as the son of Uther Pendragon. Here Uther is king of the Shades, the mysterious and veiled Being, the appointer of battles, with the rainbow as his buckler. He appears as a kind of Mars, the genius of war. In fact, Uther is here a purely mythological personage. Even when paying his addresses to Arthur's mother he assumes the form of a cloud, in Welsh *Gorlas*, which the French trouvère transforms into Gorlois, Duke of Cornwall.

In the same poem Arthur, the son of Uther Pendragon, is the chief of battles and the honour of Cornwall. Nothing can resist his valour; and they christen him " Arthur of the miraculous sword." The bardic synod chants in his praise, " Be Arthur blessed according to the rites of the assembled bards. Glory to the countenance which flashes in the fight when all around is strife." He receives from his father the

sword which this pseudo-Taliéssin calls "the great
Glaive of the Mighty Enchanter." He undertakes
great expeditions, captures cities innumerable, and
subdues tracts of country wholly unknown to modern
geographers; finally he falls at the battle of Camlan
and is seen no more. Another bard states that he was
translated to the skies and became the constellation
Ursa Major, called, in Welsh, Arthur's Chariot.

As we issue, once again, from this realm of myth
and fable, the figure of Arthur stands out in a less
unearthly light.

In the Arthurian tales in the *Mabinogion* * the
King holds his court at Caerleon. He is represented
as sitting in the centre of his hall of state on a seat
of green woven twigs, with a carpet of flame-coloured
satin under his feet, and a crimson cushion under
his elbow. There is but little etiquette observed, and
all passes in almost a bourgeois fashion. The Prince
goes to sleep on his throne. His sword, he draws
only against the wild beasts of the forest and not
against the Saxon. He exhibits no sign of religious
belief, and were it not that, occasionally, he is present
when Mass is celebrated, one would think him anything but a Christian. His courtiers eat and drink
around him in utter wantonness, passing away the

* *Vide* "The Lady of the Fountain" in Lady Guest's translation
of the *Mabinogion.*

time in telling stories, while the Queen amuses herself with her sewing in the recess of the palace
window.

In all these Cambrian or Welsh accounts, whether
historic, quasi-historic, or purely mythologic, neither
Arthur nor his knights as yet appear in the midst
of the tournament, each bearing the colours of his
favourite lady, fighting while her eyes are upon him,
and proud of having accomplished with success those
trials of skill and prowess which were necessary to
establish a title to her favour.

In other words, there is not a vestige of knight-
errantry nor those high sentiments of love and honour, none of that chivalry, in fact, which breathes
through the later romances and lends such a charm
to them. There is evidently, therefore, a gap between the Welsh ideas of Arthur and those of subsequent writers ; and presently we shall endeavour to
account for the introduction of chivalry and knight-
errantry into these famous tales.

It seems indisputable that the *romantic* Arthur is
to a great extent the creation of the Armorican
Kymry. Arthur, as depicted by the glowing fancy
of the Bretons, is neither the historic character of
the Welsh bards, nor the demi-god of later traditions,
nor the bourgeois king of the Mabinogion. He is
purely a poetic creation based on historic tradition.

The oldest Armorican poems, like the Welsh, represent him simply as a valiant warrior.   Others depict
him as protecting his country from the ravages of
giants and dragons.   With some, he even becomes
the friend of God and the *protégé* of the Saints, surpassing the bravest of his nation in valour, and the
scenes of his daring deeds are minutely pointed out.
Indeed, not content with merely singing his praises,
the popular religion sculptured him in granite and,
at the present day, in front of one of the churches
in Brittany may be seen a bas-relief representing the
ideal patriot, crown on head and sword in hand, over-
coming a dragon by the aid of St. Efflamon ; a work
clearly established as belonging to the end of the
eleventh or beginning of the twelfth century.   But
a final glory awaited Arthur in Armorica.   From
being a hero of poetry, celebrated by the popular
bards in ballads, or by less august persons in fireside
tales, he became an epic hero ; straggling tales, oral
traditions, and unwritten poems were collected and
doubtless remodelled ; more advanced notions of
chivalric heroism and Christian virtue were introduced, and the whole thrown into a fictional *Brut-y-
Brenhined* or *History of the Kings*, by some unknown
author, by the beginning of the twelfth century.

    We have already mentioned the Latin history of
Geoffrey of Monmouth.   In the introduction to his

work he states that while studying the history of the kings of Britain, and wondering why Gildas and Bede had not made mention of those who lived prior to the Christian era, nor of Arthur and many others, he was agreeably surprised by a request from Walter Calenius, Archdeacon of Oxford, to translate a book from the British tongue which Walter had brought from Brittany.

As we saw in the last chapter, Geoffrey's translation of this work created a most profound impression all over England. It was devoured with the utmost avidity by all classes, and so lasting was the effect which it produced, that even the French romancers, while writing a distinct version of the legend, still followed, (and were compelled to follow,) the outline so artistically sketched by Geoffrey.

The story as narrated by this famous Chronicler falls naturally into three sections. The first extends from the birth of King Arthur to the end of his conquest of Gaul and his second coronation as King. The second opens with the coming of the famous Roman embassy, and closes with the news of Modred's treachery and attempt to carry off queen Guinevere. The third section commences with the sudden return of Arthur to Britain, and ends with the final battle of Camlan and death of the King.

In this so-called *History*, Arthur is represented as
the son of king Uther Pendragon and Igerna, a
lady celebrated for her beauty and formerly the
wife of Gorlois, Duke of Cornwall. After Uther's
death, which happened in consequence of his drink-
ing water from a poisoned spring, Arthur, then a
youth of fifteen, is crowned King at a general assembly of the nobles at Silchester at the hands of the
holy Dubricius, Archbishop of Caerleon, the City of
Legions. Then follows a long series of his con-
quests carried on against the Saxons and Scots. He
subsequently subdues all England and Scotland with
the assistance of his nephew Hoel of Armorica, and
then proceeds to annex Ireland, Iceland, the Ork-
neys, Norway, Dacia, Aquitaine, and the two Gauls,²
finishing with Paris, which he obtains as the prize
of a duel with Flollo, the Roman tribune and governor of the city. After the lapse of nine years, during which Gaul was finally reduced, he divides the
conquered territories among his principal adherents
and then returns in triumph to England.

Two incidents occur during this period which deserve notice ; (1) shortly before his Irish expedition
the King marries Guinevere, whom Geoffrey states to
have been descended from a noble Roman family ; and
(2) he comes into possession of the celebrated sword
Caliburn or Excalibur, which our author merely states

was made in the Isle of Avalon, and that Arthur employed it with considerable effect at the battle before Bath, killing with his own hand four hundred and seventy men. Thus ends the first of the three main divisions into which all the accounts of Arthur seem naturally to fall.

The second section opens with the King's coronation for the second time together with his Queen. The place determined upon is Caerleon on Usk, and thither assemble all the crowned heads whom Arthur had made tributary, besides an immense concourse of knights and ladies, and there the ceremony is performed with the utmost magnificence by Dubricius assisted by two other Archbishops and four kings. Shortly afterwards, an unwelcome embassy arrives from Lucius Tiberius the Roman Emperor, demanding in haughty terms from Arthur, not only the restoration of kingdoms he had torn from Rome, but also payment of tribute in accordance with the custom of his less powerful ancestors. After consultation with his council, Arthur decides for war and determines himself to become the aggressor. He leaves his kingdom and his wife in charge of his nephew and natural son, Modred, and sets out with an immense fleet and army for France, having first received intelligence that Lucius and his allies were in motion towards him. During his voyage, he dreams a portentous dream of a fearful contest between a flying fiery dragon and a flying boar, ending in the destruction of the latter, an omen which he interprets in his own favour. Subsequently two engagements take place between the Britons and the Romans, in which the former are victorious though not without the loss of several important knights on the side of the Britons, among whom were Bedivere and Kay, and on the side of the Romans, the Emperor himself and several of his allies.

This victory achieved, Arthur proceeds onwards towards Rome, which, however, *he does not reach* by reason of the intelligence brought him, when *about to cross the Alps*, of Modred's treasonous revolt and carrying off of Queen Guinevere. And so the second section ends.

In the third division, Arthur returns in hot haste and a fierce contest partly naval, partly on land, takes place at Richborough where Modred attempts to oppose his Monarch's landing. It is here that Gawaine meets his death, to the great sorrow of the King. As soon as the report of his return gets abroad, the Queen flees from York to Caerleon, and takes the veil in order to avoid the possible fury of her husband, while Modred collects his forces and occupies Winchester. Arthur besieges him there and a battle ensues in which Modred is defeated. Thence, the traitor retreats to Cornwall, and makes a stand on the river Cambula where the last of Arthur's contests, that "great battle in the West," takes place. The King and Modred meet in single combat, the latter is slain outright, but Arthur is mortally wounded and all the principal knights on both sides perish in the fray. Arthur is carried from the field of battle to the Isle of Avalon to be cured of his wounds, and gives up his crown to Cador's son, Constantine, in the year of our Lord 542.

Such is a brief analysis of the account given by Geoffrey "Arturus" as he was called, and whom we have designated the first of the Chroniclers.

As this is the first collective account of poems, traditions, oral tales, and *on dits* of the Arthurian romances in Brittany and Wales, it deserves a somewhat closer scrutiny. This work was styled a *History* and soon became extensively popular. Indeed, within a century after its first appearance, it was generally adopted by writers on English history, and during several successive centuries but few dared to speak against its veracity.

But the most important question which this *History* suggests is this: To what extent are Chivalry and Knight-errantry recognised in this work? As we have seen, this, which is the most charming

feature in modern versions, is totally absent in all
previous Welsh writers.   In Geoffrey, however, it
is distinctly visible.   Here we find Arthur with the
expression, the animation, and the relief which the
poetical painting of the Armorican bards have given
him.   He retains but little of the king of the old
Welsh stories.   His thoughts, his words, his acts, are
those of a knightly king.   He enters in full panoply
into the world of chivalry, the very dawn of which
illumines his features.   He belongs not so much to
the Cambrians as to all civilised Europe.   His
knights Kai and Bedwyr become French ; one is of
La Manche, the other of Anjou.   He has the Cross
engraved on his sword, and even on his helmet he
bears the sign of the Christian as a crown.   He stands
before us in the flush of youth, perfect in form, handsome in feature, and noble in character.   The Britons
love and follow him into the thickest of dangers ; the
national saints protect him ; the pagan Saxons fear
him as their scourge, and attack him only by treason.
He is brave as the Charlemagne of story, nor is he
a less chivalric ideal of the Christian king of the
eleventh century than Charlemagne.   He is led by
love of glory and adventure beyond the limits of
his own narrow kingdom.   He holds full court in
all the cities of Western Europe, even at Paris, and
his sword glitters wherever French or Norman arms

have flashed. He is the equal of Charlemagne in point of regalia, for he has a right to thirty crowns. He chooses a queen, the superior of all the ladies of the world, a divine Beatrice, more angelic than any that poets have ever sung ; (he carries her likeness with him into the combat as a mark of affection, as a charm against disaster, as a sure token of victory. He is *the* knight *par excellence*, and when he draws the sword his cry of war is *Marie la Vièrge*.

In the so-called *History* of Geoffrey, one of the most remarkable Welshmen of the twelfth century, we thus find Arthur an ideal of the purest chivalry and surrounded by all the pomp and circumstance of knight-errantry.

If Geoffrey's statement that he translated his work from a Breton manuscript were universally acknowledged to be true, this would go far to establish the fact that the Kymry of Armorica infused into these romances, the rich colouring of adventure or knight-errantry which they have ever since possessed. But this is not the case. On the contrary, Geoffrey's statement is regarded by many critics as containing very suspicious elements. The mysterious monk of Oxford, taking an unexplained trip to France, and bringing home a priceless manuscript, which some unnamed person had found, and which had been secretly unearthed and carefully preserved until this

Oxford cleric made his appearance on the stage, all these touches were familiar devices of aspiring authors of that day, to give their fictions the semblance of fact and reality. We cannot forget the clever forgeries of Chatterton, which deceived even so acute a critic as Walpole; or the fictions of De Foe which so far misled the hard, logical mind of Lord Chatham that he actually once quoted the *Memoirs of a Cavalier* as genuine history. Still, are the circumstances connected with this manuscript really as suspicious as some would have us believe? One fact is certainly suspicious. The manuscript from which Geoffrey states that he copied the major part of his *History* cannot now be found. It is lost, hopelessly lost. But Geoffrey's translation remains, and if we cannot bring the famous manuscript itself to a critical test, we can at least cross-examine the translation.

If then, we scrutinise this *History* closely and critically, we are met by some very interesting results. We find tales, traditions, and legends imbedded in Geoffrey's narrative, which we recognise at once as Breton or Armorican, and not Welsh; for they can be traced to Breton traditions still extant and to which the Welsh have nothing similar in the whole of their literature. They are indigenous to Armorica, and their presence in Geoffrey's *History* is undeniable proof that he received these, at least, from Brittany.

On the other hand, a careful and critical analysis discloses the existence of tales, traditions, and legends, which we recognise at once as Welsh and not Breton ; for they can be traced to Welsh traditions still extant and to which the Bretons have no parallel. These, it is equally certain, were never found in any Breton manuscript.

The truth seems to be that Geoffrey did translate from some manuscript, now lost, the greater part of his Arthurian tales, but that being a Welshman and living on the borders of Wales and being familiar with Welsh traditions, he occasionally inserted tales and legends from the Welsh storehouse of fiction.

The question then recurs, was it the Kymry of Wales or the Kymry of Brittany that contributed the spirit of knight-errantry, which is so conspicuous in this work? Certainly not the Kymry of Wales. Nothing could be more remote from the British conception than knight-errantry or the spirit of adventure, neither of which had place in the Kymric character in pre-Norman times. After that period, the love of adventure gradually insinuated itself into the national character, and showed itself during the Crusades when the Cambrian knights joined the standard of religious fanatics, and mixed, on terms of intimacy, with those of other countries. But previous to the twelfth century this spirit was totally wanting.

8

It is to the Normans, and not to the Kymry, that the Arthurian Romance is indebted for its spirit of adventure and its knight-errantry. Of all the people of ancient Europe, the Normans showed themselves, during the period which preceded the rise of romance literature, to be the most intrepid and adventurous. This attribute, which they inherited from their sea-faring ancestors, they always retained, and when they settled down in Neustria, afterwards Normandy, as conquerors, this was still their ruling passion. They were, moreover, practical plagiarists, imitators, and improvers. Whenever their neighbours invented or possessed anything worthy of admiration, the sharp inquisitive Norman thrust his aquiline nose. From a Frank castle or a Lombard church to a Breton ballad or romance, there was the sharp, eager face of the Norman in the van. Moreover, the Norman invariably intermarried with the people among whom he settled and borrowed and improved their literature. From the time that he settled in Neustria, Brittany became a sort of fief of Normandy, and hence the Breton literature was made tributary. The Norman did not invent Arthurian literature, but improved and embellished what he found already invented in Brittany. It was the Norman minstrel who infused into it the spirit of adventure and knight-errantry, and hence its ap-

pearance in the history of Geoffrey and in the later
Breton and Welsh literature.

With respect to the Chivalry of these Arthurian
tales the case is somewhat different. Whence, it
may be asked, sprang a system which rendered possible the portrayal of a Lancelot, an Elaine, and a
Galahad? How comes it that the mediæval knight
should be represented as the impersonation of all
which the natural man admires and which saints
battle to become? Are we to look to the Christianised Kymry, whom Augustine found in Britain, or
even to their compatriots in Brittany, as the originals of such spotless ideality? Perhaps not. Chivalry in its least developed form belongs to Man as
the image of God. We find it in the munificence of
Joshua in his partition of the land of Canaan, and
in the courtesy of David to Saul. We find it in
classic times in the delineation of Achilles, and Hector, and Horatius. It shows itself in old Teutonic
valour and reverence for women. We find it among
the Normans, tinged with the military colouring
which Charlemagne had given to it. And finally,
we see it in Saxon England before ever the haughty
Norman had

High mettled the blood in our veins.

But to understand the full significance of the term,

as it appears in these romances, we must examine
the system as it existed in both France and England
during the twelfth century.

When these romances were being fashioned, Chivalry consisted in a double triad of Loves:

I.—The *Love of God,* and as a natural consequence the defence of Holy Church.

II.—The *Love of the Ladies,* and as a natural
consequence the defence of Woman as *woman.*

III.—The *Love of Country,* and as a natural
consequence the defence of Society at large.

But these external characteristics of chivalry had
corresponding internal laws which formed a second
triad of Loves:

I.—The *Love of Loyalty* in its broadest sense;
loyalty to God; loyalty to the Church; loyalty to
the King; loyalty to one's fellows, even though enemies, and loyalty to self.

II.—The *Love of Courtesy;* consisting not so much
in the knowledge of ceremonial customs (though this
was not disregarded) as in that true modesty, self-denial, and respect for others which flow spontaneously from the heart of the true gentleman.

III.—The *Love of Munificence,* or the despisal of
money for its own sake.

This double triad of Loves constituted the very
soul of chivalry, and formed the strongest conceiva-

ble incentive to virtue in woman, and ideal perfection in man.

At the period in question, every baronial castle of the wealthier nobles, throughout Europe, was a school of chivalry. Every child of gentle birth, at the age of seven, was taken from the custody of women and placed in charge of men of the warrior class. Henceforth he became, not only pupil, but servant and attendant. He was not only a *damoiseau*, but a page or valet (for these words had not then lost their nobility of meaning). Here, in the castle, surrounded by knights and ladies, he was taught first and foremost the duty of *obedience*, in order that he might become the true *knecht*, the true servant, the true knight. In the field, he learned to ride and guide his horse with skill; in the armoury, to use sword and lance with dexterity; on the tilting ground, to acquit himself as a miniature knight.

But let us follow the stripling into the tilting ground where the novices take their morning exercise. Close by the meadow is the massive castle with its battlements, portcullis, and drawbridge, while fringing the meadow are the pavilions of the various knights, decked with armorial flags of brilliant colours, and the knights themselves are there, watching the tyros of the lists at their morning exercise. The youthful page, armed *cap-a-pie*, in boy armour, mounted on a pony, rides full galop and with poised lance, at a large wooden figure of a man that stands in the middle of the ground. The figure is mounted on a pedestal on which it revolves when struck, the arms of the figure being stretched out at full length, while from either hand dangles a long wooden sword attached to the hand by a ring. The novice rides at the figure as at an enemy, his hand grasping firmly the tournament spear, and his boyish face a-glow with excitement. He strikes it, but not in true knightly fashion ; the figure swings round on its pivot and in doing so deals the unskilful youth a stinging blow with the wooden sword which it holds in its outstretched hand. The spectators laugh and so the rest try their skill. What a school for physical training! what a fertile soil for ambition ! How could these fledgelings fail to venerate the veteran knight whose strength and prowess had been tested in many a joust and battle?

Or, follow these valets when the military exercises of the day are ended. If there is a chase in the hunting-field, they are required to attend ; if the Baron's guests are to take an equestrian promenade, they are expected to follow. If there is a message to be delivered, they are sent on the errand. In the baronial dining-hall, they alone serve the lordly company, passing around the meats and filling the goblets with wine. But it is no menial duty they perform ; they are serving men, whom they regard as their ideals of all that is noble in manhood ; and ladies, who are the goddesses of chivalric worship, and they too, young as they are, share in the adoration paid them.

But this was not all. The lordly baron, on his part, took especial care that his *protégés* were duly instructed in all that appertained to Holy Church. The military exercises of the field and castle prepared these novices for the defence of Society. The profound reverence which on every hand they saw paid to damoiselles and ladies, trained them for the defence of Woman. But the love of God and defence of Holy Church were inculcated by the clergy. These were not duties that a knight could be expected to oversee. It took the keen wit of the priesthood, and the keen eye of the Church to train up these future barons in the dogmas of the Catholic faith, and the preservation of the hierarchy ; and the task was accomplished with marvellous thoroughness.

At the age of fourteen, the page rose to the rank of Squire, and thenceforth entered upon duties which pointed more directly to his future career. But here the Church stepped in. So important and memora-

ble an event in the life of the youth could not be
allowed to pass without religious rites. The sword
which, in future, was to be his distinguishing weapon,
was placed upon the altar of the church, solemnly
blessed, and presented to the postulant, on condition that it should be employed solely in the interest of religion and honour. His duties, henceforth,
were of a more practical character. He was escurier
or master of the stables. He broke the picked horses
to all the manœuvres of war. To him was entrusted
the sole charge and keeping of the armour of the
knight. He alone might equip the knight's horse on
all occasions ; a task of no small responsibility in
those days. If the knight rode on his palfrey and
unarmed, (which he always did when an encounter
was not imminent,) his squires followed leading the
war-horse, and bearing his armour. If a combat was
about to take place, it was the duty of the squires
to arm the knight, and see that every clasp and buckle
was firmly fastened and secure ; to lead up the *grand
cheval,* and to assist his lord when he mounted his
high horse. As soon as the battle or duel began,
the squires in attendance took up their position behind their lord, and the first shock of the encounter
past, their *rôle* commenced. If the knight was over-
borne and unhorsed, they instantly came to his rescue,
with a fresh horse if his was wounded, or if the knight

himself was hurt, shielding him from the blows of his
antagonist even at the risk of their own lives, until he
was either remounted or carried safely out of the
battle.

In the castle, the squire was permitted to penetrate
farther than the simple page within the sacred pre-
cincts of the family.   He had a recognised rank
among the inmates, and was required to be present
at private reunions or more public gatherings.   He
was the Master of Ceremonies when distinguished
guests visited the castle, and initiated foreign princes
and other noble visitors into the mysteries of national
etiquette.   If, as page, he had often sighed for the
consecrated sword and the smiles of a lady elect, so,
as squire, he looked eagerly forward to the crested
helmet, the massive armour, the heraldic coat, and
the gilded spurs which the knight wore on the field;
or to the richer silks and costlier furs which he wore
in the castle halls; perhaps, too, to the badge which
the knight displayed in tournament, the token of
his lady's favour.

At length, the severe training of another seven
years successfully past, knighthood duly followed.

On the eve of his consecration, the candidate confessed his sins.   His armour was placed on the altar
of the church, and there, alone in the sacred building, the postulant watched the livelong night in

fasting and prayer.   As soon as morning dawned, he
was led to the bath ; then the white garment was
thrown over him (a kind of chrisom), godfathers were
appointed ; a lock of hair was cut off indicating a
modified form of tonsure ; and other rites were performed, all symbolical of the purity, humility, and
loyalty which the Church required of the true knight.
Then he heard Mass ; his arms were solemnly blessed ;
and he was knighted by Bishop, priest, or some knight
of high rank, in the name of God, of St. George, and
of St. Michael the Archangel.   The newly created
knight then swore to speak the truth ; to maintain
the right ; to protect women, the poor, and the distressed ; to practice courtesy ; to pursue the Infidels ;
to despise riches and luxury ; and to maintain his
honour at every cost.   He then received the Blessed
Sacrament in confirmation of his oath, and so the
ceremony ended.

The young noble was now a knight, so far as the
Church was concerned ; but the laws of chivalry demanded something additional.   He must now " win
his spurs."   His appearance in the field was, henceforth, the same as that of the proudest knight, in
every respect save one ; his shield, unlike theirs, was
plain, unemblazoned, wanting as yet the coat-of-arms
which distinguished one knight from another, and
which was equivalent to their names being inscribed

on their shields. If the novice appeared in battle
or tournament he did so as an "unknown knight."
So Sir Lancelot, when he did not wish to be known,
borrowed Lavaine's unemblazoned shield. But as
soon as the young knight had once shown his prowess in the field, his spurs were won, and his shield
might then carry armorial bearings. "Is my son
dead, or is he hurt?" asked Edward III., at the
battle of Cressy, of those who begged him to come
to the assistance of the Black Prince. "No, sire,"
replied the barons; "but he is hardly matched."
"Well," said the King, "then suffer him to win his
spurs for, if God be pleased, I will that this day's
work be his and the honour thereof."

From this time forward the career of the knight was
considered to depend less upon himself than upon his
God and his lady. The three gems in the coronet of
knighthood—loyalty, courtesy, munificence—might
not be suffered to lose their brilliancy. Fidelity to an
engagement, whether made to the Church, to the
lady he served, or to his fellows, was the noblest
characteristic of a knight. "False" and "recreant"*
were the epithets which he had to endure who had
swerved from a plighted engagement, even toward
an enemy, and the terrible degradations and "baf-
fullings" inflicted upon the recreant knight who

* *Vide* Note K.

had broken his knightly oath, show the detestation in which such a character was held. It is true that this loyalty was, at times, carried to fantastic lengths. We read, how the knights of the respective countries, during the wars of England and France fought, as they fought at the tournament, bearing, over their armour, scarfs and devices as the livery of their ladies elect; some indeed going so far as to wear a covering over one of their eyes and vowing, for the sake of their ladies, never to see with both, until they should have signalised their prowess in the field! Still, fantastic as it was, the goddesses of this idolatry knew but too well the value of such worship to think of turning it into derision; they knew that it was the result of ideal fidelity, and that it was sure to lead to ideal heroism.

And what a grace the virtue of *courtesy* must have thrown over the stern habits of the social life of that period. Doubtless the deep reverence for the Blessed Virgin Mary, as the ideal of womanhood, had somewhat to do with this. But the strict training of the baronial castle had still more. From early boyhood, the page was taught to regard every lady as peerless; as a being, to whom adoration was due, and toward whom he was to act, on all occasions, with sterling modesty and profound respect. By a decree of the Council of Cleremont he was required at the age of

twelve to take an oath, before the Bishop of the
Diocese, that he would defend to the uttermost the
oppressed, the widow, and the orphan ; and that
women, both married and single, when in distress,
should have his special protection. A similar oath,
as we have already seen, was required of the candidate for knighthood. How could it be otherwise
than that the knight should regard woman with
ideal courtesy, since she was his especial charge ; or
that woman, in return, should regard him with feelings of loving pride, and strive to be worthy of his
worship ?

But this virtue of courtesy tended above all else to
soften down the natural roughness and cruelty of war.
The *Truce of God* and the *Peace of the King* * were
steps in the same direction. The knight, who upon
hearing that his mortal enemy was in want of wine,
stopped the siege, sent him a cask from his own sup-
plies under a flag of truce, and then continued the
war, was simply carrying out the true spirit of chivalry. It is the virtue of mediæval courtesy which
laid the basis of that indulgent treatment of prison-
ers, unknown to antiquity, but practised in modern
civilised warfare.

Valour, loyalty, courtesy, munificence, a love of
right, a hatred of oppression, these formed the code

* *Vide* Note L.

of a true knight of the twelfth century, and it is
because the essential attributes of chivalry are of
this imperishable nature, that it is laughed at only
by the half educated, and held in disrepute only
when ideality is lacking in the mind of a nation.

Chivalry was the production of no one court, and
of no one country.   It existed wherever Christianity
held sway.   It existed during the twelfth century
among all Christian nations, and resulted from a rest-
less aspiration after ideal perfection.   This craving
was due to the teachings of the Church.   Abstract-
ing a warrior from the province of history, making
him feel the impulses and speak the language of a
more civilised age, enriching him with all that cultivated minds deem good and noble, this, which we
find in the Arthurian Romance, could only have found
favour among ecclesiastics.   The fact that Arthur is
represented as having worn the image of the Virgin
on his shield and the Cross on his helmet ; that the
grandest events in his life, his coronation, and even
his wars, were hallowed by the most solemn rites of
Holy Church, these facts show an ecclesiastical influence.   It was not the bards or the chroniclers, as
such, but the clergy who gave that high religious colouring to popular traditions which has cast a pale
mellow light over subsequent romances.   It is the
infusion of the pure, the sublime, the immutable,

softening down the rugged outlines of the characters
of antique knights, and rendering more beautiful the
tournament or court festivity which, at the present
day, causes the Arthurs, the Lancelots, the Tristans,
and the Galahads to possess such a charm and fascination to the mind.

We have thus traced to their sources the three chief
elements in Geoffrey's *History*, viz.: the Adventurous,
the Chivalric, and the Religious; the first to the Normans; the second to Christianised Europe generally;
and the third to the Church; and are thus in a position to enter intelligently upon the subsequent history of this famous cyclus.

CHAPTER V.

Analysis of the Arthurian Epic.
The Romancers.

IN the last chapter we traced the Arthurian cyclus down to the time of Geoffrey of Monmouth the first of the Chroniclers. As we before said, the publication of this work marked a grand epoch in the history of romantic fiction in England and even in Europe. The Norman minstrels who, before this, had been put to their wits' end to devise new tales with which to amuse their lordly patrons, were now in possession of an inexhaustible fund of stories.

Wace, in his French metrical chronicle *Li Roman de Brut,* translating from the Latin of Geoffrey, adds little absolutely new matter, in the way of incident, to Geoffrey's account of Arthur; being content with amplifying and adorning his predecessor's prose *History.* Still, there is one point highly important to the perfection and unity of the epic on which the poems of the Welsh bards, the Welsh triads, the popular Welsh tales, the early traditions of Wales and even Geoffrey's work, maintain a profound silence; but which Wace mentions for the first time. We refer to the legend of the Round Table. It is in Wace's work that we first hear of this celebrated board. But even here, it appears only as a germ, the subject being dismissed with two short lines :

> Fist Arthur la roonde Table
> Dont Britons dient mainte fable.

Layamon, turning his back alike upon the courtly French of the palace and the scholastic Latin of the monastery, translated Wace's romance into good, native English, thus striking one of those deadly blows which ended in the triumph of the Saxon speech as the classical language of England. His version, however, unlike that of Wace, contains important additions to the story. It is in his work that we first hear of the presence of fairies at Arthur's birth. "So soon," says Layamon, "as Arthur came into the world, fairies received him ; they enchanted the child with magic most strong ; they gave him strength to be the best of all knights ; they gave him another gift, that he should be a rich king ; they gave him a third, that he should live long ; they gave to the prince virtues most good, so that he was most generous of all living men. These the fairies gave him, and thus the child thrived."

The Round Table legend, moreover, at Layamon's

9

hands, undergoes a quaint phase of development. "It saith in the tale that the king went to Cornwall; then there came to him anon one who was a crafty workman, and met the king and greeted him fairly: 'Hail, Arthur, noblest of kings, I am thine own man. I know of tree-works [carpentry]. I heard say, beyond the sea, that thy knights gan to fight at thy board; on midwinter's-day many fell, for their mickle pride wrought murderous play, and for their high lineage each would be within. But I will work thee a board exceeding fair that thereat may sit sixteen hundred and more, so that none may be without. And when thou wilt ride, thou mayest carry it with thee and set it where thou wilt, and then thou needest never fear, to the world's end, that ever any proud knight at thy board may make fight, for there shall the high be even with the low.'" Timber was brought and the board begun. In four weeks' time the work was completed. "At a high day the folk were assembled, and Arthur himself approached soon to the board and ordered all his knights to the board forth-right. When all were seated, then spake each with other; they all sate about, there were none without. Every sort of knight was there, exceeding well disposed; they were all seated, the high with the low. This was the same board that Britons boast of and say many sorts of leasing [false tales] respecting Arthur the king. Then was Arthur most high, his folk most fair; there was no knight well esteemed in Wales or in England, in Scotland or in Ireland, in Normandy or in France, in Flanders or in Denmark, or in any land, nor his deeds accounted brave unless he could discourse of Arthur and of his noble court, his weapons, and his garments, and his horsemen ; unless he could sing of Arthur the young, and of his strong knights, and of their great might, and of their wealth, and how well it became them. Then were he welcome in any place whereto he came even though he were at Rome."

The third point mentioned by Layamon, for the first time, is the romantic story of Arthur's voyage with the two ladies to Argante the Fair, in the Isle of Avalon, after the last great battle of Camlan. As the king is dying, he turns to Constantine and says: " I will fare to Avalon, to the fairest of all maidens, to Argante the queen, an elf most fair, and she shall make my wounds all sound, make me all whole with balm and healing draughts. And afterwards, I will come again to my kingdom and dwell with the Britons with mickle joy. Even with these words, there approached from the sea a little boat, floating with the waves, and two ladies therein wondrously formed, and they took Arthur anon and bare him quickly to the boat and laid him softly down, and forth they gan depart. The Britons believe yet that he is alive and dwelleth in Avalon with the fairest of all queens, and they ever yet expect when Arthur shall return."

Such, then, is the story of Arthur when stripped of all those adventures and marvels which have conferred on it as deep and undying a fascination as the venerable myths of Roman history have cast upon the earliest annals of imperial Rome. Such is the tale which our ancestors, not three centuries ago, gravely received as historical truth; yet, many a reader will doubtless find this version quite as new, perhaps more so, than many of the more marvellous editions of the story.

In no accounts which we have hitherto mentioned, do we find that array of knights surrounding Arthur, which we do in the later versions, and whose individual adventures form the greater part of the later romances. Even in the Chroniclers, Arthur stands out alone, is the true centre of the tales, and his knights occupy but subordinate positions and exercise little influence on his fortunes.

It is not till we come to the Romancers that the brilliant pageant of knightly heroes and heroines bursts into view, and it is now necessary, in order to make this sketch of the Arthurian cylus complete, to present a brief analysis of what these great writers accomplished.

We might give an abstract of that pleasantly jumbled condensation of former romances left us by Sir Thomas Malory; but we prefer to throw into the form of a connected narrative, the separate romances of the Norman trouvères, reduced to something like chronological order.

It will be remembered, that we divided the history of Arthur, as related by the Chroniclers, into three sections, the first ending with his firm establishment on the British throne and second coronation together with his queen; the second, terminating with the intelligence brought to the King, when about to cross the Alps, of Modred's treachery; and the third bringing the history of our hero to an end by the battle of Camlan. But even in this version there is an introductory chapter. There is a figure which looms forth in the dim background before ever we hear of King Arthur, or indeed of Uther Pendragon. It is the figure of Merlin, who emerges from a dark and shadowy past, just as Arthur himself, at the close of the version, vanishes into a dark and mysterious future.

This division of the cyclus into three sections, holds good with respect to the Romancers, if we make one or two important changes.* In the first place, although Merlin retains his position in the dim

* _Vide_ p. 149.

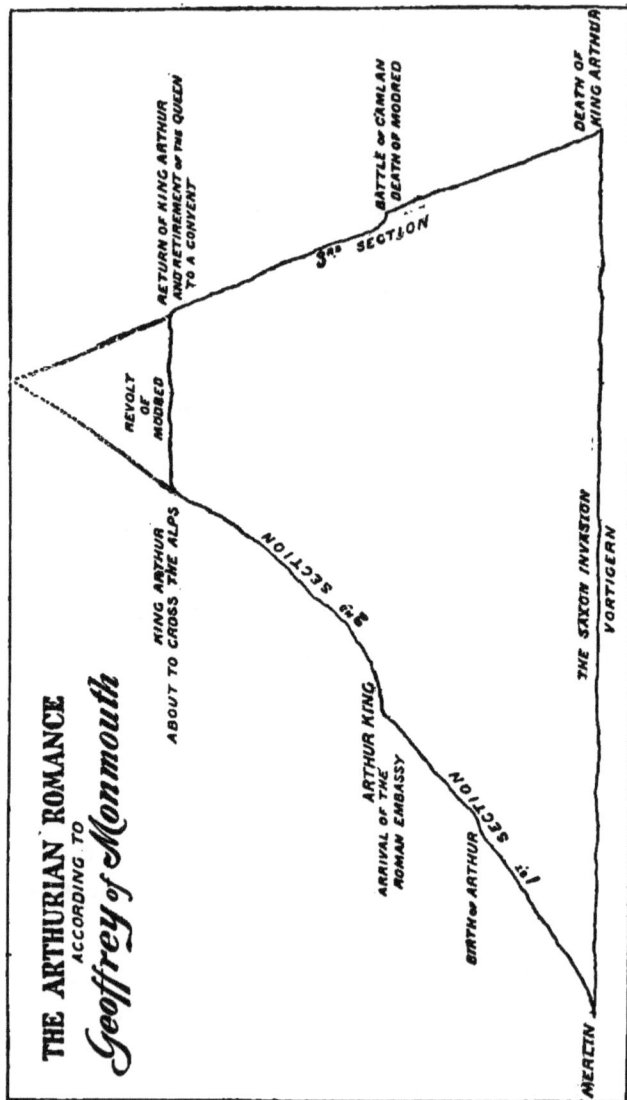

THE ARTHURIAN ROMANCE
ACCORDING TO
Geoffrey of Monmouth

MERLIN

THE SAXON INVASION

VORTIGERN

BIRTH OF ARTHUR

1ST SECTION

ARRIVAL OF THE
ROMAN EMBASSY

ARTHUR KING

2ND SECTION

KING ARTHUR
ABOUT TO CROSS THE ALPS

REVOLT
OF
MODRED

RETURN OF KING ARTHUR
AND RETIREMENT OF THE QUEEN
TO A CONVENT

3RD SECTION

BATTLE OF CAMLAN
DEATH OF MODRED

DEATH OF
KING ARTHUR

background, yet the early history of this mysterious being is not the true introduction to the Norman version. Here, there is a something which antedates even Merlin himself. It is the *Holy Graal*, the story of which connects the epic with apostolic Britain. But it is not a mere introduction; it forms the atmosphere of Norman fancy; it is the soul of the Norman romances; it is the point of unity in this Norman epic. *[it's also a lousy story]*

Moreover, in the version of the Romancers there are two additional sections. The Quest of the Holy Graal being peculiar to the tale as constructed by the Romancers, must be treated as a separate section. The adventures which compose this part of the epic, are placed by Walter Map between the conquest of Rome and the revolt of Modred, and hence, naturally, take their position as the third section; while that which we have hitherto called the third, we must henceforth style the fourth section.

Finally, the Romancers, in order to avoid the abrupt ending of the Chroniclers, have invented a concluding section reaching from the battle of Camlan, when the King fell mortally wounded, to the death of Guinevere, and the passing away of the repentant soul of Lancelot.

With this explanation, we will now proceed to the analysis of the story as told by the Romancers.

The story opens at Tintagil castle, a stronghold
of Gorlois, Duke of Cornwall. Uther Pendragon,
Arthur's father, is introduced to us as laying siege
to this castle with the avowed object of despoiling
the Duke of his beautiful wife, Igerna. But the castle is well garrisoned and resists all the forces which
Uther can bring against it. At this juncture Merlin,
with an Elijah-like suddenness, makes his appearance upon the scene and engages to bring about
Uther's marriage with Igerna on one condition,
viz.: that the king should grant him a single request.
The terms are agreed upon, and Uther is sworn
upon the four Evangelists to deliver to his (Merlin's) custody, whensoever he shall demand it, the
child, which then and there he predicts shall be born
of the marriage. By the magic arts of the great
seer the castle is taken that very night; Gorlois is
slain in the encounter, and on the morrow the king
and Igerna are wedded, to the great joy of the barons. In due time Arthur is born and Uther, in fulfilment of his oath, commands two knights and two
ladies to take the child, wrapped in a cloth of gold,
to the postern gate of the castle, and to deliver him
to a certain poor man whom they would find there
waiting to receive him. No sooner is the babe in
Merlin's possession, than the seer mysteriously disappears with his charge. Time and space present

no obstacles to him. He is no sooner gone, than we find the child in the arms of the noble wife of Sir Hector, a prince of Cornwall, and to her, as foster mother, the babe is entrusted; but not before Merlin has caused a holy man to christen him, and name him Arthur. Henceforth, we hear nothing of the royal child until Uther is lying upon his death-bed. Then, while the barons are standing around their dying chief, Merlin appears abruptly among them. " Sir," asks the crafty sage, " shall your sonne Arthur bee king after your dayes of this realme? " . . . " I give him Gods blessing and mine, and bid him pray for my soule, . . . and that he claime the crowne upon forfeiture of my blessing," said the king, in presence of his barons, and then yielded up the ghost.

After Uther's death, there was seen in the Cathedral church of London, one Sunday morning, before the high altar, a large stone with an anvil of steel upon it, and a sword fixed by its point in the anvil, and beneath, in letters of gold was the inscription : " *Who so pulleth out this sword of this stone and anvile, is rightwise king borne of England.*" By the advice of Merlin, Archbishop Dubricius proclaims a grand tournament, and knights from all quarters arrive, eager to essay the adventure of the sword, and all unsuccessful. Among them, comes Sir Hector

with his own son, Sir Kay and his foster son, the young
Arthur.   Sir Kay, having thoughtlessly left his sword
behind him, despatches Arthur to fetch it, who passing the church happens to look in, when his eye rests
upon the mystic sword, and to save himself the trouble
of riding farther, he dismounts and pulls it out of the
anvil.   Unconscious that he has performed any great
feat, he returns, and being questioned by Sir Hector,
tells how and where he had obtained it.   The knight,
convinced that his foster child is the rightful king,
is about to do " homage " when Arthur endeavours to
restrain him.   " ' Alas ! mine owne deare father . . .
why kneele you to me ? '   ' Nay, nay, my lord Arthur,' replies sir Hector, ' it is not so, I was never
your father ne of your bloud, but I wote well that
you are of an higher blood than I wende you were.' "
He then proceeds to tell him the whole story, how
Merlin had brought him, an unknown child, to the
castle, and how he and his wife had cared for him.
" Then Arthur made great mone when hee understood that sir Hector was not his father."   Time and
again, in the presence of the assembled barons, does
this unknown youth draw forth the mysterious sword,
the only one of them all, capable of performing the
adventure.   Time and again, do the barons, envious
and angry, succeed in getting the final award post-
poned.   But no delays avail them, and finally they

swear formal allegiance to Arthur and he is crowned
King.

After his coronation, however, there were many to
dispute his title to the throne. Many a battle rolled
across the plains of England before the young King
assured his sovereignty; in fact, a series of battles,
the counterparts of those detailed in the first section
of what we have called the History. In the romance,
however, we meet with a far less uniformity of success on the part of Arthur, who is indebted for his
life, more than once, to Merlin's skill.

Two foreign sovereigns, moreover, king Ban and
king Bors, also lend him powerful aid against an alli-
ance of eleven British potentates who refuse to recognise, in the beardless Arthur, the successor to the
mighty Uther Pendragon.

These enemies being at length subdued, Arthur
proceeds to Cameliard to succour his friend Leodegraunce against his mortal foe king Rience of North
Wales, and while there, meets for the first time the
beautiful Guinevere.

Subsequently, he obtains Excalibur from the Lady
of the Lake with its scabbard, which was of more
potent virtue than the sword itself. As the King and
Merlin are riding through the country in search of
adventures, Arthur tells the sage, " ' I have no sword.'
' No force,' [no matter,] said Merlin, ' here by is a

sword that shall be yours and I may.' So they rode til they came to a lake, which was a faire water and a broade, and in the middes of the lake king Arthur was ware of an arme clothed in white samite, that held a faire sword in the hand. 'Lo,' said Merlin to the king, 'yonder is the sword that I spake of.' With that they saw a damosell going upon the lake. 'What damosell is that?' said the king. 'That is the lady of the lake,' said Merlin, 'and within that lake is a roch, and therein is as faire a place as any is on earth, and richly beseene, and this damosell will come to you anone, and then speak faire to her that she will give you that sword.' Therewith came the damosell to king Arthur and saluted him, and he her againe. 'Damosel,' said the king, 'what sword is that which the arme holdeth yonder above the water? I would it were mine, for I have no sword.' 'Sir king,' said the damosell of the lake, 'that sword is mine, and if yee wil give me a gift when I aske it you, yee shal have it.' 'By my faith,' said king Arthur, 'I will give you any gift that you will aske or desire.' 'Well,' said the damosell, 'goe ye into yonder barge, and rowe yourselfe unto the sword, and take it and the scabbard with you, and I will aske my gift when I see my time.' So king Arthur and Merlin alighted, tyed their horses to two trees, and so they went into the barge. And when they came to the sword that the hand held, king Arthur tooke it up by the handles and tooke it with him ; and the arme and the hand went under the water ; and so came to the land and rode forth."

Afterwards, he marries Guinevere, the daughter of Leodegraunce, king of Cameliard, and receives with her, as a present, the famous Round Table, which, it seems, could seat any number of knights up to one hundred and fifty.

At the ceremony of the marriage and coronation, the order of the Round Table is instituted, and comprises thirty-two seats, including that of the King and the "siege perillous," the latter being reserved for the best knight in the world, till whose appearance it was to remain vacant, on pain of mysterious punishment to any less noble one who should presume to occupy it.

In this first section, Arthur appears chiefly in the character of an ordinary knight-errant seeking adventures, relieving distressed damsels, and not infrequently getting sorely mauled by older hands than himself. At times, his very life is endangered by the machinations of some hostile enchantress, from whose malice he is saved only by the interposition of Merlin or the Lady of the Lake. Occasionally, too, he acts as commander-in-chief of an army, as in the battle against the eleven confederate kings in the

forest of Bedegrayne, where, however, he appears to
have owed more to his miraculous sword than to his
skill as a tactician.

There are two incidents, connected with this section, which are highly important in their bearing on
the epic unity of these romances. After the departure of kings Ban and Bors, Morgause, the wife of
king Lot of Orkney, mother of Gawaine, and therefore Arthur's half-sister, came to Arthur, sent thither
by her husband to espy the Court of the young King,
though ostensibly on a message of state, "and she
was a passing fayre lady, wherefore the king cast
great love unto her, .   .   .   and she was his sister
on his mothers side.   .   .   .   But all this time king
Arthur knewe not that king Lots wife was his
sister." The result of this *mésalliance* was the advent of Modred, whose history to the very last cast
its dark shadow over Arthur's life, until in the fulness of time the King made a terrible atonement for
this inexpiable sin at the hand of the very wretch
whom he had begotten !

What Æschylean Ate dogging the footsteps of its
victim in silent vengeance could throw a more tragic
colouring over a tale than does this incestuous curse
over the Arthurian Romance ?

One other point. With this section closes the
history of Merlin. The famous magician, seer, and

prophet is made love-prisoner by Vivienne, the pure, the affectionate nymph of the Lake, and henceforth disappears from the scene, yet not until he had accomplished the great object of his life, the establishment of Arthur as King.

The next section opens with the arrival of the famous Roman embassy. The King is holding a royal feast with his allies of kings, princes, and noble knights, and is seated on his throne, when twelve ancient men, each bearing an olive branch, enter the hall, bringing a message from Lucius, " Dictator of the Public Weal of Rome." The message is couched in haughty terms, demanding fealty and tribute, and closing with a threat of war in case of refusal. The King, in spite of his offended dignity and the murmured menaces of his barons, entertains the ambassadors as a true knight. Meanwhile, a Round Table council is held at which the claim set up by Rome is indignantly repudiated and war determined upon. On both sides, the preparations for the conflict are on the grandest scale. The Emperor summons his vassals from countries not yet known to any geographical society, to say nothing of India, Arabia, Africa, Turkey, Greece, etc., etc., while King Arthur assembles a vast army, crosses the Channel, and himself becomes the aggressor. At length, the two armies meet and a stubborn battle is fought. For a long time victory hovered, now over the Romans, now over the Britons, till finally, "king Arthur espied where Lucius fought and did wonder with his owne hands, and anon he rode to him and either smote other fiersly; and at the last, Lucius smote king Arthur overthwart the visage and gave him a large wound, and when king Arthur felt himself hurt, anon hee smote him [Lucius] againe with Excalibur that it cleft his head from the somet of his helm and stinted not till it came beneath the brest. And then the emperour fell downe dead, and there ended he his life." This, of course, throws the Romans and their allies into confusion; they take to flight, pursued by the Britons, who put over one hundred thousand to the sword!

In Geoffrey's *History* it is stated that the King, after this decisive victory, was *about to cross the Alps*, but was prevented from doing so in consequence of receiving news of Modred's revolt. In the Romance, the treason of Modred does not occur until many years later, and accordingly the Norman writer states that "Arthur entred into Loraine, Braband, and Flaunders, and sithen returned into hie Almaine, and so over the mountaines into Lumbardy and after into Tuskaine." During his triumphal march to Rome all the cities around send great sums of money, proffering him their allegiance, and do homage for the

lands they hold. Even before he reaches Rome, all
the senators that were left alive, and all the noblest
cardinals, come forth to meet him and pray that they
may " crowne him emperour with holy creme." On
the day appointed for the ceremony, he enters Rome
in triumph, "and there he was crowned emperour by
the popes owne hands with all the solemnitie that
could be made, and sojourned there a certaine time
and established all his lands from Rome unto France,
and hee gave lands and realmes unto his servants and
knights, to every each after his deserving, in such wise
that none of them complained.

"Then after this all his lords and knights and all
the great men of estate assembled them together
afore the triumphant conquerour, king Arthur, and
said, 'Noble emperour, blessed be the eternal God!
your mortall warre is all finished, and your conquest
is achieved in so much that we know no man so great
nor mightie that dare make any warre against you.'"
They then request leave to return to their homes,
which Arthur grants : grand preparations are made,
and finally King and knights pass over the sea
and land at Sandwich, " against whom came queene
Guenever and met with him and made great joy of
his comming."

So far as we have gone, (i. e., in the first two sections), whatever difference there may be between the

History and the Romance, whether in the plot, the incidents, or the epic soul of the tale, the two versions are sufficiently similar to enable us to recognise a common origin for both. And this statement holds equally true of the third, or as we must now call it, the fourth section, in both History and Romance, as we shall presently see.

But in the Romance, there is an additional section, as we before noticed, and it is this increment to the story which gives to the Romance or Epic its distinctive character. So important indeed are these additions, that from them alone, we are warranted in regarding the Romance as a totally distinct version from the History. This section, peculiar to the Romance, has, moreover, a distinguishing mark which stamps it, and which leaves its imprint upon the whole version. That mark is the famous tale of the *Quest of the Holy Graal.* No other version contains it. As we said in a previous chapter, this Quest is *the* adventure *par excellence.* Its achievement forms the culminating point of the whole story. It is the one point towards which every incident tends, and which renders intelligible all that goes before and all that follows. Even if we grant that the deepest interest gathers around the tragic ending of King and knights, still, this is simply because we can appreciate better the widespread ruin after an earthquake, than the silently working forces which produce so stupendous a result.

The Quest of the Saint Graal, however, does not stand alone in this section. It is simply a central point around which a number of other adventures cluster; adventures, as essential to the unity of the Graal legend as the Graal legend itself is essential to the unity of the Arthurian epic.

That the reader may thoroughly grasp this important point, on which hinges the right understanding of these romances as a whole, let us picture to the mind a mountain, rising from the plain in a gentle sweeping slope till it reaches a pointed summit, while the opposite side presents an almost perpendicular line from summit to base. Let the sloping side represent the Arthurian epic as it gradually and slowly unfolds, rising in ever-increasing grandeur till it reaches its culminating point; and let the steep precipitous side represent the Romance in its swift and rapid *finale*. As we leave the plain and climb the sloping ascent our first halting-place is where Arthur is crowned *King;* thence we proceed to our second halting-place, where he is crowned *Emperor;* then commences the steepest part of the ascent, the *Quest* of the Holy Graal; but we advance and reach the apex or summit of the mountain, the *Achievement* of the adventure of the Holy Graal. Thence we de-

scend on the other side and reach the first of our
two halting-places in the descent, the point where
Modred revolts; thence we follow the steep downward path till we come to the point where Arthur
falls and dies; and finally, we reach the plain once
again, the death of Queen and Lancelot and the end
of the Romance.

This third section then, reaching from Arthur's
coronation as " Emperor " to the revolt of Modred,
falls naturally into three parts : (1) The events immediately preceding the Quest ; (2) the Quest itself ;
(3) the events subsequent to the Quest and introductory to the fourth section or the revolt of
Modred.

In this part of the narrative, which occupies a considerable length of time and by far the largest amount
of space in the epic, Arthur retires somewhat into
the background. He is now Emperor of the civilised world, and chief of a brotherhood of knights
which numbers in its ranks the flower of the chivalry
of Christendom, but, as he takes no active part in
the actual Quest of the Holy Graal, the narrative is
more especially occupied with the deeds of those
who acquired celebrity by participating in this noble
adventure. Among the personages who now stand
prominently forward, no one has so great a share in
this section of the legend, and indeed in all that fol-

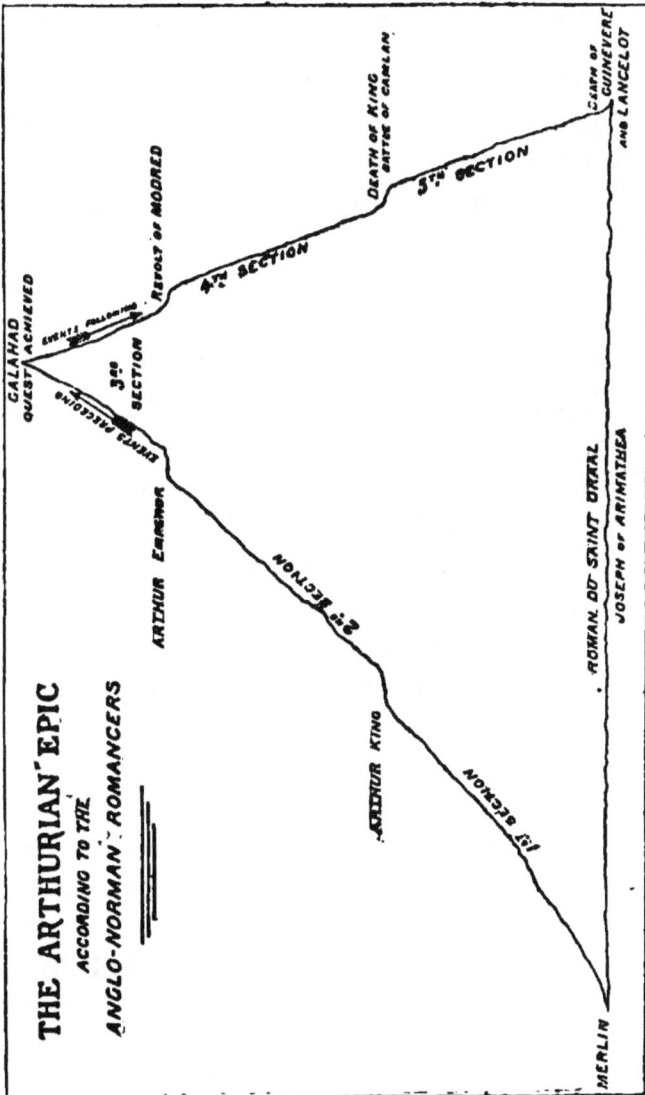

THE ARTHURIAN EPIC

ACCORDING TO THE

ANGLO-NORMAN ROMANCERS

GALAHAD
QUEST ACHIEVED

EVENTS FOLLOWING

REVOLT OF MODRED

4TH SECTION

DEATH OF KING
BATTLE OF CAMLAN

3TH SECTION

DEATH OF
GUINEVERE
AND LANCELOT

EVENTS PRECEDING

3RD SECTION

ARTHUR EMPEROR

2ND SECTION

ARTHUR KING

1ST SECTION

ROMAN DU SAINT GRAAL

JOSEPH OF ARIMATHEA

MERLIN

149

lows, as Sir Lancelot of the Lake. After the conquest of Italy, he returns to England with the
victorious army, but soon growing weary of the ease
and luxury of Court life, goes forth in search of adventures, which, as we shall subsequently see, he
finds to his heart's content. It was during one of
these adventures, that he stayed at the castle of a
certain king Pelles, a lineal descendant of Joseph of
Arimathea. This knight, it appears, knew that his
daughter, Elaine (not her of Astolat), was destined
to be the mother of the peerless hero who should accomplish the Quest of the Holy Graal, and accordingly, he endeavours his utmost to bring about a
match between his daughter and Lancelot. Failing
in this, he procures the aid of an enchantress and by
magical deception attains the desired end. In course
of time Galahad is born; but of his subsequent
career we hear but little until we arrive at the eve of
the great Quest.

Meantime, we find, now and again, new knightly
members elected to the Order of the Round Table.
It is at this stage of the story that the episode of
Gareth and dame Liones occurs, which Tennyson
reset in one of the *Idylls of the King*. It is now for
the first time that we read of Tristan and La Beal
Isoude, one of the most exquisite pieces of mediæval
romance which we possess. The introduction of this

knight at Arthur's Court is extremely quaint and
beautiful. Lancelot and Tristan meet on the field
and engage in single combat, neither knowing who
or of what degree his antagonist is. The contest is
fierce and long. At length Sir Tristan discovers
during the fight that his foe is Sir Lancelot du Lac.
"'Alas!' cried sir Tristram, putting an end to the
duel, 'what have I done? for ye are the man in the
world that I most love.' 'Now, faire knight,' said
sir Launcelot, 'tell me your name.' 'Truely,' said
he, 'my name is sir Tristram de Lyones.' 'Oh
Jesu,' said sir Launcelot, 'what adventure is now
befallen mee.' And therewithall sir Launcelot
kneeled downe, and yeelded him up his sword, and so
either gave other the degree." Then Sir Tristan is
persuaded to go to Arthur's Court. And the King
when the knight was come, took Sir Tristan by the
hand. "Then came queene Guenever and many
ladies with her, and all these ladies said, all with one
voice, 'Welcome, sir Tristram'; 'Welcome,' said
the damosels; 'Welcome,' said the knights; 'Welcome,' said king Arthur, 'for one of the best knights
and gentilest of the world and a knight of the most
worship.'" Then he is led to the Round Table and
duly installed one of their Order. Another famous
knight is brought forward at this period, Sir Percival, who is treated with especial marks of favour by

the romancer. After he is knighted by the King and has taken his seat among the less renowned members of the Round Table, a maiden in the Queen's court, who was dumb, enters the hall, " and went unto Percivale and tooke him by the hand and said aloud, that the king and all the knights might heare it, 'Arise, sir Percivale, the noble knight and Goddes knight.' . . . And there shee brought him unto the right side of the siege perillous and said, 'Faire knight, take here thy siege, for that appertaineth unto thee, and unto none other.'"

In this way, the Court of King Arthur became the centre of all that was imperial in empire and knightly in knighthood. If the Roman ambassadors could report to the Emperor that Arthur's estate was " the royallest that ever wee saw in our dayes for he was served at the table with nine kings, and the noblest fellowship of other princes, lords, and knights that bee in all the world, and every knight approved and like a lord," what must that estate have been when he had made tributary the whole country " from Rome to France," and had assembled around himself the most valiant barons and beauteous ladies of these his conquered territories? But this was not all. Even knights like Tristan, whose proud spirit might have refused to bow to Arthur as conqueror, or others, like Lancelot, whose prowess might

have made them formidable rivals, were allured by
the splendour of a Court which eclipsed that of all
former dynasties, and were irresistibly drawn within
the magic circle of an Order which raised its members to the highest pinnacle of worldly fame.

Such is the glowing picture which the Romancers
have drawn of Arthur's Court as an introduction to
the Quest of the Holy Graal.

And yet, throughout all these episodes, when
Arthur's glory rises to its highest pitch by his invasion of Italy, by the brilliant splendour of his wedding feast; in all his high festivals of Pentecost and
Easter, when, from far and near, the chivalry of the
world comes to honour him, the handwriting on the
wall is distinctly seen, casting over all, the spectral
glare of retribution in consequence of previous sin.

And now, a new scene opens before us. The peerless Galahad, having been knighted, is in due time
admitted to the fellowship of the Round Table. At
the hour when the knights were seated for dinner,
the Sangraal appears, and Galahad, at the bidding of
the "holy maiden," places himself in the "siege
perillous." The vision of the mystic Vessel causes
profound astonishment, and when it has vanished,
Gawaine avows his determination to go forth on the
Quest. The proposition is immediately caught up
by all the boldest knights present. Arthur's grief at

this sudden resolution is beyond bounds. He knows, he has a presentiment that this would be the last time that all the members of the Order would meet at the Round Table. But his entreaties are ineffectual, and the hall is soon deserted by the brilliant assemblage, never to meet there in equal numbers and splendour again.

All the knights, with the exception of Lancelot, Percival, Bors, and Galahad, soon abandon the Quest, being thwarted by foes both fiendish and human, and also by holy hermits who tell them that without purity of life they will not be able to obtain even a vision of the Sangraal. Sir Galahad, and his two companions in arms, Percival and Bors, proceed under the direction of the "holy maiden," and at length the adventure is achieved. Sir Galahad is translated to heaven in the sight of his friends. Sir Bors returns to Arthur's Court to relate the story of their miraculous achievement, and Percival becomes a hermit, and no longer appears in the romance.

The reunion of the knights after this adventure is a melancholy one. Sad gaps may be seen at the Round Table, and many seats formerly occupied by those who bore names of high renown are now empty. The golden names of Tristan, Lamorak, Percival, and Galahad are there ; but they are gone. The King's darkest forebodings fall far short of the reality, but the guiding star of his reign had reached its highest point, and was now beginning to set.

No sooner was the Quest of the Holy Graal ended than Sir Lancelot, forgetful of the solemn vows which had procured for him a vision of the Sacred Cup, and unable to resist the smiles of the Queen, fell back into his old ways of false fidelity.

At this point in his career downward, a *second* Elaine crosses his path—Elaine, the "lily maid of Astolat." But not even could the purity of her character or the intensity of her love, restrain him from the ruin into which he was about to plunge his King and country. Sinister rumours concerning the Queen, begin to be whispered on every side, and symptoms of the approaching end are plainly visible. The curse which hangs over Arthur and his family is slowly gathering strength as each of the greater knights adds, by his indiscretion or sin, to the fast approaching and almost imminent doom which threatens the Court. Thrice does Lancelot save the life of queen Guinevere, when condemned to be burnt as an adulteress, by presenting himself at the nick of time and so averting the death penalty from his royal mistress by his bravery in single combat. In the last of these affrays, Lancelot kills unwittingly, two brothers of Gawaine, a man who, hitherto, had been foremost in defending Lancelot, and preventing war between him and the King. But now Gawaine becomes Lancelot's mortal enemy, and at his instigation the King crosses the sea, besieges Lancelot in his French castle of Joyous Gard, and surrounds the adjacent town with his army.

In the History, as we have seen, it is on the breaking out of the Roman war that Arthur leaves his Queen and kingdom in charge of Modred. In the Romance this does not take place till the King determines upon the siege of Joyous Gard. "And there king Arthur made sir Modred chiefe ruler of all England ; and also hee put queene Guenever under his governauce because sir Modred was king Arthurs sonne, for hee gave him the rule of all his land and of his queene. And so king Arthur passed over the sea, and landed upon sir Launcelots land."

The war which ensued might have been ended time and again, had it not been for the implacable hatred and bitter vengeance of Gawaine, who urges the King on, in spite of his still deep love for the knight who had most wronged him. At length, news of Modred's treachery and violation of his trust compels the King to raise the siege of Joyous Gard, and return to chastise the traitor. And so the third section ends.

The final act in this mediæval tragedy, both in the appalling grandeur of the closing scene and in the

chastened simplicity of the narrative, is perhaps un-
equalled by any writing in the English tongue.

"And there (at Dover) was sir Modred ready
waiting . . . to let his owne father to land
upon the land that he was king off." But Arthur,
in spite of all opposition, effects a landing and puts
the rebel army to flight.

Poor Gawaine! when the battle is over, he is found
" in a great boate lying more than halfe dead " to
the great sorrow of the King his uncle. As Arthur
holds the dying knight in his arms, his royal heart
overflows, and he sobs aloud : " In sir Launcelot and
you I most had my joy and mine affiance, and now
have I lost my joy of you both, wherefore all mine
earthly joy is gone from me." Gawaine, when it is
too late, sees the madness of the course he has been
pursuing, and a priest, having been summoned,
writes to Sir Lancelot this letter, indited by Gawaine in broken and fast-failing accents :

" Floure of all noble knights that ever I heard of
or saw in my dayes ; I, sir Gawaine, king Lots sonne
of Orkeney, sisters sonne unto the noble king Arthur, send unto thee greeting, and let thee have
knowledge, that the tenth day of May, I was smitten
upon the old wound which thou gavest mee before the
citie of Benwicke, and through the same wound that
thou gavest mee, I am come unto my death day,
and I will that all the world wit that I sir Gawaine

knight of the round table, sought my death and not
through thy deserving ; but it was mine owne seeking ; wherefore I beseech thee, sir Launcelot . . .
for all the love that ever was betweene us, . . .
make no tarying but come over the sea in all the hast
that thou maiest, with thy noble knights, and rescew
that noble king that made thee knight . . . for
he is full straightly bestood with a false traitour
. . . sir Modred, and he hath let crowne himselfe
king, and he would have wedded my lady queene
Guenever . . . if shee had not put her selfe in
the toure of London." And so in deep penitence
he dies.*

Arthur pursues Modred from place to place, till at
length, unable to escape, the traitor is forced to
stand his ground and fight. On the eve of the
battle, however, the ghost of Gawaine appears to
Arthur, warning him not to fight the next day or he
would be slain. A truce is accordingly proposed
and accepted ; but mutual distrust exists, and each
commander strictly charges his army that if any man
sees a sword drawn in the enemy's ranks to rush at
once to the attack. On the very day, against which
Gawaine had cautioned him, and just as the truce is
being ratified, a snake issues from a bush hard by,
and stings one of the knights on the foot. In an
unguarded moment the knight draws his sword to

* *Vide* Note M.

kill the reptile, but his action is taken as a signal of battle ; the heralds sound their trumpets, the knights retire each to his own side, and the battle of Camlan begins. The contest lasts the livelong day till, at last, Modred stands alone, the sole survivor of all the rebel knights who sided with him : and Arthur, with but two of his fellowship, Sir Lucan and Sir Bedivere. Then follows a deadly duel between the King and the arch-traitor. Modred falls dead upon the field of battle, but ere he sinks in death he summons, by one mighty effort, his fast ebbing strength, and, grasping his sword with both his hands, strikes his King to the ground and dies exultant.

Arthur, mortally wounded, is carried from the field by Sir Bedivere. Sir Lucan, though groaning with a wide-gaping wound, seeks to help lift his fallen King, but even as he stoops, he drops lifeless at his monarch's feet.

At the command of the dying King, Excalibur is restored to its mysterious owner by the hands of Sir Bedivere, and Arthur is translated to the Isle of Avalon, there to be healed of his wounds by Argante the Fair, and await the fulfilment of his epitaph :

HIC JACET ARTHURUS, REX QUONDAM, REXQUE FUTURUS.*

And so the fourth section ends.

* *Vide* Note N.

But, as if the terrible curse had not even yet worked itself thoroughly out, the mediæval roman- cer continues to paint the closing scene of all, in ever darkening colours, piling ruin upon ruin, until the once glowing halls of many towered Camelot disap- pear in utter blackness, and neither King nor Queen nor knight is left, nought save the lonely gloom of direst desolation.

The romance must be read as it came from the imaginative brain and skilful touch of the Norman trouvère, if we would realise to the full extent, its exquisite beauty, its artistic perfection, and its mar- vellous power.

In the special studies which follow, we shall enter more fully into the consideration of many of the in- cidents of the story, than has been possible in such a summary sketch as we have here given of the Arthurian Epic.

CHAPTER VI.

Merlin and Vivienne.

THE personage first in chronological order, though perhaps not first in importance, in the Arthurian Romance, is Merlin the prophet and enchanter. In point of time, he appears upon the stage long before King Arthur, his famous exploits reaching back even to the reign of Vortigern. He also represents the *intellect* of the world as depicted in these poems, while Arthur represents simply its *physical force.* It is to the necromantic skill and wise counsels of Merlin that the King owes his birth, his crown, his order of Round Table knights, and his victories. It is Merlin who, as Court prophet and counsellor, predicts the grandest events in the life of his sovereign, and without whose advice no affair of moment is undertaken.

But the legend of this prophet, protector, and counsellor is involved in no little obscurity. We must therefore now, retrace our steps back through the dazzling period of the Romancers, where the brilliant imagination of the mediæval writer has clothed all the scenes he depicts with a glow of noonday splendour; back through the sombre era of the Chroniclers, where, in the grey dawn of early romance, the grand outlines of the more prominent figures can be discerned with tolerable accuracy; back to the thick misty shades of bardic times, where amid the darkness of pre-historic days, the figures of heroes and enchanters loom colossally forth, like dim supernatural forms, the very haze which obscures them, magnifying their true proportions.

As we peer into the dim past, the figure of Merlin stands out, at one time as a Welsh bard, at another as a Roman king, at another as magician, prophet, and enchanter; one form or the other appearing in bolder relief as a chance ray of historic or bardic light, shooting far into the thick darkness, illuminates this or that side of the character of this mysterious being.

It appears to be historically certain, that about the sixth century, there lived a personage who under the name of Myrdhin or, as it is written in the oldest Welsh form Myrthin, acquired celebrity as a bard, if not as one gifted with supernatual powers. In the *Myvyrian Archaiology* there are six poems attributed to this bard, none of which, perhaps, belong to him, unless they have been altered from their

original form by later interpolators. Even Nennius,
who mentions Aneurin, Taliéssin, and Lywarch Hên
among the bards of the sixth century, makes no
mention of Myrdhin. The conclusion seems inevit-
able, that whatever Merlin the bard, may have written
had, by the ninth century, become lost, and that his
poetic or prophetic skill had passed by that time
into the airy world of tradition. According to the
Welsh genealogies this Merlin, called Merlin the Cale-
donian or Merlin the Wild, belonged to the same
Northern clan which furnished nearly all the heroes
of Welsh romance ; and his pedigree, so far from
being mysterious, is as well ascertained as that of
any other British celebrity. The event which was
the source of his fame as a prophet, was the fact of
his having become insane (and consequently an object of superstitious veneration), after a disastrous
battle which the bard had assisted to provoke, in
which he was himself engaged, and at which he witnessed the terrible slaughter of his own kinsmen.
After this calamity, he is described as frequently
sitting by the side of a fountain of healing waters.
This Merlin is said to have been buried at Bardsey,
the island of the Welsh saints in North Wales.

But there comes to us, from this far past, accounts
of another Merlin who possesses far less of an earthly
character than the preceding one. According to

very early authority, the prophetic child, who was afterwards to develop into Merlin the enchanter, was called Ambrosius, the name Merlin being then unknown. And here we are met by a curious confusion of two totally distinct characters. At the time when Ambrosius the enchanter was at the height of his fame as a magician, Ambrosius the king was a renowned ruler of Britain, at least so says the *History*. Indeed, the historic Ambrosius (Ambrosius Aurelianus) was the brother of king Uther Pendragon, and hence Arthur's uncle, and according to Geoffrey of Monmouth, he preceded Uther as king in Britain, the name Ambrose being at the time of the account a well-known and common appellation. Moreover, the birth and parentage of both Ambrose the king and Ambrose the magician were involved in obscurity and fable, and consequently it is no wonder that a writer, narrating events which occurred many years before his own time, should confound the two, Ambrose the king and Ambrose the enchanter, and attribute to the enchanter, tradition current respecting the king. Whatever of a kingly character therefore, early accounts of Merlin Ambrose may contain, we may throw out of consideration as the result of confounding two totally distinct personages.

The earliest account of Ambrose the enchanter is in the history of Nennius. Vortigern, by the advice

of his twelve wise men, resolved to build and fortify
a city in which to defend himself against his Saxon
foes. After travelling far and wide, he came to a
certain mountain (Snowdon) which seemed adapted
to his purpose. He then collected together work-
men and materials, but the whole of the latter disappeared in one night. A second and a third time
materials were collected, but these vanished in like
manner. Then the wise men advised Vortigern to
" find a child born without an earthly father, to put
him to death and to sprinkle with his blood the site
on which the proposed citadel was to be built."
Messengers were accordingly despatched throughout
Britain in search of the required child, and at last
one was found and taken to the king. " Why have
thy men dragged me hither?" inquired the youth
when brought into the presence of the king. " That
thou mayest be put to death, and that thy blood
may be sprinkled around the site of my citadel,"
replied the king. " Who did show thee this thing ? "
asked the youth. " My wise men," said Vortigern.
" Let them be summoned into my presence," said
the mysterious child. So they were brought in.
" Now," said the youth, " I ask these thy wise men
what there is under the soil in this spot." They
answered, " We know not." " I know," replied the
boy, " there is a pool in the midst of the ground ;

dig and ye shall find it." Accordingly, they dug and
found as the boy had predicted. Again he spoke:
" Disclose to me what is in the pool." The wise men
were silent. " There are two vessels buried within,"
said the prophetic child. Then they searched and
found the vessels. " What is there enclosed in the
vessels ? " asked the youth. Again, the wise men
were silent. " There is a tent in the midst of them,"
said Ambrose ; " separate the vessels and ye shall
find it." Then the vessels, at the king's command,
were separated, and there they found a tent rolled
up. " What is there within the tent ? " asked the
child ; but no one could tell. " Two dragons are in
it," said the young prophet ; " one red and one
white." So they opened the tent and there they
found two dragons asleep. " Now," said the boy,
" watch and observe what the dragons will do."
Then the dragons, aroused from their torpor, began
each to attack the other and expel his fellow from
the tent. At length, after a protracted and often
doubtful battle, the red dragon expelled the white
one, and took sole possession of the field. " To me,"
said the youth, " is this mystery revealed. The pool
is an emblem of the world ; the tent is a figure of
thy kingdom, O Vortigern ; the red dragon is thy
dragon, but the white dragon has occupied many regions in Britain, and ere long shall hold almost from

sea to sea, but afterwards our nation shall arise and
shall cast out the Saxons for ever."

" What is thy name?" asked the king, astonished
at the wisdom of the child.

" I am called Ambrosius," was the reply.

At once the question arises, how did Ambrosius,
the enchanter, obtain the name of Merlin?

In later traditions this child is stated to have been
the "sun of a nun," in Welsh Mab-leian, and this
afterwards took the latinised form of Merlinus, and
hence the identity in name. Both Merlin the bard
and Merlin the enchanter are stated to have lived at
the same time and in the same locality, namely, the
north of Britain, and their fame was doubtless transplanted into Brittany by the refugees from the Saxon
conquest, and so moulded into the romances with
which we have been made acquainted by Geoffrey
of Monmouth and by the Norman trouvères. The
figure of the great enchanter is doubtless a pure work
of fiction, woven in with the historical threads which
belong to the epoch of the Saxon wars in Britain,
and the identity of name caused the two primarily
distinct personages to be treated as one, and the acts
and attributes of the enchanter to be transferred to
the bard.

This view is corroborated by the later bardic poems,
where the two Merlins are again kept distinct, and

it is the enchanter who especially becomes a mythologic hero. He was supposed to know the past, the
present, and the future, and to be able to assume the
form of any being animate or inanimate. Before
history began, he ruled in Britain, then a delightful
island of flower-bedecked meadows. His subjects
were fairies, and their lives were a continued festival
of singing, playing and enjoyment. He also possessed a sub-lacual kingdom, where everything was
of the richest character, the inhabitants being charming little creatures, with waves of long hair falling in
massive curls on their shoulders, and the only want
felt was the full, soft light of the sun, which, coming
to them through the water, was but faint and cast
no shadow. Here was the famous workshop where
Merlin forged the enchanted sword Excalibur, and
where alone the stones were found by which the
sword could be sharpened. It was to this region
that Excalibur was restored at Arthur's dying
request, and where it will remain until his future
return. At some time, not specified in history, this
Merlin quitted the earth. He was last seen by some
Irish monks sailing away westward in a skiff of crystal. One thing is curious: these poets state that it
was his blind passion for one who did not reciprocate
his devotion that caused him to sail in the fatal
vessel.

The bardic poems, which seem to reproduce very ancient traditions, reveal to us a fact as interesting as it is important, viz.: that many years before the production of the *Roman de Merlin*, the principal facts in his history had already been related by the bards. In respect to Merlin, the enchanter, they refer to his mysterious birth; his triumph over the wise men; his attachment to Ambrose, the king, and they call him "son of the Vestal virgin," Commander-in-chief of the army of Ambrose, and prince of prophets.

With respect to Merlin, the bard, they make him prophesy the advent of Arthur, and the glorious future of the Britons. They represent him as fleeing to the woods to live there in seclusion. They speak of a nymph of the woods, companion of his solitude, who could render herself invisible at will, and who was deeply versed in the magic art, who eventually made him captive, and whom they call Vivlian, a name which the romancers have converted into Vivienne. Indeed the palace or skiff of crystal was doubtless the germ out of which the later romancers fabricated Merlin's enchanted prison. Hence, the prototype both of Vivienne, and of the Enchanter of the romance, are evidently to be traced back to the bardic poems.

In the later Welsh traditions, Merlin appears as

a *Christian* character. According to the Welsh legend, St. Columba came from Ireland and presented himself to the unhappy seer. The saint's mantle was black, his hair dark, his complexion swarthy, and he was mounted on a black steed. Merlin, at once recognised the great Irish saint, and after some conversation, confessed that he had once burned a church, that he had flung the holy Book into a river, and had done other heterodox things. However, as we might suppose, he repents, and after absolution and reception of the Holy Eucharist, becomes a good Christian.

The tale as related by the Armorican Kymry, is somewhat different but extremely beautiful. St. Cadoc, who previously had evinced so much anxiety for the salvation of Virgil, being himself a poet, took the deepest interest in the future wellbeing of all of the poetic family. Hearing of the deplorable condition of Merlin in the wilds of Caledonia, he made a pilgrimage thither, and succeeded in his self-imposed mission ; he found the maniac bard, and restored him to reason and to the bosom of the Church. The same story, whether related by Welsh or Armorican writers, differs only as to the personality of the missionary ; the circumstances of the reconciliation of the poor bard or prophet to Holy Church being nearly the same in both versions. This legend of the conversion of Merlin, is of course an ecclesiastical addition to the tale, and accounts for the fact that in all subsequent chronicles or romances Merlin, while performing pagan feats, is represented as holding Christian views and associating with and advising dignitaries of the Church.

In Geoffrey, the first of the Chroniclers, the story of Merlin's birth is repeated as in the bards, with the addition already quoted, that he is said to have been the "son of a nun." Then follows the same story of Vortigern and of the white and red dragons. We are then treated with a long prophecy by Merlin respecting the future of Britain and the appearance of Arthur. Subsequently, Merlin brings about the marriage of Uther Pendragon and Igerna, and renders the father of our hero other important services. He displaces by certain magic words, the huge stones of the "Giants' Ring" in Ireland, and, taking them to his native land, builds a grand funeral monument at Stonehenge on Salisbury Plain, in honour of the British warriors who had fallen in previous battles. As before, he frequents sylvan fountains, and then suddenly disappears from the history.

Wace and Layamon, following the Latin history of Geoffrey, relate the same story, Layamon, as usual, adding certain poetic touches. The nun, for example, is represented by him as the daughter of a

king. She sits at Vortigern's side when questioned
as to her son, and while telling her story she " hangs
down her head and bends it towards her breast and
covers her features." Indeed, in the period between
the earlier Welsh bards and the Chroniclers, Merlin
the bard and Merlin the enchanter had become
identical, although the character of enchanter and
prophet seems to have retained the predominance.

So far as we have gone, all accounts, whether
Welsh or Breton, whether of Bards or Chroniclers,
agree in three important points: 1. Merlin's miraculous birth; 2. His possession of supernatural powers; and, 3. His retirement to the woods and final
captivity; although between these points the various
narratives diverge widely.

We now come to the Romancers, to Walter Map
and Robert de Borron, whose *Roman de Merlin* contains the fullest account we possess of the achievements of the great seer.

And here, at the very outset, we may state that
the Merlin of romance is a purely poetic creation,
and though still retaining the general characteristics
which he possessed in previous poems, legends, and
histories, is a grander and more perfect conception
than he was in earlier times. The weird Keltic bard,
prophet, and enchanter, subject to magnetic trances,
had to undergo a civilising process before he was

deemed presentable to Norman lords and ladies; and as Malory's work gives but an imperfect reflection of the original romance, we will go to the fountain-head for our information.

As in all the earliest traditions, the romancer gives Merlin a spirit (*incubus*) for father, but in addition he makes him a genuine demon of evil. Innate wickedness is, however, driven out by baptism, and being aware at a very early age that his life would be one of wonders, he makes the quaint request of a holy hermit named Blaise,* with whom he had become acquainted, that he would make a book in which to write his life as it proceeds. "Many of those who shall read this book or shall hear it read," explains Merlin, "will be the better for it, and will be on their guard against sin." The saint complies, but not until he has made Merlin swear "by the Father, the Son, and the Holy Ghost, one God in three Persons, by the blessed Virgin Mary, by the angels, apostles, saints, and all who serve and love our Lord, . . . to do nothing contrary to the will of Jesus Christ, and Merlin sware it;" whereupon the holy man went to the woods of Northumberland, there to accomplish the task unmolested.

* This personage is none other than Lupus, Bishop of Troyes, and apostle to Britain in the fifth century, whose Latin name was translated into Blaidd (pronounced Blaiz) in the Welsh legend.

After the death of Vortigern, Merlin joins his
biographer in the forest, but he has not been there
long before the kings Ambrose and Uther send to
consult him.   Merlin, possessing the powers of a
magician, no sooner arrives at Court than he diverts
himself by mystifying those who had sent for him.
At first he assumes the guise of a woodman with a
long, shaggy beard, then of an idiot tending a flock,
then of a wretched-looking beggar, and finally of a
charming little boy.   He tells them, however, in
what manner they may banish their Saxon foes, and
this done, suddenly quits the Court for his favourite
woods.

During the subsequent battle, in which Ambrose is
slain, a terrible dragon appears in the air, vomiting
out smoke and flame.   All the seers are dumb, the
Saxons are dismayed.   At this juncture, Merlin appears and addressing himself to Uther exclaims:
" Hasten, O Uther, attack the enemy ; all the island
shall submit to thee for thou art the fiery dragon."
Uther, from this circumstance named " Pendragon "
or Dragonhead, causes two winged serpents to be
cast in gold, and one to be placed in the cathedral,
the other to be borne at the head of his forces.   The
pious Blaise having chronicled these events, Merlin
announces the greatest of his extraordinary deeds:
" I am going to speak a mystery, that of the Round

Table; the table at which our Lord ate and drank
with his disciples. It was lost, but I have found it,
and must establish it during the reign of king Uther
Pendragon. He shall seat thereat fifty of the most
valiant and virtuous knights of his kingdom, but
those who shall occupy it during the reign of his son
Arthur, shall be still better and more famous men."
And accordingly, he departs and performs his enterprise.

After this, Merlin, by his enchantments, brings
about the marriage between Uther and Igerna, and
stipulates as the reward of his services, that the edu-
cation of the young prince should be left in his hands.
Accordingly, he is no sooner born than he is spirited
away, not even his parents knowing whither he is
taken. After Uther's death, the Britons left without
a king, seek out Merlin, who had meantime returned
to the woods, and entreat his advice. He accordingly composes the following prayer which he commands all the people to repeat: "O Lord God
Almighty, who didst deign to be born of the Virgin
Mary, King of Kings and Lord of Lords, be pleased
to show which of us thy servants is worthy to be
king, for the wise government of the nation and its
establishment in the Christian faith. Grant that a
sign may appear in the presence of us all, showing
which is the most worthy to reign over us."

Just as the Archbishop had finished the break-of-day Mass there appears before the high altar of the cathedral a marble stand supporting an anvil, and a sword fast in the anvil, while on the guard of the sword is the inscription :

"Celui qui me retirera
De par Jésus-Christ roi sera."

A boy, known to no mortal man but Merlin, performs the feat of drawing it out, and the Archbishop raising him in his arms, so as to be seen by all the people, commences to chant the *Te Deum*. Subsequently, at a grand solemnity convened at Caerleon by the Archbishop, (by the advice of Merlin,) the boy is crowned King ; but the barons and chiefs break into open rebellion, refuse to acknowledge his sovereignty, and besiege the young King in his fortress. While the siege is in progress, Merlin attempts to end the insurrection by telling the confederate kings that Arthur is truly Uther Pendragon's son and rightful heir to the crown, but they deride him and the siege continues. At length, the Archbishop excommunicates the rebels from the walls, while Merlin, at the same time, by his enchantments, rains showers of fire upon them from the summit of a high tower and their overthrow is complete.

It is by Merlin's aid, as we saw in the last chapter,

that Arthur obtains Excalibur from the Lady of the Lake, with its scabbard of more potent value than the sword itself. Even the King's marriage is brought about by the diplomacy of Merlin. One day the King explains to his trusty adviser. * " ' My barons will let me have no rest, but needes they will have that I take a wife, and I will none take but by thy counsaile and by thine advise.' ' It is well done,' said Merlin, ' that ye take a wife, for a man of your bountie and noblenesse should not be without a wife. Now is there any faire lady that yee love better than another ? ' ' Yes,' said king Arthur, ' I love Guenever, the king's daughter Leodegrance of the land of Camelyard, which Leodegrance holdeth in his house the table round that ye told he had of my father Uther. And this damosell is the most gentilest and fairest lady that I know living, or yet that ever I could find.' ' Sir,' said Merlin, ' as of her beautie and fairenesse she is one of the fairest that live ; but and you loved her not so well as ye doe, I would finde you a damosell of beautie and of goodnesse that should like you and please you, and your heart were not set. But there as a mans heart is set, he will be loth to returne.' ' That is truth,' said king Arthur. But Merlin warned the king

* We have here given Malory's rendering of the conversation because of the charm of its quaintness.

privily that Guenever was not wholesome for him to take to wife, for he warned him that Lancelot should love her and shee him againe. . . . Then Merlin desired of the king to have men with him that should enquire of Guenever. And so the king graunted him."

Merlin is accordingly despatched as ambassador to king Leodegraunce to ask his daughter Guinevere in marriage. The king, honoured by the request, delivers his daughter to Merlin, together with an escort of a hundred knights. On the evening of the wedding day, Guinevere, having to cross the palace garden, attended only by her maids of honour, is attacked by some villains lying in wait behind a thicket. Merlin, aware of their designs, was waiting in ambush, attended by a superior force, thwarts their designs and saves the future Queen.

We find the patriot sage continually thus guarding the interests of his King in his own fantastic fashion. He is always Arthur's adviser, and the ruling spirit in the councils of war, so that nothing of importance is ever undertaken without his approval and sanction. He is also the prophet of the Court. He predicts that Lancelot should love the Queen and she him again; that he who should kill the King should be born on May-day; he warns Arthur that he keep well the scabbard of Excalibur, since he shall lose no blood as long as he has the scabbard with him, though he be covered with wounds ; and finally, he predicts that only three of all the knights who should go in quest of the Holy Graal should be present when it was carried up into heaven.

At times, he amused and mystified the Court by his powers as a magician. Once, he entered the hall as a blind boy playing on the harp and led by a greyhound, and demanding as recompense, to be allowed to carry the King's banner in an approaching battle. Being refused on account of his blindness, he vanished. Shortly after, there entered the hall a poor child with shaved head, features of livid tint, eyes light gray, bare-footed and bare-legged, speaking and looking like an idiot, and asking the King's permission to bear the royal ensign at the approaching battle. The courtiers laughed, and Arthur, suspecting that it was a joke of the witty enchanter, granted the request, when instantly the man of magic power stood in his proper person before the company. Of course, possessing such supreme command over the laws of nature, he, at times, excited the impotent jealousy of those less gifted ; he was called a "witch," a "dreeme-reader," and it was even said that he performed his marvels by "devils-craft."

At length he discloses to the hermit Blaise, the secret which was in his heart : "I go," he said, "to

12

the land which I have reason to dread, sweet and lovely as it is. The fairy is there in the forest. She will secure me with chains neither of iron, nor steel, nor gold, nor silver, nor tin, nor lead, nor wood, nor anything produced by earth, air, or water, and she will bind me so straitly that I shall never be able to stir." We next find him in Brittany seated alone at the celebrated fountain of Broceliande, with the countenance of a youth of twenty, and in the attire of a student. Near this fountain dwelt a nobleman who was married to a beauteous fairy. Their daughter, the lovely Vivienne, also had received the endowments of a fairy at her birth. While Merlin tarried near the fountain the fair Vivienne approached. He admired her grace of form and movement, while she, in turn, seemed captivated by the manly beauty of the stranger. Courteous salutes were exchanged; the lady announced herself the daughter of a knight whose castle was in the neighborhood; the youth represented himself as a student in search of a teacher.

"What have you learned up to this time?" asked Vivienne. "Many things," replied the seer. "I can raise a château before your eyes, and fill it with ladies and knights; I can produce lake or river where drop of water never flowed, and I can walk on the same water without wetting my ancle." "Certes,

you are deeply learned," rejoined Vivienne, "I
would give much for such power." "All this," said
Merlin, "is but child's play. I can perform higher
wonders than these to entertain mighty kings and
barons." "In truth, Sieur student," exclaimed Vivienne, "I am desirous of witnessing your power. In
return I will grant you my friendship." "By my
faith, fair lady," said Merlin, "your speech is so gentle and pleasing that I will freely show you a proof
of my art. For my trouble I claim your friendship
alone." "I grant it," said Vivienne. Merlin made
a circle on the grass, and then came and sat beside
the damsel, and in a few seconds they saw troops of
knights and ladies approaching from the neighbouring
woods, and as they entered the enchanted circle,
dancing to the sounds of various musical instruments,
minstrels sang to a soft melody :

> " L'amour arrive en chantant
> Et s'en retourne en pleurant."

Behind the groups of knights and ladies, were seen
the choicest plants and flowers and fruit-trees, and a
lawn of softest verdure, and a charming château
gently arising at the rear of this delightful garden.
The rich foliage of the trees and the harmonious
blending of the thousand hues of myriad flowers,

charmed the sight, and a sweet odour, expanding on every side, reached to the fountain. When the company were fatigued, they retired to the garden and refreshed themselves under the agreeable shade of the trees. At the approach of evening, they departed dancing and singing, and as they disappeared amidst the forest, the château vanished from view. At Vivienne's request the garden remained an enchanted spot.

The gratification of Vivienne was extreme, but in expressing it, she reminded the young sage that he had not instructed her in the art of producing any wonder as yet. He replied, that she should be qualified to do these and much greater charms when he was certain of possessing her affections. Meantime, it was necessary that he should depart to Britain on affairs of state. "But when will you return?" "In a year, sweet friend," said Merlin, " on the vigil of St. John in summer "; and so they parted.

Having done the State good service during his absence, and having received fruitless warnings innumerable from his pious biographer, Merlin returned to Brittany on St. John's eve to keep his promise. How long the time had seemed to Vivienne! She sat expectantly by the fountain, whither she had so often gone during his absence, and now saw her young student approach, joy and earnestness playing on his features. She hastened to meet him, took his hand and conducted him to the enchanted garden, where, in the grateful shade, she had prepared a delicious repast at the foot of the fountain. Merlin had had no such love affair in his youth, and his new passion carried him completely away. Vivienne now appeared ten times more fascinating than at the former interview, and he, all absorbed by his mighty though pure passion, taught her how to cause lake to rise, or river to flow where water had never been, to change her form at pleasure, and to lay whom she would in magnetic sleep. With womanly diplomacy, she asked this last gift, blushing, because, she urged, her parents would kill her if they found out her attachment to him, and she desired the possession of the power in order to leave them wrapped in slumber whenever she wished to meet him.

A second parting took place at the end of a week, of course more affectionate and lingering than the former one.

The sage then returned to Britain and assisted his monarch once more. Still, under the irresistible sway of his love for Vivienne, yet incensed against himself for his weakness, he sped from the Court to the forest, notwithstanding the entreaties of his sorrowing King and master to remain. From the forest he sped to the sea, and across the sea to Rome; then, after many adventures, he hastened home to the woods of Northumberland and to his faithful counsellor again, hoping that he had outstripped his love in his headlong race. It was only a delusion; he awoke the next morning to find his passion as strong and imperious as ever. Making a virtue of necessity, he resigned himself at once to that which he knew was his fate; he took a final farewell of Blaise, and crossed the sea for the last time. In the enchanted garden of Broceliande he found his Vivienne as lovely and loving as ever.

Before taking up the final scene in the romance, we will compare Tennyson's Vivien with her of the Norman trouvère.

In framing his Idyll of *Merlin and Vivien*, Tennyson had the alternative before him, either of building up an independent and original tale on the weird Keltic or Armorican tradition, or of resetting the episode as it stood in the Anglo-Norman romance of Merlin. As a matter of fact, the poet, in this instance, has utterly ignored poems, traditions, and romances, and has departed most widely from all pre-existing versions of the legend. In fact, he has invented a Vivienne unknown to any previous writer, the creature and invention of his own brain. We shall now see the truth of the statement before made, that his pictures are deficient in beauty in

proportion to his departure from a strict fidelity to
his originals.

In the romance, the culminating point of the whole
story is, of course, the *possession of the charm*, leading to the final captivity of Merlin. And this is
true of Tennyson's Idyll; it is in the possession of
the charm that all the interest of the poem centres.
But apart from this bare fact, the two versions have
little, if anything, in common. Vivienne of the
romance, as we have seen, is not a creation of the
Norman trouvère; on the contrary, she can be found
in the writings of the bards as far back as Merlin or
Arthur. But we are naturally led to ask, who and
what is she as depicted by the Romancers? Is she
the Vivlian of the Bards, or is she (the high-born
Roman beauty of the Chroniclers?) She is neither,
but, like Merlin, she is simply a poetic creation ; she
is the Lady of the Lake, the queen of a sub-lacual
kingdom, the foster mother of Lancelot of the Lake ;
and her portrait, as drawn by Walter Map, is one of
love, womanly, parental love, the purest, the most
ardent that the brain of man could conceive. Her
character is depicted as that of a female Galahad, a
picture of chaste, refined, ideally perfect womanhood,
with no gross admixture, no repulsive traits of character or action. She talks to Merlin at the fountain,
as we have seen, with all the openness of an un-

sophisticated nature, and expresses unreservedly her admiration and pleasure in the scenes which his magic power creates. She has not a suspicion of man's awful perfidy, and sits at the fountain on St. John's eve, or subsequently, in the enchanted garden, without doubting for an instant that her lover will return according to his promise; and, by her secret interviews, she discovers a heart as yet as true and pure as the air she breathes.

Nothing, however, can be plainer than the fact that Vivien of the Idyll no longer retains this character. She knows of love, only as a growth of the rankest kind, only as a hideous mask to conceal a fiendish desire to blot out the very name of the great seer of the time.

Indeed, at a single glance of the Idyll, we can see how she degenerates in Tennyson's hands. The poet's favourite epithet is "wily Vivien," or "lissome Vivien." He speaks of her as "Vivien smiling saucily." He calls her a "lovely, baleful star," even "a wanton" and "a harlot"; and the whole of the poem directly or by *innuendo* is but the development of Vivien's wiles.

But let us descend to particulars. The mainspring of the two versions being thus the two poles of human conduct, namely, ideal purity on the one hand, and the limit of deformity of character on the other, we need not be surprised to find in Tennyson, actions, words, and characteristics attributed to Vivien in harmony with the poet's own conception of her moral degradation. In the romance, Merlin, as we have seen, crosses the sea alone, and finds Vivienne wandering near the grounds of her castle home, a sweet, lovely girl, in all the innocence, freshness, and beauty of youth ; a second and a third time he makes the lonely voyage to meet her at the fountain of Broceliande, where she is waiting to receive and welcome him.

According to Sir Thomas Malory, the sage meets her at Arthur's Court, and, continues Malory, " Merlin would let her have no rest, but always he would be with her in every place " ; for " hee was so sore assotted upon her that he might not be from her. . . . And, within a while, the damosell of the lake departed, and Merlin went evermore with her wheresoever she went. . . . So she and Merlin went over the sea together."

In the Idyll, Tennyson has given a far different version of this incident :

> So leaving Arthur's court he gain'd the beach ;
> There found a little boat, and stept into it ;
> *And Vivien follow'd, but he mark'd her not.*
> She took the helm and he the sail ; the boat
> Drave with a sudden wind across the deeps,

And touching Breton sands, they disembark'd.
And then she follow'd Merlin all the way,
Ev'n to the wild woods of Broceliande.*

And afterwards, when she reproaches him for his unknightly conduct during the voyage, she says :

But yesterday you never open'd lip,
Except indeed to drink : no cup had we :
In mine own lady palms I cull'd the spring
That gather'd trickling dropwise from the cleft,
And made a pretty cup of both my hands
And offer'd you it kneeling : then you drank
And knew no more, *nor gave me one poor word ;*

.   .   .   .

And when we halted at that other well,
And I was faint to swooning, and you lay
Foot-gilt with all the blossom-dust of those
Deep meadows we had traversed, did you know
That Vivien bathed your feet before her own ?

Subsequently, the Seer explains his brusque behaviour, but tells her

You follow'd me unask'd ;
And when I look'd, and saw you following still,
My mind involved yourself the nearest thing
In that mind-mist :

* It is scarcely necessary to say that wherever in this and the following chapters any single words, lines, or passages are italicised, the italics are our own, and are used simply to call especial attention to some important point under discussion.

In the romance it is Merlin who, impelled by
the all-absorbing power of his love, follows Vivienne
whithersoever she went; but in the Idyll it is Vivien
who, unwomanlike, follows Merlin, and this in spite
of his evident wish to be alone.   But this is only
one, and that a very slight indication of her true
self.   Presently, the poet gives a still further insight
into the depravity of his heroine.

The wily Vivien
    .   .   .   .   .   .

    hated all the knights, and heard in thought
Their lavish comment when her name was named.
For once, when Arthur walking all alone,
Vext at a rumour issued from herself .
Of some corruption crept among his knights,
Had met her, Vivien, being greeted fair,
Would fain have wrought upon his cloudy mood
With reverent eyes mock-loyal, shaken voice,
And flutter'd adoration, and at last
With dark sweet hints of some who prized him more
Than who should prize him most; at which the King
Had gazed upon her blankly and gone by :
    .   .   .   .   .

It made the laughter of an afternoon
That Vivien should attempt the blameless King.

During the journey with Merlin this unchaste
side of her character comes out in still bolder relief.
In the forest, when they stop to rest, Tennyson
tells us :

> There lay she all her length and kiss'd his feet,
> As if in deepest reverence and in love.
> A twist of gold was round her hair ; a robe
> Of samite without price, that more exprest
> Than hid her, clung about her lissome limbs,

And shortly after he tells us :

> And lissome Vivien, holding by his heel,
> Writhed toward him, slided up his knee and sat
> Behind his ankle twined her hollow feet
> Together, curved an arm about his neck,
> *Clung like a snake ;* and letting her left hand
> Droop from his mighty shoulder, as a leaf,
> Made with her right a comb of pearl to part
> The lists of such a beard as youth gone out
> Had left in ashes ·

Nor can we fail to note with what artistic skill Tennyson has made her words to correspond with her unchaste actions. In the Anglo-Norman romance, not a single word does the trouvère put into Vivienne's lips which is not spotless and untainted, and might not be uttered by the purest-hearted Christian lady. In Tennyson, however, when Merlin, unwilling to disclose to her the charm, says :

> " Ask no more :
> For tho' you should not prove it upon me,
> But keep that oath ye sware, ye might, perchance,
> Assay it on some one of the Table Round,
> And all because ye dream they babble of you."

Then

> Vivien, frowning in true anger, said :
> "What dare the full-fed liars say of me ?
> *They* ride abroad redressing human wrongs !
>
> .　　　.　　　.　　　.　　　.　　　.　　　.
>
> *They* bound to holy vows of chastity !
> *Were I not woman, I could tell a tale.*
> *But you are man, you well can understand*
> *The shame that cannot be explain'd for shame.*
> *Not one of all the drove should touch me : swine !*"

And so when Merlin retorts :

> "You breathe but accusation vast and vague,
> Spleen-born, I think, and proofless. If ye know,
> Set up the charge ye know, to stand or fall ! "

Vivien replies :

> "*What say ye then to fair Sir Percivale*
> *And of the horrid foulness that he wrought,*
> The saintly youth, the spotless lamb of Christ,
> Or some black wether of St. Satan's fold.
> What, in the precincts of the chapel-yard,
> Among the knightly brasses of the graves,
> And by the cold Hic Jacets of the dead ! "

Then

> deeming Merlin overborne
> By instance, recommenced, and *let her tongue*
> *Rage like a fire among the noblest names,*
> *Polluting, and imputing her whole self,*
> *Defaming and defacing, till she left*
> *Not even Lancelot brave, nor Galahad clean.*

Now and again, even her consummate artfulness cannot conceal the anger which is burning within her
breast. After Merlin has told her that he has the
book in which the charm is written :

> Vivien answer'd smiling saucily :
> " Ye have the book : the charm is written in it :
> Good : take thy counsel : let me know it at once :
> For keep it like a puzzle chest in chest,
> With each chest lock'd and padlock'd thirty-fold,
> And whelm all this beneath as vast a mound
> As after furious battle turfs the slain
>
> .   .   .   .
>
> I yet should strike upon a sudden means
> To dig, pick, open, find and read the charm :
> Then, if I tried it, who should blame me then ? "

And upon Merlin expostulating, she answers in true
anger :

> " Have I not sworn ?   I am not trusted.   Good !
> Well, hide it, hide it ; I shall find it out ;
> And being found take heed of Vivien."

But this is not all.   Not only does Tennyson make
her unchaste and unlovely, he actually proceeds to
depict her, Medea-like, as a murderess at heart, one
who would have stabbed Merlin had she found the
weapon at hand.   After one of her petulent, unlovely moods, Merlin mutters unutterable things to
himself :

He spoke in words part heard, in whispers part,
Half-suffocated in the hoary fell
And many-winter'd fleece of throat and chin.
But Vivien, gathering somewhat of his mood,
And hearing " harlot " mutter'd twice or thrice,
Leapt from her session on his lap, and stood
Stiff as a viper frozen ; loathsome sight,
How from the rosy lips of life and love,
Flash'd the bare-grinning skeleton of death !
White was her cheek ; sharp breaths of anger puff'd
Her fairy nostril out ; *her hand half-clench'd*
Went faltering sideways downward to her belt,
And feeling ; had she found a dagger there

. . . . .

She would have stabb'd him ; but she found it not :
His eye was calm, and suddenly she took
To bitter weeping like a beaten child.

Strange contrast this, to the ethereal lovely nymph
of the tale ! In the latter, Vivienne is perfectly love-
able ; we meet with no repulsive traits in her character, no repulsive actions ; hers is a portrait of ideal
loveliness ; all that divides the high-born gentlewoman from the bourgeoise counterfeit is hers.
Her nobility does not exist merely by comparison ; she is not great simply because others are
small ; she is essentially pure, and therefore essentially grand.

And what a contrast there is between the Merlin
of the romance and the Seer of the Idyll ! In

the romance, his attachment to Vivienne is represented as tender almost to a fault ; it is the utter
self-forgetfulness of real affection. De Borron tells us
that Merlin " had never loved anyone but with a
pure and loyal heart " ; and so intense was his love
for Vivienne that he did not attempt to conceal it
even from his confessor and biographer, for in spite
of the saint's remonstrances, Merlin tells the holy
man, in reference to the charm, " she shall know all
that I know, for though I might refuse her yet I will
not." But Merlin of the Idyll, though at times attracted and lured on by the wily ways of Vivien, is
far oftener disgusted with her actions, and expresses
in no measured terms the disdainful feeling of his
heart.   Indeed, at times he must have even hated
her.   When she had been calumniating the knights
he mutters to himself :

" *I well believe she tempted them and fail'd,*
    Being so bitter : for fine plots may fail,
    Tho' harlots paint their talk as well as face
    With colors of the heart that are not theirs.
    I will not let her know : nine tithes of times
    Face-flatterer and backbiter are the same."

.   .   .   .

            " Tell *her* the charm !
    So, if she had it, would she rail on me
    To snare the next, and if she have it not
    So will she rail.   *What did the wanton say ?* "

and he ends his musings with the exclamation :

" I am weary of her."

But the crowning point of dissimilarity between the two versions, lies in the difference of *motive* which causes Vivienne to desire the knowledge of the charm; and in the difference of *incentive* which induces Merlin finally to disclose the secret.

In the romance, Vivienne longs to gain possession of the charm, from a wish amounting almost to a passion and necessity to have Merlin always near her, so that he might not leave for Britian and parts unknown. "She felt wretched and lonely," says the romancer, " at the very thought of having him leave her again, and tried to discover some means by which she might keep him close to her and always as young and handsome as he now was ; she thought, though in vain, of twenty schemes and in vain tried them all." " My sweet friend," said Vivienne at their third meeting, "there is one thing which I know not yet, and I beg you to teach it to me." " What is it, my heart," said Merlin, although he divined her thought. " I wish to know, sweet friend," replied Vivienne, " how to imprison a person without stone or wood or iron, simply by a charm." (Merlin sighs.) " Why do you sigh?" " I know, sweet girl," said Merlin, " what you intend, and that

13

you desire to keep me as your own, I have not
strength to resist. Willing or not, I grant your request." "Sweet friend," continued Vivienne, throwing her arms around his neck, "is it not just that
you should be wholly mine as I am wholly thine?
Have I not left father and mother for you? Are
not you my only desire, my only thought? Have I
any joy or hope but in you, and since we love, why
should you not obey me as I obey you?" * "It is
but just, my sweet," replied Merlin, "*I will do it
with all my heart. Ask what you will.*" "I will,"
said Vivienne, passionately, "that this garden never
be destroyed, that we two live here alway *without
growing old or parting or ceasing to love and be happy.*"
"It shall be as you wish," said Merlin. "But I
must work the charm myself," replied Vivienne;
"teach it to me." So he taught her the charm, and
the substance of the spell."

One day as they were walking side by side and
hand in hand, under the young foliage at Broceliande,
they found a wide spreading bush of white thorn in
blossom. In the shade of the flowers they sat down
on the green sward, and Merlin rested his head in
Vivienne's lap; she lovingly ran her fingers through
his white hair and put him asleep, she then arose

* The author of the romance tells us : " elle l'aimait d' amour
sincère."

and wound her scarf nine times around the thorn,
and nine times whispered the charm she had learned.
She then returned and again placed his head on her
knee, doubtful as yet of the power of the enchant-
ment. But when Merlin opened his eyes and looked
around, forest, garden, white thorn, all had disappeared. He was in an enchanted castle reposing on
a couch of flowers, love prisoner to Vivienne. "Ah,
Vivienne," he cried, " I will consider you falsest of
lovers if you ever forsake me." "My sweet friend,"
answered she to her dear, voluntary captive, "could
you imagine it? could I ever leave you?" And
Vivienne kept her word ; she did not leave him.

How conspicuously is this tender pathos wanting
in the Idyll! In the poem, this motive of pure impassioned affection is transformed to one of cruel
selfishness :

> *And Vivien ever sought to work the charm*
> *Upon the great Enchanter of the Time,*
> *As fancying that her glory would be great*
> *According to his greatness whom she quench'd.*

Indeed, the artistic delineation of this ignoble passion in its many phases, masked though it may be by
craft and wily art, is one of the leading characteristics
of the poem from first to last. At the very opening
of the story, as we have just seen, the poet does not

scruple to depict Vivien as intent on her own ag-
grandisement at the expense of Merlin's great fame;
and when the tale is nearing its close, the same
ignoble trait is equally conspicuous.   During the
storm in the woods of Broceliande she stood,

> Upright and flushed before him :
> A virtuous gentlewoman deeply wrong'd :

but one thought ever uppermost in her mind, viz.:
the inflaming of her own ambitious pride by the
conquest of the great Seer.

> " I will go," (she said.)
> " In truth, but one thing now—better have died
> Thrice than have asked it once—could make me stay—
> That proof of trust—so often ask'd in vain !
> .   .   .   .
> *Lo ! what was once to me*
> *Mere matter of the fancy, now hath grown*
> *The vast necessity of heart and life.*
> Farewell ! "

Every word, every thought, every image in these
many lines is but the artistic outpouring of a soul
steeped in self and craft and hate.

We have not to go far to discover the exact incentive which the poet would have us understand
induced Merlin finally to disclose the charm to the
" wily " Vivien.

Early in the tale, when she had chided the great
Seer for his churlish silence during the journey, he
tells her:

> " Shall I tell you truth ?
> *You* seem'd that wave about to break upon me
> And sweep me from my hold upon the world,
> My use and name and fame."

And shortly after this, when her desire to know
the charm began to take more definite utterance, he
replies :

> *"If I fear,*
> Giving you power upon me thro' this charm,
> *That you might play me falsely, having power,*
> However well ye think ye love me now,
>
> .   .   .   .
>
> I rather dread the loss of use than fame ;
> If you—and not so much from wickedness,
> As some wild turn of anger, or a mood
> Of overstrain'd affection, it may be,
> To keep me all to your own self,—or else
> A sudden spurt of woman's jealousy,—
> Should try this charm *on whom ye say ye love."*

After an outburst of unlovely anger during which
Vivien threatens,

> To dig, pick, open, find and read the charm ;

the Seer changes his tactics, and tells her somewhat
sharply

> " Ask no more :
> For tho' you should not prove it upon me,
> But keep that oath ye sware, *ye might, perchance,*
> *Assay it on some one of the Table Round,*
> And all because ye dream they babble of you."

Thus repulsed, Vivien indulges in a graceless tirade of basest vituperation and detraction, but

> Her words had issue other than she will'd.
> He dragg'd his eyebrow bushes down, and made
> A snowy penthouse for his hollow eyes,
> And mutter'd in himself, " Tell *her* the charm !
> So, if she had it, would she rail on me
> To snare the next.
>
>   .   .   .   .   .   .
>   I will not let her know.
>
>   .   .   .   .   .   .
>   I am weary of her."

The question recurs, what then was the irresistible incentive which compelled the Seer finally to disclose the secret ?

Tennyson gives us little more than dark hints of the fatal truth which seems to lurk beneath his words. In the opening of the Idyll, the poet makes Vivien exclaim :

> " O Merlin, teach it me.
> The charm so taught will charm us both to rest."
>
>   .   .   .   .   .
>   " *Yield my boon,*
> *Till which I scarce can yield you all I am ;*
> And grant my re-reiterated wish,
> The great proof of your love : "

Subsequently, after Merlin had been muttering unutterable things, "harlot, twice or thrice," the poet tells us that Vivien,

> Leapt from her session on his lap

and, in harmony with the fury of the storm, which at that moment was gathering over the woodlands, broke forth into an impassioned semi-soliloquy in which she cries:

> "O God, that I had loved a smaller man !
> I should have found in him a greater heart."

> .   .   .   .

> She paused, she turn'd away, she hung her head,

> .   .   .   .

> She wept afresh.

Meanwhile Merlin's anger

> slowly died
> Within him, till he let his wisdom go
> For ease of heart, and half believed her true :

While in this changed mood the poet tells us that the Seer

> Call'd her to shelter in the hollow oak,
> "Come from the storm,"

> .   .   .   .

> Then thrice essay'd, by tenderest-touching terms,
> To sleek her ruffled peace of mind, in vain.
> At last she let herself be conquer'd by him,
> And as the cageling newly flown returns,

The seeming-injured simple-hearted thing
Came to her old perch back, and settled there.

At the very moment that she was calling heaven to
witness that she had never schemed against Merlin's
peace,

. . . a bolt
(For now the storm was close above them) struck,
Furrowing a giant oak,

.   .   .   .

But Vivien, fearing heaven had heard her oath,

.   .   .   .

and crying out,
" O Merlin, tho' you do not love me, save,
Yet save me ! " *clung to him and hugg'd him close ;*
And call'd him dear protector in her fright,
Nor yet forgot her practice in her fright,
But wrought upon his mood and hugg'd him close.
The pale blood of the wizard at her touch
Took gayer colours.

.   .   .   .

She call'd him lord and liege,
Her seer, her bard, her silver star of eve,
Her God, her Merlin, the one passionate love
Of her whole life ;

.   .   .   .

And what should not have been had been, *
For Merlin, overtalk'd and overworn,
Had yielded, told her all the charm, and slept.

* The writer of the romance tells us that Merlin " ait jamais aimé
personne autrement que d'amour loyale."

The concluding lines of the Idyll show but too clearly the strangely distorted view of Vivien's character which the poet must have had in mind throughout the writing of this tale.

> Then, in one moment, she put forth the charm
> Of woven paces and of waving hands,
> And in the hollow oak he lay as dead,
> And lost to life and use and name and fame.

> Then crying " *I have made his glory mine,*"
> *And shrieking out* " *O fool!*" *the harlot* leapt
> Adown the forest, and the thicket closed
> Behind her, and the forest echo'd "fool."

If the French adapter did not seize the wild and weird spirit of the Keltic tradition, and if he took unwarrantable liberties with the latter part of the narrative, he at least infused a tender and romantic spirit into the story. Under his hands the character of the attachment between Merlin and Vivienne is as pure as ideal fancy could make it, rather a rare merit among the minstrels of the twelfth century! It is strange that the muse of Tennyson, as a rule, so pure and chaste, should have preferred the Vivien who figures so disadvantageously in the Idyll, to the spotless, ethereal, and affectionate Vivienne of the Norman romancer. It is a mystery. The Idyll may be a fine study for old worldlings

with a lifelong experience of that which makes for
vice ; but what a glorious poem would the Anglo-
Norman romance have produced had it passed
through the tender, glowing, and chastened fancy
of the author of Elaine.　It might have rivalled the
finest of his poems, and even have surpassed them
all, in its delineation of ideal womanly love.　The
only way in which we can assign to Tennyson a
niche in our Pantheon of poets as the peer of England's noblest masters of song, is by mentally obliter-
ating the poem of Merlin and Vivien from the *Idylls
of the King.*

CHAPTER VII.

Lancelot, Guinevere, and Elaine.

IN a former chapter we called the romances relating to Arthur and his knights of the Round Table an epic cyclus. By the commencement of the fifteenth century at the latest, these novels of our forefathers had reached their highest point of development and perfection. They were the production of no one man and of no one age. Like the classic tales in the Æneid and the Iliad, they had existed for centuries as floating traditions, at first, orally transmitted, and gaining additions at the capricious will of subsequent narrators, till at length, this or that incident, or series of incidents, was seized upon by some poetic imagination which transformed the original crude conception or plain historic fact into the airiest phantom of chivalric romance. Thus, simple, neural-tint incidents became highly coloured, until the original outlines of the original figures became scarcely recognisable under the glowing tints of Norman painting.

The central figure, though not the true hero of this cyclus, is Arthur, and, revolving around him in an eccentric orbit, we observe the figure of Merlin, whose history to the very last exerts so palpable an influence upon that of the King that, next to Arthur, he becomes one of the most important personages in the romantic system. But, moving in outer, concentric circles, we find the knights of Arthur's Court, each of whose history seems to keep the universe of romance in a state of unstable equilibrium. Of these, no knight (as the romances have descended to us) is more famous than Lancelot du Lac. For although Sir Gawaine was the pet of the old traditions, and Galahad the virgin knight of the world, the model of pure Christianised chivalry, yet the heroic bravery and manly character of Lancelot have thrown a charm over his eventful history that renders him the Achilles, the Hector, or the Sir Philip Sidney of Arthurian Romance. Moreover, the sad story of Queen Guinevere, and that gem of beauty, the episode of Elaine, the maid of Astolat, have been cut and set with such exquisite skill by the old romancer around that of Lancelot, that the three form a cluster of remarkable brilliancy and beauty in the diadem of romantic fiction.

Guinevere, or as the bards call her, Gwenhwyvar, was, according to Taliéssin, " of a haughty disposition even in her youth, and still more haughty in her womanhood." A bard of the tenth century has left to posterity a dialogue in which she is represented as contradicting her future husband at every turn.

In the lays of the later bards she proves faithless and elopes with Modred. "She was punished," writes one ; " she languished in a cloister, and was subjected to ecclesiastical authority." Indeed, in these later bardic poems her character is represented just as it is in the French romances, though in an undeveloped form.

Geoffrey of Monmouth, and the chroniclers Wace and Layamon, simply state that Arthur took to wife Guanhumara, descended from a noble family of Romans ; that she was educated under Duke Cador of Cornwall, and in beauty surpassed all the women of the island. At the second coronation of Arthur, together with his Queen, the chronicler tells us that Guinevere, dressed in her richest ornaments, was conducted by the Archbishops and Bishops to the " Temple of Virgins," four queens bearing before her four white doves, according to ancient custom, and after her there followed a retinue of women making all imaginable demonstrations of joy ; and, when the ceremony was over at both churches, the King and Queen put off their crowns, and, putting on their lighter ornaments, went to the banquet.

Upon the breaking out of the Roman wars Arthur, according to this account, committed the government of his kingdom to his nephew, Modred, and also queen Guanhumara, and then proceeds to Gaul, where he conquers the Roman Emperor Lucius, and is about to proceed to Rome, when he hears of Modred's treachery and attempt to carry off the Queen, who had been left in his charge. After Arthur's return, and successive defeats of Modred, the Queen, says Geoffrey, fled to Caerleon "where she resolved to pass her life among the nuns of the church of S. Julius the Martyr, and enter herself one of their order."

In Robert de Borron's *Roman de Merlin*, while the young King and his sage counsellor were rescuing Leodegraunce from the attacks of a terrible giant, and Arthur was valiantly contending with one of his colossal captains, the princess Guinevere, looking from a window, admired his person and prowess, and whispered to herself, "Happy the lady whose love is sought by such a hero, and shame on her who gives him refusal." Merlin, who himself was passing through a love affair with Vivienne, "noticed that Arthur was far from indifferent to the charms of Guinevere," and, as he did not consider her of sufficiently high rank to be the King's wife, he persuades Arthur to leave the castle and go to the assistance of his cousin, the king of Little Britain, who was hard pressed by enemies.

According to Malory, Arthur informs Merlin that his barons will let him have no rest, but importune him to take a wife. He consequently confesses to Merlin that he loves Guinevere, daughter of Leodegraunce, king of Cameliard, the possessor of the mystic Round Table, which this king had received from Uther Pendragon. The sage warns Arthur of her true character, but all being, of course, in vain, he is despatched as ambassador to the king of Cameliard to ask the hand of his daughter. The monarch, feeling highly flattered by the proposal, Guinevere is delivered to Merlin, together with the Round Table and an escort of a hundred knights. "Then was the high feast made ready, and the king was wedded at Camelot unto dame Guenever in the church of Saint Stevens with great solemnitie."

As we hear no more of Guinevere until the appearance of Lancelot, we will now turn to the history of our hero.

All the personages hitherto brought forward have had historical prototypes; in other words, though their characters as romantic heroes or heroines are fictitious and ideal, still there is a germ of real fact, viz.: their historic existence, underlying the superstructure of romantic creation. But in the case of Lancelot this is apparently wanting.

In the first place, the very name is French, while

14

those we have before mentioned are pure Keltic. But M. de la Villemarqué believes that he has found the original of Map's Lancelot in a certain king Mael who figures conspicuously in Welsh poems. In the oldest French manuscript of the romance, the name is written L'Ancelot, where the first letter represents the definite article. The word Ancel (Latin, *Ancilla*) means a servant, and Ancelot is its diminutive. Also, Mael is Welsh for a servant. Lancelot is, therefore, says the Vicomte, the Welsh Mael translated into the Romance tongue and means " a darling servant " or knight. But this is not all. King Mael is said to have lived in the sixth century, and is spoken of as redoubtable for arms and gallantry though of a barbaric kind. One writer actually states that he carried off Guinevere and was, in consequence, besieged by Arthur. Mael is also said, like Lancelot, to have ended his days in a monastery. This wild hero, who at times assumed the form of a satyr, was, according to this theory, transmuted, by the · genius of Walter Map, into an ornament of spiritual chivalry and brought into the world once again, generous and brave, the very same king Mael of Cambrian fame, but in courtlier form, and, like him, closing his days in the bosom of the Church. This theory, though highly ingenious, does not seem, on critical grounds, to rest on anything more solid

than mere conjecture. Whether or not Map constructed the character of this famous knight on that
of any pre-existing Kymric model is, of course, an
open question; but the theory of M. de la Villemarqué does not accord with what we know of
Map's method of invention in name giving, if we
may judge him by the use he has made of Kymric
prototypes in his other romances.*   We cannot but
think that Lancelot, like Galahad, is the creation
both in name and character of Walter Map, and em-
bodies his idea of the purely heroic, chivalric knight
of the twelfth century.

Following Map's romance, Lancelot was the son
of king Ban, one of the two foreign potentates
whom Arthur, by Merlin's advice, called in to assist
him in conquering the eleven confederate kings who
refused to acknowledge his title to the throne.
This king Ban, while besieged by his inveterate
enemy Claudas, escapes from his castle under the
cover of night to seek the assistance of Arthur, to
whom, in former years, he had rendered such valuable aid.   No sooner is he without the castle gates,
than the seneschal traitorously betrays his trust and
admits the besiegers.   The castle is fired, and the
flames of his burning citadel reaching the eyes of
the unfortunate monarch during his flight, he ex-

* *Vide* Note O.

pires with grief. His distracted wife, the Lady
Helen, who had been the companion of his journey,
abandoning for a moment the care of her infant
son, flies to the assistance of her husband, and on
her return finds the little Lancelot in the arms of
the beautiful nymph Vivienne, who had previously
shown her deep, womanly affection by confining
her lover, Merlin, in an enchanted castle in order
that he might always be near her. On the approach
of the mother, the nymph suddenly springs with
the child into a deep lake and instantly disappears;
and hence her adopted child is afterwards known
as Lancelot du Lac. *≈ the Sangstel which is older in
avoid mercies to Maiden-law*

The fairy, when her *protégé* had attained the age
of eighteen, takes him to Arthur's Court in order
that he may receive the honour of knighthood. At
the first appearance of the youthful novice in his
white armour, which the nymph had expressly made
for him, the graces of his person, and the manifest
bravery of his nature, make an instantaneous and indelible impression on the heart of the Queen; while
her beauty fascinates him in spite of his nobler
feelings.

According to another version, it is Lancelot, and
not Merlin, who is sent as ambassador to ask the
hand of Guinevere, and then commenced that fatal
love which, though it appeared at first only as a tiny

cloud on the horizon of romance, afterwards cast its
shadow over Arthur's whole life and darkened his
end.

According to Map's account, Lancelot is no sooner
knighted than he seeks adventures to prove himself
worthy of the honour conferred upon him.

During one of these adventures he is assailed by
forty knights, and although not overcome, yields
himself to the lady of the manor, who traitorously
treats him as a captive, and he pines miserably in
the lady's custody. While confined in her castle, a
war breaks out between Arthur and a certain king
Galiot. Sir Lancelot, hearing of this, craves leave
of the lady to be allowed to take part in the next
battle, and his request is granted on condition of his
promise to return to his prison after the fight. She
then provides him with a complete suit of red
armour, in which he appears at the second battle
and is "the head and comfort of the field." He
then returns to his castle prison according to
promise, and his fair captor, well pleased at hearing
the reports of his famous deeds, visits him when
asleep, out of curiosity to observe his appearance
after the fight. Again, he obtains permission to be
present at the third battle, choosing this time to be
arrayed in arms of black. The black knight utterly
eclipses the red knight, and his deeds of prowess ex-

cite the wonder and admiration of all. Towards evening, as he is attempting to make his way back to the castle secretly, Galiot confronts him and compels him to go to his tent to rest.

Subsequently, Lancelot brings about a reconciliation between the King and Galiot, though Arthur is not aware at the time how or by whom the reconciliation is effected. During the interview which takes place between Arthur and Galiot, the latter asks the King what price he would pay to have the black knight's perpetual friendship, to which Arthur replies that he would gladly share with him all he possessed. The question is next put to Gawaine, who replies that he would wish to be the most beautiful woman in the world so as to be beloved by the black knight. Next, it is put to Guinevere, who remarks " that Sir Gawaine had anticipated all that a lady could possibly wish," an answer which is received with much laughter. The Queen then obtains a conference with Galiot, and prays him to obtain for her an interview with the black knight, and he promises to do his utmost to effect it. He accordingly sounds Lancelot upon the subject, and, finding him agreeable, he arranges that they shall meet that evening. Galiot, his seneschal, and Lancelot arrive. At first the Queen cannot think which is the black knight, but one is so modest, almost bashful, that

she fixes on him.   After a searching cross-examina-
tion, Guinevere discovers that he is the black knight
and, what is more, that he is the famous knight, Sir
Lancelot.   The love which had been smouldering in
her heart since his first appearance at Court is re-
kindled, and she promises, then and there, to give
him her love and to become his loyal lady all her life.

Tired of the ease and inactivity of Court life,
Lancelot again goes forth in search of adventures,
and, as we shall see, succeeds to his heart's desire.
It happened, during one of these excursions, that
Lancelot is one day received hospitably at a castle
where dwelt king Pelles, a cousin, in some distant
degree, of Joseph of Arimathea.   While at table, a
dove enters at the window bearing a golden censor
in its mouth, whence a delicious odour diffused
itself.   Next, appears a maiden bearing a golden
bowl, before which the king falls on his knees and
worships devoutly, while the table is suddenly covered with every sort of delicate food.   Then the
apparition vanishes, and the king explains to his
mystified and astonished guest that this was the
Holy Graal.

He then informs Lancelot that there is a prediction that when the Holy Graal went about the
world, the Round Table should shortly be dissolved,
and that the achievement of this adventure was re-

served for a knight yet unborn, who should sit in the
" siege perillous," and be the best knight in the
world both in arms and purity of life.   During
Lancelot's stay at the castle, the king is very desirous of arranging a match between their guest and
his daughter Elaine, knowing well that she was the
destined mother of the peerless hero who was to.
achieve the Saint Graal : but as Lancelot takes but
little notice of the somewhat violent love made to
him, magic is resorted to in order to effect so de-
sirable a match.

Shortly after this adventure, Elaine visits Arthur's
Court, and her great beauty, added to the rumour of
Lancelot's previous attachment to the daughter of
king Pelles, arouses the passionate jealousy of queen
Guinevere.   Unable to bear the tempest of reproaches which the Queen showers upon him, Lancelot leaves the Court and for two years wanders about
the land, melancholy in mood and studiously eluding
the quest of several knights whom both King and
Queen send to seek him.   At last, after a terrible
encounter with caitiff knights who wound him,
(though he sorely punishes them in the fray,) he
rushes into a garden, weary and bleeding, and falls
asleep.   The garden turns out to be that of the
castle of king Pelles, whose daughter Elaine finds
him, and by her care he is restored to health.

Tired of adventures, Lancelot returns to Court, and, when the time arrives, joins the famous Quest of the Sangraal. In this Quest his fate is different from that of any of the other more prominent knights. He, like them, is several times discomfited by foes human and superhuman. Like them, he has visions, and meets with several very plain-spoken hermits; but, unlike most of the knights, he repents, does penance, and at length, after a multitude of adventures, is vouchsafed a wondrous vision of the Sangraal clothed in samite. Upon his attempting, in spite of a warning voice, to approach too near the sacred Vessel, a blast of fiery wind prostrates him, and for twenty-four days he remains unconscious and entranced. On awakening, he asks where he is, and learns that it is the castle of king Pelles, and that Elaine is dead.

Before the Quest is over he meets and converses long with his saintly son Galahad shortly before his death. Then, knowing that the achievement of the Quest of the Holy Graal was not for him, he returns to Camelot, where he hears the details of the final achievement of the Sangraal and the passing away of Galahad into heaven.

The end glares on us with such visible fire from the moment of Lancelot's return to the Court of Arthur and Guinevere, after the achievement of this adventure, that we have scarce a thought for the tale of Elaine la Blaunch, Elaine, the maid of Astolat ; yet it makes a belt of pale, pure light across the deep red, lurid way that might have kept Sir Lancelot within its radiance as he hurried on to the goal of ruin beyond. Poet and painter have made us familiar with the story of Elaine " the fayrest mayde that myght be founde." We cannot now follow her through the whole of her tearful history, but must be content to trace the leading incidents of the episode, as these will clearly show what we have before stated, that Tennyson's pictures are beautiful only in proportion as he copies, in an unaltered form, the pathetic touches of the Norman trouvère.

Before comparing parallel passages from the romance of Map and the Idyll of Tennyson, we may state in passing that the poem of *Lancelot and Elaine*, in our estimation, is one of the finest, if not the finest, of the whole of the series of Tennyson's Arthurian poems.

This estimate is based chiefly on the fact, that in this instance the poet has followed strictly the lines of the original romance ; but in addition to this, it is based on the further fact, that he has reproduced the tale with such exquisite beauty of thought and additional touches of fancy, that we can imagine what the delight of the Norman romancer would be, could

he read his own narrative as reset in artistic verse by
the nineteenth century trouvère. But to return.

After the achievement of the adventure of the
Sangraal, a tournament is proclaimed at Camelot.
Arthur and his knights proceed thither, leaving
Lancelot behind with the Queen ; but by her advice
he resolves to be present at the jousts and determines, in his own mind, to appear as an *unknown*
knight. After a long ride he arrives at the castle of
Astolat where the King and his court are staying,
but he manages to conceal himself so well, that not
one of the Round Table knights recognises him. Sir
Bernard, the lord of Astolat, receives his stranger
guest with every mark of distinction. "This old
baron had a daughter that time, that was called the
faire maide of Astolat ; and ever shee beheld sir
Launcelot wonderfully ; and she cast such a love
unto sir Launcelot that shee could not withdraw her
love, wherefore she died ; and her name was Elaine
la Blaunch. So . . . shee besought sir Launcelot to weare upon him at the justs a token of hers.
' Faire damosell,' said sir Launcelot, ' and if I graunt
you that, yee may say I doe more for your love than
ever I did for lady or damosell.' Then hee remem-
bred him, that hee would ride unto the justs dis-
guised, and for because he had never before that
time borne no manner of token of no damosell, then

he bethought him that he would beare on of hers, that none of his blood thereby might know him. And then hee said 'Faire damosell, I will graunt you to weare a token of yours upon my helmet and therefore what it is shew me.' ' Sir,' said shee, ' it is *a red sleeve of mine, of scarlet, well embroadered with great pearles.*' And so shee brought it him. So sir Launcelot received it and said : ' Never or this time did I so much for no damosell.' And then sir Launcelot betooke the faire damosell his shield in keeping, and prayed her to keepe it untill he came againe.' "

With what power do the full, deep strains of Tennyson's verse resound the simple music of Map's prose.

. she stood

Rapt on his face as if it were a God's.
Suddenly flash'd on her a wild desire,
That he should wear her favour at the tilt.
She braved a riotous heart in asking for it.
" Fair lord, whose name I know not—noble it is,
I well believe, the noblest—will you wear
My favour at this tourney ? "   " Nay," said he,
" Fair lady, since I never yet have worn
Favour of any lady in the lists.
Such is my wont, as those, who know me, know."
"Yea, so," she answer'd ; " then in wearing mine
Needs must be lesser likelihood, noble lord,
That those who know should know you." And he turn'd

Her counsel up and down within his mind,
And found it true, and answer'd, " True, my child.
Well, I will wear it : fetch it out to me :
What is it ? " and she told him " *A red sleeve*
Broider'd with pearls," and brought it : then he bound
Her token on his helmet, with a smile
Saying, " I never yet have done so much
For any maiden living," and the blood
Sprang to her face and filled her with delight.

Lancelot and Sir Bernard's son, Sir Lavaine, then start for the tournament, and upon their arrival attract little or no attention, Lancelot wearing, as he does, the unemblazoned shield. But soon he enters the lists and performs such deeds of valour that

> King, duke, earl,
> Count, baron—whom he smote, he overthrew.

At length, a spear piercing his armour enters his side and, breaking off, leaves the spear-head embedded in the wound. Then the heralds, by the King's order, blow the trumpets, and the prize is awarded to " the knight with the white shield and that beare the red sleeve." But, forgetful of the prize he had won, Lancelot gallops from the field, and having reached the woods, he turns to Elaine's brother and beseeches him : " ' O gentle knight, sir Lavaine, helpe me that this trunchion were out of my side, for it sticheth so sore that it almost sleyeth mee.' ' O, mine owne lord,' said sir Lavaine, 'I would faine helpe you but it dreads me sore and I draw out the trunchion that yee shall bee in perill of death.' ' I charge you,' said sir Launcelot, ' as yee love mee, draw it out.' . . . and forthwith sir Lavaine drew the trunchion out of his side; and sir Launcelot gave a great shrieke and a mervailous, ghastly grone, and his blood brast out . . . that at the last hee sanke downe . . . and sowned paile and deadly.' "

Here, again, the poet follows closely the very wording of the old romance. Sir Lancelot, gasping, charges Sir Lavaine

> " Draw the lance-head : "
> " Ah my sweet lord Sir Lancelot," said Lavaine,
> " I dread me, if I draw it, you will die."
> But he, " I die already with it : draw—
> Draw,"—and Lavaine drew, and Sir Lancelot gave
> A marvellous great shriek and ghastly groan,
> And half his blood burst forth, and down he sank
> For the pure pain, and wholly swoon'd away.

Sir Gawaine is sent by King Arthur to seek the unknown and mysterious knight, and, after a fruitless attempt, he comes by chance to the castle of Astolat. Then, in consequence of Elaine's questioning him about the champion of the jousts, she discovers that it is the unknown knight who had worn her favour, and whom she loved, who had carried off the prize. So she tells Sir Gawaine that, because his shield was too well known among the noble knights, he had borrowed her brother's and had left his own with her. "' Ah, faire damosell,' said sir Gawaine, 'please it you for to let me have a sight of that shield.' ' Sir,' said she, ' it is in my chamber *covered with a case*, and if it will please you to come in with me, ye shall see it.' ' Not so,' said sir Bernard unto his daughter; 'let send for it.' So when the shield was come, sir Gawaine took off the case, and when he beheld that shield he knew anon that it was sir Launcelots shield, and his owne armes."

With what beauty the poet has clothed this incipient idea of the case :

> Elaine the fair, Elaine the loveable,
> Elaine, the lily maid of Astolat,
> High in her chamber up a tower to the east
> Guarded the sacred shield of Lancelot ;
> Which first she placed where morning's earliest ray
> Might strike it, and awake her with the gleam ;
> Then fearing rust or soilure fashion'd for it
> A case of silk, and braided thereupon
> All the devices blazon'd on the shield
> In their own tinct, and added, of her wit,
> A border fantasy of branch and flower,
> A yellow-throated nestling in the nest.
> Nor rested thus content, but day by day,
> Leaving her household and good father, climb'd

That eastern tower, and entering barr'd her door,
Stript off the case, and read the naked shield.

After Gawaine's departure for the Court, Elaine
obtains her father's permission to seek Sir Lancelot,
and accordingly goes forth, accompanied only by her
younger brother. Erelong, they meet Sir Lavaine,
who, learning the object of their journey, leads them
to the hermitage where Sir Lancelot is lying sick of
his grievous wound, "And when shee saw him lie so
sicke and pale in his bed, shee might not speake, but
sodainly shee fell unto the ground in a sowne, and
there shee lay a great while."

Nothing could surpass the power with which this
is told in the Idyll of *Lancelot and Elaine :*

> There first she saw the casque
> Of Lancelot on the wall : her scarlet sleeve,
> Tho' carved and cut, and half the pearls away,
> Stream'd from it still ; and in her heart she laugh'd,
> Because he had not loosed it from his helm,
> But meant once more perchance to tourney in it.
> And when they gain'd the cell wherein he slept,
> His battle-writhen arms and mighty hands
> Lay naked on the wolfskin, and a dream
> Of dragging down his enemy made them move.
> Then she that saw him lying unsleek, unshorn,
> Gaunt as it were the skeleton of himself,
> Utter'd a little tender dolorous cry.
>
> .   .   .   .
>
> And slipt like water to the floor.

After his recovery, they all three bid adieu to the
good hermit and return to the old baron's castle.
There, Lancelot stays some time, but at last determines to leave for the Court, and, when about to
depart, Elaine says : "' My lord sir Launcelot, now
I see that yee will depart ; faire and curteous knight,
have mercy upon me, and suffer mee not to die for
your love.' 'What would yee that I did?' said
sir Launcelot. 'I would have you unto my husband,' said the maide Elaine. 'Faire damosell, I
thanke you,' said sir Launcelot, 'but certainely,'
said hee, 'I cast mee never to bee married.' . . .
'Alas!' said she, 'then must I needes die for your
love. ' 'Ye shall not,' said sir Launcelot, 'for wit
yee well, faire damosell, that I might have beene
married and I had would, but I never applyed mee
to bee married ; but because, faire damosell, that yee
will love mee as yee say yee doe, I will, for your good
love and kindnesse, shew you some goodnesse, and
that is this : that wheresoever yee will set your heart
upon some good knight that will wed you, I shall
give you together a thousand pound yearely to you
and to your heires ; thus much will I give you, faire
maide, for your kindnesse. And alway while I live
to be your owne knight.' '*Of all this*,' said the
damosell, '*I will none*.' . . . Then she shriked
shrilly, and fell downe to the ground in a sowne ;
15

and then gentlewomen beare her into her chamber,
and there she made ever much sorrow."

How tenderly and faithfully has Tennyson described this scene:

"   . . . and do not shun
To speak the wish most near to your true heart ;
Such service have ye done me, that I make
My will of yours, and Prince and Lord am I
In mine own land, and what I will I can."
Then like a ghost she lifted up her face,
But like a ghost without the power to speak.
And Lancelot saw that she withheld her wish,

.   .   .   .

And said, " Delay no longer, speak your wish,
Seeing I go to-day : " then out she brake :
" Going ? and we shall never see you more.
And I must die for want of one bold word."
" Speak : that I live to hear," he said, " is yours."
Then suddenly and passionately she spoke :
" I have gone mad.   I love you : let me die."
" Ah, sister," answer'd Lancelot, " what is this ? "
And innocently extending her white arms,
" Your love," she said, " your love—to be your wife."
And Lancelot answer'd, " Had I chosen to wed,
I had been wedded earlier, sweet Elaine :
But now there never will be wife of mine."

. . . And she said,
" Not to be with you, not to see your face—
Alas for me then, my good days are done."
" Nay, noble maid," he answer'd, " ten times nay !

This is not love : but love's first flash in youth,
Most common : yea, I know it of mine own self :
And you yourself will smile at your own self
Hereafter, when you yield your flower of life
To one more fitly yours, not thrice your age :
And then will I, for true you are and sweet
Beyond mine old belief in womanhood,
More specially should your good knight be poor,
Endow you with broad land and territory
Even to the half my realm beyond the seas,
So that would make you happy : furthermore,
Ev'n to the death, as tho' ye were my blood,
In all your quarrels will I be your knight.
This will I do, dear damsel, for your sake,
And more than this I cannot."

                    While he spoke
She neither blush'd nor shook, but deathly-pale
Stood grasping what was nearest, then replied :
" *Of all this will I nothing ;* " and so fell,
And thus they bore her swooning to her tower.

And so Lancelot departs ; and so the maiden
pines and pines, week after week, for eleven long
weeks, till

    Death, like a friend's voice from a distant field
    Approaching thro' the darkness, call'd.

" And then she called her father . . . and heartely
shee praied her father that her brother might write a
letter like as she would endite it.   And so his father

graunted her. And when the letter was written,
word by word, like as shee had devised, then shee
prayed her father that shee might bee watched untill she were dead. 'And while my body is whole,
let this letter be put into my *right hand*, and my
hand bound fast with the letter untill that I bee
cold, and let me be put in a faire bed with all the
richest clothes that I have about me, and so let my
bed and all my rich clothes be laide with me in a
chariot to the next place where as the Thamse is,
and there let me bee put in a barge, *and but one man
with me*, such as yee trust, to stere me thither, and
that my barge be covered with blacke samite over
and over. Thus father, I beseech you let me be
done.' . . . [and] anon shee died. And so when
shee was dead, the corps and the bed and all was led
the next way unto the Thamse, and there a man
and the corps, and all were put in a barge on the
Thamse, and so the man steered the barge to Westminster."

In the solemn, funeral music of Tennyson's verse
we read:

> So when the ghostly man had come and gone,
> She with a face, bright as for sin forgiven,
> Besought Lavaine to write as she devised
> A letter, word for word ; and when he asked
> " Is it for Lancelot, is it for my dear lord ?

Then will I bear it gladly " ; she replied,
" For Lancelot and the Queen and all the world,
But I myself must bear it." Then he wrote
The letter she devised ; which being writ
And folded, " O sweet father, tender and true,
Deny me not," she said—" ye never yet
Denied my fancies—this, however strange,
My latest : lay the letter in my hand
A little ere I die, and close the hand
Upon it ; I shall guard it even in death.
And when the heat is gone from out my heart,
Then take the little bed on which I died
For Lancelot's love, and deck·it like the Queen's
For richness, and me also like the Queen
In all I have of rich, and lay me on it.
And let there be prepared a chariot-bier
To take me to the river, and a barge
Be ready on the river, clothed in black.
I go in state to court, to meet the Queen.

And when her spirit had flown to where the weary
are at rest, her brothers follow the procession to the
waterside :

And on the black decks laid her in her bed,
Set in her hand a lily, o'er her hung
The silken case with braided blazonings,
And kiss'd her quiet brows, and saying to her
" Sister, farewell for ever," and again
" Farewell, sweet sister," parted all in tears.
Then rose the dumb old servitor, and the dead,
Oar'd by the dumb, went upward with the flood—

In her right hand the lily, in her left *
The letter—all her bright hair streaming down—
And all the coverlid was cloth of gold
Drawn to her waist, and she herself in white
All but her face, and that clear-featured face
Was lovely, for she did not seem as dead,
But fast asleep, *and lay as tho' she smiled.*

As the King and Guinevere (or according to Tennyson, as Lancelot and the Queen) are talking at the palace window overlooking the river, a barge is seen slowly drifting to the royal landing. "'That faire corps will I see,' said king Arthur. 'And then the king tooke the queene by the hand and went thither. . . . Then the king and the queene went in [to the barge], with certaine knights with them, and ther they saw a faire gentlewoman lying in a rich bed . . . and all was of cloth of gold; *and shee lay as though she had smiled. Then the queene espied the letter in the right hand; and told the king thereof.* Then the king tooke it in his hand, and said, 'Now I am sure this letter will tell what she was and why shee is come hither.' Then the king and the queene went out of the barge; . . . and so when the king was come within his chamber, he called many knights about him." Then the letter is opened and read as follows: "'Most noble knight, my lord sir Launcelot du Lake, now hath death made us two at debate for your love;

* *Vide* Note P.

I was your lover, that men called the faire maiden of
Astolat; therefore unto all ladies I make my moone;
yet for my soule that yee pray, and bury me at the
least, *and offer ye my masse peny. This is my last
request. . . . Pray for my soule, sir Launcelot, as
thou art a knight pearles.'*"

Here, Tennyson has at times retained the very
wording of the old romance:

> . . . the King
> Came girt with knights : then turn'd the tongueless man
> From the half-face to the full eye, and rose
> And pointed to the damsel, and the doors.
> *So Arthur bad the meek Sir Percivale** see at Q
> *And pure Sir Galahad to uplift the maid ;*
> And reverently they bore her into hall.
> Then came the fine Gawain and wonder'd at her,
> And Lancelot later came and mused at her,
> And last the Queen herself, and pited her :
> *But Arthur spied the letter in her hand,*
> Stoopt, took, brake seal, and read it ; this was all :

> " Most noble lord, Sir Lancelot of the Lake,
> I, sometime call'd the maid of Astolat,
> Come, for you left me taking no farewell,
> Hither, to take my last farewell of you.
> I loved you, and my love had no return,
> And therefore my true love has been my death.
> And therefore to our Lady Guinevere,
> And to all other ladies, I make moan :

* *Vide* Note Q.

Pray for my soul, and yield me burial.
Pray for my soul thou too, Sir Lancelot,
As thou art a knight peerless."

"And when sir Launcelot had heard it word by word, hee said: 'My lord king Arthur, wit you well that I am right heavy of the death of this faire damosell; God knoweth I was never causer of her death by my will. . . . Shee was both faire and good and much I was beholden unto her, but shee loved me out of measure.' 'Yee might have shewed her,' said the queene, 'some bountie and gentlenesse, that ye might have preserved her life.' "

Equally beautiful is the description in Tennyson:

> Thus he read;
> And ever in the reading, lords and dames
> Wept, looking often from his face who read
> To hers which lay so silent, and at times,
> So touch'd were they, half-thinking that her lips,
> Who had devised the letter, moved again.
>
> Then freely spoke Sir Lancelot to them all:
> "My lord liege Arthur, and all ye that hear,
> Know that for this most gentle maiden's death
> Right heavy am I; for good she was and true.
> But loved me with a love beyond all love
> In woman, whomsoever I have known.
> . . . .
> Then said the Queen

" Ye might at least have done her so much grace,
Fair lord, as would have help'd her from her death."
He raised his head, their eyes met and hers fell.

Lancelot, after showing to the satisfaction of the
Queen, at least, that such was impossible, " Then
said the king unto sir Launcelot, 'It will be your
worship that ye oversee that shee bee buried worshipfully.' 'Sir,' said sir Launcelot, 'that shall
bee done as I can best devise.' And so did the
knight,

" *Not knowing he should die a holy man.*"

But heaven was now shut to Sir Lancelot, and
much must happen ere he can pray again. Through
tourney and joust the shadow darkens on Arthur's
Court. Day by day, Guinevere's love and angry
jealousies bind the falling knight in closer bands,
until even his worldly honour is sullied in her cause.

At last, the threatening cloud breaks over the
Court. The Queen's disloyalty to her husband and
Lancelot's part in it are made manifest.

Through the treachery of Sir Agravaine and Sir
Modred, a trap is laid for the lovers, which succeeds,
but Lancelot takes stern vengeance on the spies who
discover his ill doing, and out of a party of twelve,
Modred alone survives to tell the tale.

In the *Idyll of Guinevere*, beautiful as it is, Tennyson has not kept strictly to the old romance.   Here
the Queen exhorts Sir Lancelot :

"O Lancelot, if thou love me get thee hence."
And then they were agreed upon a night
(When the good King should not be there) to meet
And part for ever.
.   .   .   Passion-pale they met
And greeted. Hands in hands, and eye to eye,
Low on the border of her couch they sat
Stammering and staring.   *It was their last hour,*
A madness of farewells.

But, in the romance, it is not their last meeting.   In
the next lines the poet is faithful to his original:

And Modred brought
His creatures to the basement of the tower
For testimony ; and crying with full voice
"Traitor, come out, ye are trapt at last," aroused
Lancelot, who rushing outward lionlike
Leapt on him, and hurl'd him headlong, and he fell
Stunn'd, and his creatures took and bare him off.

Arthur's fury at this information of the truth of
the report is unbounded.   His Queen, he declares,
shall have the law. She is doomed to be burned, and
few knights will attend to witness her execution.
Many side with Sir Lancelot, and join him in the
rescue of the Queen.   She must have been a sight to

move pity, her proud and perfect beauty, shorn of
its rays and sinking in such lurid clouds ; but, like a
sudden storm-rift, Lancelot tears apart the imminent
shade of death and carries her off to his castle of
Joyous Gard.   Even in victory, the blood of his
friends, the two brothers of Gawaine, struck down
defenceless in the fray, reddens Lancelot's hands,
and Gawaine turns on his old friend, to whom, up
to this time, he had been loyal.

The result is a war between Lancelot and the King,
or, rather, a siege by Arthur, of Lancelot's castle of
Joyous Gard.   In vain, Sir Lancelot restores his
Queen to Arthur under the safe conduct of a Papal
Bull, and prays for pardon.   In vain, he offers what
reparation he can to his outraged master, and proves
all the patience and courtesy of his strong heart, for-
bearing the King and humbling himself to Gawaine.
Wars sway to and fro between the King and Lancelot.   The scene is shifted from England to France,
and marches and sieges, defiances and knightly deeds,
follow each other as we may imagine the Plantagenet
wars to have ebbed and flowed on the plains of Anjou
and Guienne. At length, Lancelot meets Sir Gawaine
in single combat, and the latter knight is compelled
to relinquish the single combat he has provoked with
a dangerous wound. Scarcely has he time to recover,
before news of worse evils force Arthur to raise the

siege and return to England. The cause is Modred's treachery. The traitor had not only usurped regal power, but had even insolently proposed marriage to queen Guinevere, and had laid siege to the tower of London to which she had fled for safety. Finally, Arthur is slain, and the proud, passionful Queen, struck to the ground by remorse, bows her head low in Almesbury Convent.*

In the romance, the Queen *does not enter the convent until after she hears of her husband's death;* and hence in neither chronicle nor romance is Arthur ever represented as visiting his Queen after her retirement. This episode, which forms *the chief feature* in the *Idyll of Guinevere,* is the invention of Tennyson's own imagination. Still, much of the poem—especially that which describes her reception by the nuns—is so naturally beautiful, that it may be taken as a faithful picture of her convent life.

No sooner had Arthur raised the siege of Joyous Gard than Lancelot, hearing of the King's distress, hurries to England, not however to continue the fight, but to succour his lord. It is too late; he finds consummated the ruin he himself had entailed on those he loved best, and learns that even Arthur is dead. Leaving his kings and knights, he rides in

---

* This was the famed Abbey at Almesbury, an abbey of nuns of the Benedictine order, which was in high repute during the Middle Ages.

search of her who had been the false light of his eventful life.

We will follow the language of the old romance to describe their last meeting. " And at the last hee [Sir Lancelot] came to a nunry. And then was queene Guenever ware of sir Launcelot as hee walked in the cloyster ; and when shee saw him there, shee sowned three times. . . . And when sir Launcelot was brought unto her, then shee said [turning to the nuns] : ' Through this knight and mee all these warres were wrought, and the death of the most noble knights of the world ; for through our love that wee have loved together, is my most noble lord slaine.' " . . . Then turning to Sir Lancelot, she exclaims : " ' Therefore, sir Launcelot, I require thee and beseech thee heartely, for all the love that ever was betweene us two, that thou never looke mee more in the visage. . . . For as well as I have loved thee, sir Launcelot, now mine heart will not once serve mee to see thee ; for through mee and thee is the floure of kings and knights destroyed. Therefore, sir Launcelot, goe, goe thou unto thy realme, and there take thee a wife, and live with her in joy and blisse. And I beseech you heartely pray for mee.' . . . ' Nay, madame,' said sir Launce-lot, ' wit yee well, that I will never while I live ; for I shall never bee so false to you of that I have promised, but the same desteny that yee have taken you unto I will take mee unto.' . . . And so they departed. But there was never so hard a hearted man but hee would have wept to see the sorrow that they made, for there was a lamentation as though they had beene stungen with speares and many times they sowned and the ladies beare the queene to her chamber ; and sir Launcelot awoke, and went and tooke his horse and rode all that day and all that night in a forest weeping." * ꜱₑₑ ᵢ₊ₜ ₓ

Lancélot and seven of his knights, in fulfilment of his promise, remain for six years in penance as postulants, and then he took the habit of priesthood and for twelve months he sang the Mass. "And thus upon a night there came a vision unto sir Launcelot, and charged him, . . . to hast him towards Almesbury 'and by that time thou come there thou shalt finde queene Guenever dead . . . and bring you the corps of her, and bury it by her lord and husband, the noble king Arthur.'" He started ere it was day, but his fellows were weak and weary, and when he reached her bedside Guinevere had been dead a half hour. Her constant prayer for two long days before her death being that she might be spared the trial of another meeting with Lance-lot. "I beseech Almighty God that I may never

* *Vide* Note R.

have power to see sir Launcelot with my worldly
eyes."

To the dregs Sir Lancelot drank the cup of suffering. He led the funeral to Glastonbury, and when the
Queen was put into the earth, Sir Lancelot swooned
and lay long upon the ground. For six weeks he
lay "grovelling" and praying continually upon the
tomb of Arthur and Guinevere; but, at last, rest
came to the weary penitent. During the night the
bishop of the monastery has a vision. "I saw," he
said, "the angels heave up sir Launcelot towards
heaven, and the gates of heaven opened against
him," and going to the knight's cell "hee lay as hee
had smiled." He had died in the night alone.

We cannot look upon Lancelot as a mere embodiment of chivalric ideas. If, during his early career,
he was but part of Arthur's pageant, in his grief and
death a human interest gathers around him, and the
hero of the old trouvères seems to us warm with the
same life that we live. There are Lancelots on the
field of battle; there are Lancelots in society; men
so strong, yet so weak, offering noble qualities at an
evil shrine. It is not through weakness of heart or
sinew that Lancelot fails to accomplish the high
ends of his existence; he is the one peerless knight,
peerless in joust and tournament, peerless in strength
and courage and endurance; peerless in generosity

and courtesy, and forgetfulness of self ; but in purity, in humility, in obedience, he fails. Which of our novelists would leave their hero a feeble and stricken beggar at Heaven's porch without at least surrounding him with the halo of religious joy ? No theatrical deathbed scene makes us almost rejoice in the crime which requires such a display of redeeming grace. In sombre shade Lancelot creeps to his grave hidden from the wonder of men. No light is granted to him till Death draws aside the veil, Death the evening star that rose on his night when all other lights of mortal life were quenched.

The romance is an ennobling study, teaching the grand truth of our incapacity to fulfil our highest aspirations if they are not hallowed by those virtues which form the Christian's crown.

CHAPTER VIII.

Galahad and the Quest of the Holy Graal.

A S we ascend the steps and enter the portals of the amphitheatre of Arthurian Romance, the leading object that strikes the eye is the Holy Graal. There, in the midst, raised high above the concourse of noble knights and peerless ladies, high above the arena where armed warriors, in the pride of manly strength, tourney and joust, high above the throne where King and princes sit, hovers the mystic Vessel, clothed in white samite, tinged with a roseate hue, and refulgent with the sheen of its own glory.

Beneath the wondrous cup stands Galahad, his eyes raised from the brilliant assemblage beneath, and fixed in beatific rapture upon the heavenly prize which he has won. As we gaze upon the holy youth, he looks like a second St. Michael, a conqueror, yet passionless in the hour of triumph, piercing the dragon Evil, yet unsullied by its fiendish breath. There is no shadow upon him of coming death. He wears his immortality with the calm of perfect faith. There is no dint of conflict on his white shield, no

16   241

blood-stains on his glistening armour, and if he has fought with Satan, no soilure mars the perfection of his form, and as he stands there, his whole body is enwrapped in the mellow rays which dart downwards from the Holy Graal.

But this subject of Galahad and the famous Quest, of which he is the hero, is beset by innumerable difficulties. In this part of the tale we find ourselves wandering amid the phantoms of an epic allegory. At times, as we read, it is difficult to dispel the illusion that we are being led into some hitherto unexplored region of the *Faerie Queene*, so ideal, so ethereal are the scenes which surround us. But this allegorical garb, in which the romance is clothed, presents but slight difficulty. There are other and weightier ones lurking behind.

We have seen that this Graal romance has no existence in the Cambrian version, and that it is unknown to the Armorican story. In other words, it is peculiar to the Norman *epopoiia* and is the production of Walter Map, wit, poet, scholar, priest, and theologian. We might therefore expect, *à priori*, that this romance would contain a great deal which only hard, patient study could unfold. And such we find to be the actual case. To understand this romance in all its fulness and depth of meaning, it is necessary to have read the apocryphal gospels; to be familiar with the Talmud and the fanciful legends of the Rabbis ; to be well versed in ecclesiastical history, the traditions of the Church, and Catholic theology ; and, moreover, we must be willing to analyse quaint fables and strange mystic conceits. These are difficulties. Still, it is not necessary to go thus deeply into the subject in simply tracing the Arthurian narrative as told by the trouvères, since the interest of the story is not wholly dependent upon the understanding of the subtle meaning which lies beneath the surface. Many have, doubtless, read *Gulliver's Travels* and others of Swift's writings, at a period of life when the terms Whig and Tory were scarcely less mythic than those of Gog and Magog. Hundreds, read *Don Quixote* as a clever, amusing creation, who are innocent of any knowledge of chivalry or of the difference between an Idealist and a Realist. Even Voltaire's philosophical romances may be perused with pleasure without the reader being aware that there is such an axiom in philosophy as the relativity of human knowledge. And so, the Quest of the Holy Graal will afford gratification, even though the fancies and legends and mystic meaning which lie concealed beneath the glittering pageant are but faintly perceived.

Now, this adventure is not only the culminating point, but the essential feature, of the whole narra-

tive as told by the trouvères. It permeates every
part, it colours every incident, and it gives soul to
every scene, from the advent of Merlin to the translation of Arthur ; and the question arises, what object could Map have had in thus spiritualising the
tale ; in thus changing so essentially its whole scope,
motive, or aim, as to render it a distinct and independent version ?

A glance at the origin of the English drama will,
at once, give a clue to this apparent anomaly. It is
a curious fact, that the oldest English plays known
to us, were written during the same century in
which Walter Map wrote his romances, though
somewhat earlier in that century. They are what
are technically known as Miracle plays, *i. e.*, some
Scripture narrative, say, the *Raising of Lazarus*, was
taken from the New Testament, thrown into the
form of a dialogue, with additional touches suggested by the fancy of the writer, and so modernised as to suit the customs and habits of thought of
an uneducated audience. On the day of the per-
formance, the town church was turned into a temporary theatre, and the clergy into amateur actors.
The slightest acquaintance with twelfth century life,
renders it certain that the clergy assumed the *rôle*
of playrights and actors, not simply for the amuse-
ment of the people, but for their instruction. What

audience that had ever witnessed a Miracle play
could fail to carry away an indelible remembrance
of the facts thus represented? What oral instruction could ever equal this pictorial teaching of the
rude, ignorant ceorls and villeins?

Now, what the secular clergy endeavoured to accomplish, on behalf of the unlettered masses, by
means of Miracle plays, that did Walter Map, the
University Archdeacon, attempt to accomplish on
behalf of the warrior class, by means of the tales of
chivalry. There was this distinction, however, that
while the Miracle plays taught principally the *facts*
of the Holy Gospel, the romance dealt chiefly with
the *doctrines* of Holy Church. The object of each
was to familiarise the truths of religion and to instruct the people. On the one hand, to instruct the
masses in the facts of Scripture by means of plays;
and on the other, to instruct the *knightly class* in
the doctrines of Christianity by means of the romances of chivalry. It was a shrewd, far-sighted idea
of this witty priest; a grand idea for that age, and
carried out with the artistic finish of genius. How
delighted the clergy must have been, as they met
with the old, familiar dogmas of the Church, decked
out in all the pomp and glitter of knighthood for
the delectation of the barons; and how big with
importance the knights must have felt, when they

saw members of their own Order represented as the heroes of an adventure which eclipsed even the highest possible glory of the Crusades. Little did the noble lords and gentle ladies dream, as they followed with breathless interest the fortunes of Galahad and the questing knights, that they were listening to a sermon on the " Quest of Eternal Life." And yet, that such is the fact, will appear in a very clear light as we advance in the examination of the romance itself.

On the vigil of the feast of Pentecost, which Arthur always celebrated with royal magnificence, there entered into the hall of the palace at Camelot, a fair gentlewoman who desired to see Sir Lancelot, and when that famous knight is pointed out to her, she requests him, on king Pelles' behalf, to follow her on an adventure into a neighbouring forest. Lancelot accordingly accompanies her, not knowing why or whither he is going, till they come to an " abbey of nuns," and the two enter within the sacred enclosure. No sooner has the knight rested himself, than there enter into the room where he is awaiting them, three of the sisters, leading by the hand a young squire of noble mien and bearing, and entreat Sir Lancelot to make him a knight. The request is granted, and at the hour of prime next morning, the youth, who proves to be Galahad, re-

ceives the honour of knighthood at the hands of his
own father. This, then, is the first glimpse which we
get of the virgin knight, the hero of the romance.
He had been committed to the care of this sister-
hood upon the death of his mother Elaine (king
Pelles' daughter, not her of Astolat), and having
been nourished by them, suddenly appears in the
narrative at this point.

The same morning, being Whitsunday, Sir Lancelot returns to Court, arriving there while the King
and Queen are at Mass. But service being ended, a
strange sight is seen in Camelot. Letters of gold,
as if produced by miracle, are discovered in the
seats of the Round Table, and in the " siege perillous " is an inscription stating that that siege should
be fulfilled that very day. Scarcely have King and
knights recovered from their astonishment, when a
squire rushes breathless into the hall, announcing
that he has just seen, floating on the river near by, a
large stone and a sword fast therein by the point.
The hall is immediately deserted by King and knights
who hasten to the river side, and there see the mysterious sword. Urged by the King, one after another
of the company attempts to draw out the sword,
but all are unsuccessful, and finally relinquish the
adventure for the time being.

Shortly after this, while the knights are seated at

dinner, there enters the palace " an old man and
an ancient " clothed in white, but no member of
the Round Table knows his name or whence he
comes.   Accompanying him is a young knight in red
armour but without shield or sword ; only an empty
scabbard dangles at his side.   Then the old man addresses King Arthur : " Sir, I bring you heere a young
knight, that is of kings lineage, and of the kindred
of Joseph of Arimathy, whereby the mervailes of
this court and of strang realmes shall be fully accomplished."   The King welcomes him, and then,
at the bidding of his companion, the youth places
himself in the "siege perillous," to the astonishment
of the assembled knights, who fear lest his temerity
be punished by sudden malady or death.   No evil,
however, befalling him, a whisper passes around the
board, that the unknown youth is doubtless he whom
Merlin had long before foretold, should achieve the
adventure of the Holy Graal and fill the long vacant
seat.   All doubt on this point is soon set at rest.
The dinner ended, the King raises the silken covering of the " siege perillous," and there, written in
letters of gold, is seen the name of " Galahad."   The
King then takes the youthful knight by the hand,
and, accompanied by the Court, leads the way to the
river to show Sir Galahad the mystic sword.   No
sooner does the latter touch the weapon than it in-

stantly yields to his hand, and, more wonderful yet, it is found upon trial to fit exactly the empty scabbard which dangles at his side. The report spreads, lightning-like, over Camelot, that the hour has arrived for the adventure of the Sangraal, and that the long-expected hero, who is to achieve the adventure, has at length made his appearance. The halls of Camelot ring with excitement and merriment. The Queen, hearing the commotion, enquires the cause, and is told of the strange things that are occurring. On his return from the river, the King bids the knights of the Round Table to assemble in the meadow to joust and tourney and to see Galahad "proved." The Queen's curiosity is excited; she attends the tournament, and when the young knight has "won his spurs" by overthrowing all of the noblest warriors save two, Sir Lancelot and Sir Percival, he is summoned into the presence of queen Guinevere to receive the guerdon of praise from her own lips.

That very night, in the banquet hall, is revealed to Arthur's Court the mystery which Galahad is come to solve. As the knights are sitting at supper, there is heard a mighty blast, and the next moment a beam of heavenly light darts athwart the hall, disclosing the presence of the Holy Graal, clothed in white samite, while delicious odours diffuse themselves on every side, and the tables are spread with the choicest of earthly gifts. It appears but for a second, then vanishes, and the hall, deserted by the supernatural light, looks dark and drear. The King is the first to break the death-like silence which succeeds, and utters in trembling tones an ascription of praise to God.

Gawaine next speaks : " I will make heere avow," he exclaims, in ringing tones, "that tomorrow without any longer abiding, I shall labour in the quest of the sancgreall, that I shall hold me out a twelve moneths and a day, or more if neede bee and never shal I returne againe unto the court *til I have seene it* [the Graal] *more openly than it hath beene seene heere ;* and if I may not speed, I shall returne againe as hee that may not bee against the will of our Lord Jesu Christ."

The majority of the knights present, when they hear Gawaine's resolve, join in the avow. Arthur is greatly displeased at this sudden resolve, and turning sharply upon his nephew, Gawaine, he exclaims, "Alas! yee have nigh slaine me with the vow and promise that yee have made; for through you yee have beereft mee of the fairest fellowship and the truest of knighthood that ever were seene together in any realme of the world. For when they shall depart from hence, I am sure that all shall never meete more in this world, for there shall many die, in the quest. . . . And therewith the teares fell into his eyes." The whole Court is thrown into a state of deepest mourning by this fatal vow. "I mervaile," cries queen Guinevere with her accustomed impetuosity, when told of what has happened, "I mervaile my lord will suffer them to depart from him."

On Whitmonday, the morning of their departure, "as soon as it was daylight, the king arose, for hee had taken no rest of all that night for sorrow." Then, seeing Gawaine chatting with Lancelot, while biding the hour of Mass, he approaches him, and in sorrowful terms bewails the Quest. "'Ah, sir Gawaine, sir Gawaine,'" he exclaims, "'yee have betraied me. . . . Yee will never be sory for me as I am for you,' and therewith the teares began to runne downe by his visage." After Mass at the Minster, the King commands that those who have taken the vow be numbered, and the tale is found to amount to a hundred and fifty knights, all of the Round Table. Then follows a busy scene of arming and preparing for departure, after which the knights and attendant squires mount their horses, and the brilliant cavalcade rides through the streets of Camelot. And as they pass, elated with hope, and glorying in their strength, throngs of weeping men and weeping women and weeping children mourn their departure.

And so the Quest of the Holy Graal is begun.

One point we may notice before passing on. It must be borne in mind, that the presence of the sacred Vessel in Britain, in Apostolic times, is represented by the romancer as having produced so profound an impression upon the national mind, that when it was seen no more by mortal eyes, the story of its wonder-working power still survived as a vivid tradition, handed down from generation to generation, but never for a moment absent from the national imagination ; and that the hope of its reappearance and final realisation retained its hold on the national heart throughout all the vicissitudes of its history. This traditional expectation, moreover, is represented as having taken a more tangible form after Merlin's famous prediction : " By them that shall be fellowes of the round table the truth of the sancgreall shall be knowne " ; and when asked " how men might know them that should best do in the achieveing of the sancgreall," he said, " there shall be three white bulls that shall achieve it, and the two shall be maidens and the third shall be chaste ; and one of the three shall passe his father as much as the lyon passeth his libbard both of strength and of hardinesse." But that which is depicted as having raised national expectation to the highest possible pitch, was the fact that, on many occasions, the Sangraal, clothed in samite, had actually appeared to some of the knights before the Quest began, and that more than one miracle had been performed by its instrumentality.

These considerations will render intelligible the otherwise inexplicable fact, that Arthur and his knights should at once identify the vision which appeared in the banquet hall, with the Holy Graal, and should have entered upon the Quest with an eagerness that brooked no delay.

We shall pause here, at the end of this introductory section, and consider Tennyson's version of this part of the romance.

The form in which the poet has thrown his Idyll, that of a dialogue, is pardonable, since to have given it in the narrative form of the romance, would have required dramatic power of a high order; a power conspicuously absent in Tennyson, as his dramas clearly prove. The parties to this dialogue are Sir Percival, after his retirement to the monastery, and a brother monk; a most unfortunate selection, as we shall now see. In no version with which we are acquainted, is Percival represented as returning to Arthur's Court after the termination of the Quest. On the contrary, we are distinctly told that he "yeelded him to an hermitage oute of the city" (Sarras), immediately after the Quest; whereas Ten-

nyson depicts him as accompanying Sir Bors back
to Britain, visiting the Court, and relating to the
monk what had happened at that time. With regard to the monk himself we are at a loss to know
where Tennyson found his prototype. This worthy,
it seems, had scarcely so much as heard of the Holy
Graal, and when it is mentioned by Percival he
exclaims:

> " The Holy Grail !—I trust
> We are green in Heaven's eyes ; but here too much
> We moulder—as to things without I mean—
> Yet one of your own knights, a guest of ours,
> Told us of this in our refectory.
>
> .   .   .   .
>
> *What is it ?*
> *The phantom of a cup that comes and goes ? "*

Is it not strange that a *monk* should be represented
as hearing, for the first time, of this ecclesiastical
legend from a knight ? Moreover, what could Tennyson mean, when he makes the monk say respecting the Graal:

> " From our old books I know
> That Joseph came of old to Glastonbury,
>
> .   .   .   .
>
> For so they say, these books of ours, *but seem*
> *Mute of this miracle, far as I have read,"*

when every abbot, monk, and hermit introduced in
this romance is represented, not only as perfectly

familiar with the history of the sacred Vessel, but
also with all the predictions respecting it. Indeed,
wherever Galahad goes, he is at once recognised by
the religious Orders as *the* knight whose advent has
long been expected, and in connection with whom
the adventure of the Holy Graal is to be achieved.

But we will now proceed to the poem itself:

Tennyson, in dealing with this section of the
romance, has wandered very materially from his
original. The Idyll opens with the story of the
Graal, which, however, is dismissed with a few
masterly touches. Then Galahad is brought forward, not by any means as a newly made knight of
the Round Table, but as one whose white armour is
already well known at Court. The marvel of the
sword is entirely omitted, and the tournament,
which, in the romance, is proclaimed to "prove" the
young knight, (an indispensable custom of chivalry,)
is transformed, by Tennyson, into a grand reunion
of the Court previous to the Quest.

In the episode of the appearance of the Sangraal
in the banquet hall, which immediately follows this
tournament, Tennyson strictly follows the old romance:

"Then anon they heard cracking, and crying of
thunder, that hem thought the place should all to-
rive: in the midst of the blast entred a sunne beame

more clear by seaven times than ever they saw day,
and all they were alighted of the grace of the holy
Ghost. Then began every knight to behold other,
and either saw other by their seeming fairer then
ever they saw afore, not for then [nevertheless] there
was no knight that might speake any word a great
while, and so they looked every man on other as
they had beene dombe. Then there entred into
the hall the holy grale covered with white samite,
but there was none that might see it nor who beare it
and there was all the hall fulfilled with good odours
. . . and when the holy grale had beene borne
through the hall then the holy vessel departed sud-
enly, that they wist not where it became."

So in Tennyson :

> " And all at once, as there we sat, we heard
> A cracking and a riving of the roofs,
> And rending, and a blast, and overhead
> Thunder, and in the thunder was a cry.
> And in the blast there smote along the hall
> A beam of light seven times more clear than day :
> And down the long beam stole the Holy Grail
> All over cover'd with a luminous cloud,
> And none might see who bare it, and it past.
> But every knight beheld his fellow's face
> As in a glory, and all the knights arose,
> And staring each at other like dumb men
> Stood."

In the romance, as we have seen, it is Gawaine who first takes upon himself the avow; but in Tennyson this distinction is claimed by Percival:

> " I sware a vow before them all, that I,
> Because I had not seen the Grail, would ride
> A twelvemonth and a day in quest of it,
> Until I found and saw it, as the nun
> My sister saw it ; and Galahad sware the vow."

According to Tennyson, the King is absent when this vision appears; he had been called away to avenge a maiden who had been assaulted by bandits, and returns only just in time to witness the commotion caused by the vision, and to learn the sad news of the vow which the knights had taken upon themselves during his absence. As we have before observed, the moment Tennyson leaves the beaten path of the old romance, the beauty, unity, and consistency of the epic immediately suffer. It is difficult to see why Arthur, who is now represented as Emperor of the civilised world, should go in person,

> " to smoke the scandalous hive of those wild bees,"

a bandit stronghold not far from Camelot. What skilful narrator would have made the King absent, not only on a festival which Arthur always kept with

17

regal splendour, but on that grandest of all festivals,
which was to reveal the crowning glory of his reign
and to be the culminating point of knightly adventure? However, the King returns and expostulates
with the knights for their discourtesy in not awaiting
his return before taking the vow. After his somewhat bitter reproof, and while Sir Percival is relating
very courteously all the facts connected with the
vision, the King brusquely interrupts him, and with
marked petulance exclaims:

> " ' Yea, yea,
> Art thou so bold and hast not seen the Grail ? '

> " ' Nay, lord, I heard the sound, I saw the light,
> But since I did not see the Holy Thing,
> I sware a vow to follow it till I saw.'

> " Then, when he ask'd us, knight by knight, if any
> Had seen it, all their answers were as one :
> ' Nay, lord, and therefore have we sworn our vows.'

> .   .   .   .

> " Then Galahad on the sudden, and in a voice
> Shrilling along the hall to Arthur, call'd,
> *' But I, Sir Arthur, saw the Holy Grail,*
> *I saw the Holy Grail and heard a cry—*
> *" O Galahad, and O Galahad, follow me."* ' "

In the romance, to *see* the Graal is tantamount to
the achievement of the Quest; for, as we shall sub-

previously seen the Graal have already achieved
the [...] cycle and Malory. But this is not
[...] then in not seek it out

sequently find, not even Galahad is allowed to *see* the Graal until the Quest is virtually at an end. It was because Gawaine and the other knights had *not* seen it, they made the vow. It was because Galahad had *not* seen it that *he* took upon himself the vow. If Galahad had *seen* the Holy Graal there was no longer any need of a vow, for, to him, the Quest was achieved. Tennyson, not recognising the fact that to *see* the Holy Vessel is equivalent to the *achievement of the adventure*, has first transferred to his pages the very words of the vow as they stand in the romance, viz.: "to follow till they see," and then has added this exclamation of Galahad,

"But I, Sir Arthur, *saw* the Holy Grail," as a fanciful touch of his own, thus stultifying the whole story.

We have said that this Romance is an allegory. It is an allegory of *Justification*, and, as we proceed, this point will come out very fully. The Holy Graal is an image of *Salvation*, or Eternal Life. The appearance of the Holy Graal on Whitsunday, the baptismal day, represents the Divine *call* to Salvation, and the Quest of the Holy Graal is a figure of the *quest* of Salvation, or Eternal Life. With this allegory in his mind, the romancer could never, for one moment, have represented Galahad as having *seen* Eternal life, before he had so much as started on the Quest. Galahad, simply does what all the knights do; he swears to go on the Quest of the Graal because it has not been seen, and to pursue it till it is revealed in the full effulgence of the True Blood which it enshrines. *

Tennyson had before him in this allegorical romance one of the most exquisite conceptions and most artistic productions in literature, which he might have rendered still more beautiful by the grace of his poetic skill; but unfortunately he missed the allegory and has produced the tale, shorn of its unique fascination and bereft of its deep spiritual meaning.

The only remaining point that we need notice is the start from Camelot.

" And then they put on their helmes and departed, recommanded them all wholy unto the queene, and there was weeping and great sorrow. Then the queene *departed into her chamber*, so that no man should perceive her great sorrowes. When sir Launcelot missed the queene hee went into her chamber, and when shee saw him, she cried aloud, ' O, sir Launcelot, ye have betraied me, and put mee to death, for to leave thus my lord.' ' A! madame,' said sir Launcelot, ' I pray you bee not displeased,

* *Vide* Note S.

for I shall come againe as soone as I may with my
worship.' ' Alas,' said shee, ' that ever I saw you !
but he that suffred death upon the crosse for all
mankind, bee to you good conduct and safetie, and
all the whole fellowship.' Right so departed sir
Launcelot, and found his fellowship that abod his
comming ; and so they mounted upon their horses,
and rode through the streetes of Camelot, and there
was weeping of the rich and poore, and the king returned away, and might not speake for weeping."

In Tennyson, the cavalcade passes rich galleries,
lady laden, who shower flowers upon them, and in
the streets :

> " . . . men and boys astride
> On wyvern, lion, dragon, griffin, swan,
> At all the corners, named us each by name,
> Calling ' God speed ! ' but in the ways below
> The knights and ladies wept, and rich and poor
> Wept, and the King himself could hardly speak
> For grief, *and all in middle street the Queen,*
> *Who rode by Lancelot, wail'd and shriek'd aloud,*
> ' This madness has come on us for our sins.'
> So to the Gate of the three Queens we came,
> Where Arthur's wars are render'd mystically,
> And thence departed every one his way."

To our way of thinking, the simplicity of the
romancer's " chamber scene," and a queen retiring
thither alone, to hide her great sorrows, is far more

artistic and far truer to nature than Tennyson's picture of a shrieking queen riding by the side of Sir
Lancelot in middle street.

The next section of the romance covers the whole
period, from the beginning of the Quest to the return to Arthur's Court of Gawaine and the rest of
the noble knights, with the exception of Galahad,
Percival, Bors, and Lancelot. To give an analysis
of this part of the tale is simply impossible. Every
page contains some knightly adventure, beautiful in
idea, and exquisitely narrated; or some strange
dream or fantastic vision, too ethereal to allow of its
being taken out of its original setting. As the adventure proceeds, we follow noble knights over a
kind of dreamland of forest and meadow, hill and
valley, mountain and plain; we see them entertained
at fair castles, and rich abbeys, and lonely hermit-
ages; we watch them in the brilliant tournament or
jousting in single combat in unfrequented spots; we
hear of them taking up the gauntlet in defence
of oppressed gentlewomen, and restoring the disin-
herited to their estates; we find them battling with
fiends who attack them in human shapes, or allure
them by their blandishments from solemn vows;
we see them at confession and at Mass, or listening
to the advice of plain-spoken hermits; the whole
so delicately interwoven, that no analysis will do

justice to the romance, or give any adequate idea of
its beauty.

But whithersoever we follow these knights, it is the
achievement of the Quest which inflames their hearts
and prompts them to noble actions. Their superhuman efforts to achieve the adventure, vividly image
forth the strivings of the soul after communion with
the True Blood, after Eternal Life; and the opposition which the knights experience from fiends who
would destroy them, or from Cyprians who would
dazzle their senses, is but an idealised portrayal of
the temptations which beset the Christian knight of
every age.

But we will descend to particulars. On the departure of the knights from Camelot, they journey
in different directions, each one taking the road
which his fancy points out. Galahad, after four
days' wandering, comes to a white abbey, *i. e.*, an
abbey of white or Augustine monks, and while there
becomes the possessor of a white shield, embla-
zoned with a cross of blood that comes and goes; a
miraculous shield, which Joseph, "son of the gentle knight that tooke downe our lord from the
crosse," gave to a certain pagan king who accompanied him into Britain. This miraculous shield, on
the death of its owner, was left in charge of these
monks, for them to have in keeping until the advent

of the best knight of the world ; and, accordingly, when Galahad appears, it is at once taken from its hiding-place behind the altar and presented to him. Armed with this shield, and with the mystic sword won at Camelot, the maiden knight proceeds on the Quest, accompanied by a young prince as his sole attendant. They have not journeyed far, when they see facing them a huge cross which marks the point where the road branches off into two paths. Inscribed on the cross, they read the following warning: "Yee knights arraunt, the which goeth for to seeke adventures, see here two waies, that one way defendeth thee that thou goe not that way, for hee shall not goe out of that way againe, but if hee bee a good man and a worthy knight ; and if thou goe on the left hand, thou shalt not there lightly win prowesse, for thou shalt in this way be soone assayed."

The young prince, Galahad's attendant, eager to show his prowess, obtains Galahad's reluctant permission to travel this perilous path, and so they part. Soon the youth comes to a fair meadow, where he espies a shady bower, and a rich banquet spread upon the grass, and near by, lying on a throne of boughs, a crown of gold. The novice, dazzled by the splendour of the jewel, seizes it, and rides off, but scarcely is he out of sight when two knights, who are the owners of the treasure, pursue him and give him battle.   The novice is worsted ; left on the field apparently dead, and might have perished had not Galahad, at that moment, come to his succour, vanquished his assailants, and carried the wounded man off to a neighbouring convent.   The holy hermit, who there undertakes to cure him of his wounds, administers at the same time some wholesome advice.   " I mervaile," said the good man, "how ye durst take upon you so rich a thing as the high order of knighthood without cleane confession ; and that was the cause yee were so bitterly wounded."   He then proceeds to explain the mystery of the two roads.   " The way on the right hand betokneth the hieway of our Lord Jesu Christ, and the way of a true and good liver, and the other way betokneth the way of sinners and misbeleevers . . . and pride is the head of all deadly sinnes that caused you to depart sir Galahad, and where thou tookest the crowne of gold thou sinned in coveteousnesse and in theft, and these were no knights deeds."

Leaving his companion to the care and blunt reproofs of the holy man, Galahad proceeds on the Quest alone, and meets with many and strange adventures.   At one time he comes to a strong castle, strongly guarded, called the " Castle of Maidens." As he approaches it, bent on destroying the wicked

customs of the place, he is attacked by seven armed
knights at once. But he overthrows them single-
handed, and so enters the fortress unopposed. A
strange sight now meets his eyes. The court of the
castle is filled with a multitude of people, and the
dungeons crowded with captives, who hail him as
their deliverer, and whom he releases from thraldom.

We have noticed this adventure simply because it
is allegorical of the mediæval legend known as the
"Harrowing of Hell." "The castle of Maidens,"
says a hermit, who is introduced here, as elsewhere,
to explain the allegory, "betokeneth the good
soules that were in prison afore the incarnation of
Christ; and the seaven knights betoken the seaven
deadly sinnes, which reigned that time in the world.
And I may liken the good knight sir Galahad unto
the sonne of the high father that . . . brought
all the soules out of thraldome."

In this part of the romance, although the allegory is
never dropped for any length of time, yet we occasionally meet with a plain matter-of-fact adventure
which forms a kind of link between the romance
proper and the allegory. Thus : shortly after the
preceding adventure, Sir Galahad meets Sir Lancelot
and Sir Percival, the two most famous knights of the
Round Table ; but they, failing to recognise the

vanishing arms on Galahad's shield, offer to joust, and are successively smitten to the earth by their unknown enemy. It is only after Galahad has put spurs to his horse and disappeared, that they guess the truth with regard to their antagonist.

Even in such cases, where an allegorical meaning is wanting, there is an evident purpose, viz. : to show Galahad forth as the one peerless knight of the world, and this, as the consequence of his unapproachable purity of character.

In addition, however, to the romantic and allegorical elements in this part of the narrative, elements which are intertwined throughout the whole work with consummate skill, there is a charm which is peculiar to this part of the story. As Percival and Bors and Lancelot ride through city, hill, and plain, on this ideal Quest, we may imagine them jogging along the country, at times faint, at times weary, at times despairing, but ever dreaming of foes human and superhuman which may at any moment become realities and require to be overcome. These daydreams of the knights, these phantom adventures which have no existence outside of the fervid brain of the knights, which come and go like castles in the air, are inserted in the romance, and so skilfully are they woven into the warp and woof of the tale, that, like the story of *Alice in Wonderland*, it is often difficult to see where the reality ends and the dreamland begins. Indeed, so perfect is the illusion, that in reading the Romance of the Quest for the first time one often fails to recognise the transition from real adventure to dream adventure, until by some accident the knight is awakened from his dream and the whole scene vanishes into air. What increases the illusion still more, is the allegorical nature of these day-dreams or phantom adventures; for, dreams though they be, they form an essential part of the tale; they have a direct bearing on the character of the knights, and possess as subtle and spiritual a meaning as any other portion of the legend.

Let us take an example. As Sir Bors is riding through the country, he overtakes a man clothed in a religious habit and mounted on a strong, black horse. As they are going in the same direction they join company, and soon knight and monk become absorbed in an all-engrossing conversation. At length they come to a castle with a high tower, and the monk invites Sir Bors to enter. Wearied with the day's journey, he accepts the proffered hospitality and, on entering, finds there a brilliant assemblage of knights and fair ladies, who give him a hearty welcome and assist him to unarm. Presently, knowing that he is hungry, they make him such cheer that he forgets all his sorrows and anguish, and, oblivious of all besides, abandons himself to the delights and dainties placed before him. While thus engaged, the lady of the castle approaches " more richer beseene then ever he saw queene Guinever," and by her he is treated with all the consideration which pertains to a knight of the Round Table. But during the evening this lady makes such violent love to Sir Bors that at last the knight " was right evill at ease " and wishes himself well away. Finally, seeing that all her more delicate manœuvres are lost upon the sturdy knight, she tells him point blank : " Ah, sir Bors, . . . I have loved you for the great beautie I have seen in you and the great hardinesse I have heard of you, therefore I pray you graunt it mee [his love]." But Sir Bors, whose soul is wrapped up in the Quest of the Sangraal, courteously excuses himself. Therewith, wounded in pride, she leaves the company, goes up into a high battlement, taking with her her twelve gentlewomen, and when they reach the summit of the tower one of the ladies cries : " Ah ! sir Bors, gentle knight, have mercy on us all, and suffer my lady to have her will, and if yee doe not, wee must suffer death with our lady, for to fall downe from this high tower." Sir Bors raises his eyes to the battlement and there sees these gentlewomen on the point of being dashed to the ground. He pities them, but is inexorable, and the next moment they are hurled from the tower and fall to the earth dead. Filled with horror at such a deed, the knight makes the sign of the cross on his forehead, when instantly, "he heard a full great noyse and a great crie as though all the feends of hell had beene about him; and therewith he saw neither tower, nor lady, nor gentlewomen. . . . Then he heard a clocke smite on his right hand, and thither hee came to an abbey on his right hand closed with high walls, and there hee was let in."

This is evidently a day-dream or phantom adventure, which has no existence outside the brain of the knight. At the same time, it is an allegory, as the writer himself expounds it, of the temptations of "the world, the flesh and the devil," which a saintly knight must overcome if he would attain to the communion of the Sangraal; and hence essential to the unfolding of the character of the true Christian knight and to the unity of the story.

On a similar occasion, when Sir Percival is grievously tempted, the *finale* is more striking yet. The knight had been wandering three whole days without food or rest, his whole being absorbed in the sanctities of the Quest; ever toiling, fighting, striving to aid the right and punish wrong, when he finds himself in a rich pavilion surrounded by all thc beauties of an ideal landscape, and there lies down to rest. Scarcely has he slept sufficient time to refresh himself, when he is aroused by a sense of his criminal sluggishness in thus relaxing his ardour, and is about to put on his armour, when there is miracuously set before him " all maner of meats and wines that he could thinke of." Yielding to this fresh temptation, he partakes of the food, and drinks freely of the wine. Again a feeling of lassitude takes possession of him. He throws himself, a second time, on the luxurious couch and abandons himself to ease and effeminacy, forgetful of the Holy Quest. Temptation after temptation assails him, each succeeding trial being of graver and more seductive character than the preceding one. He lies sunk in sensuality, an easy prey to any deadlier lust that may assault him, but at length, when on the point of yielding, his eye rests on his naked sword which lies on the ground at his side. He sees the pommel of that sword on which was a red cross and the sign of the crucifix. Instantly he thinks of his knighthood, his vow, his holy vocation, and, rising from the couch, he crosses himself, when pavilion, banquet, all turn to smoke and black cloud and the air is filled with fiendish yellings.

What need to explain such an allegory as this?

The adventures in this romance, as we before

noticed, have but one end or aim, viz. : to show in the clearest possible light the Catholic doctrine of Justification.

In the previous section we had an allegory of *Preventing Grace ;* the appearance of the Graal in the banquet hall being an image of the *divine Call to Salvation ;* the eager start on the Quest being an emblem of the feverish thirst in the heart of man for Eternal Life, and man's *Free Will* being mirrored forth in the starting of a hundred and fifty knights, while only three attain the object of the Quest.

In this second division of the romance, under a complexity of adventures lies hidden the doctrine of *Penance.* In every case the knights are required to evince true contrition, to confess, and to seek absolution as a pre-requisite to success, and to make satisfaction as a condition no less necessary. Then, the cure of the soul is attended to. Chastity and all Christian virtues are held forth as essential, and adventure is cumulated upon adventure only to bring out, in strong relief, the necessity of sanctification and good works that man, through the infinite satisfaction of the Cross, may become really just in the sight of God.

This section, so distinctly marked in the romance as one most important stage in the Quest of Salvation, has scarcely any counterpart in Tenny-

son's Idyll. The reason of this is readily seen.
Tennyson either failed to recognise or intentionally
ignored the spiritual meaning underlying the romance, and hence it would have been superfluous
to reproduce adventures essential only to the perfection of the allegory. The Quest of the Sangraal
in Walter Map's hands is not only the culmination
of all previous knightly adventures, it is a reflection of the highest spiritual aspirations of man and
of his mortal conflict with the powers of darkness. It is impossible, however, to read the Idyll of
the *Holy Grail* without feeling that Tennyson must
have viewed the romance simply as a quaint, mediæval conceit, without any organic connection with the
rest of the epic ; an appendage, so to speak, and inserted because, for some inexplicable reason, the
knights of the Round Table figure in it. In the
Idyll, the Holy Graal itself is little more than a
poetic will-o'-the-wisp. In the opening of the poem
the King asks Sir Percival :

> " ' Have ye seen a *cloud* ?
> What go ye into the wilderness to see ? ' "

and he tells the knights that the

> " ' Chance of noble deeds will' come and go
> Unchallenged, while *ye follow wandering fires*
> *Lost in the quagmire.*' "
>
> 18

True to this view of the tale, Tennyson has left unnoticed the phantom adventures in the romance and has supplied their places with creations of his own. We shall now see whether he has improved upon the story.

> " And then behold a woman at a door
> Spinning; and fair the house whereby she sat,
> And kind the woman's eyes and innocent,
> And all her bearing gracious ; and she rose
> Opening her arms to meet me, as who should say,
> ' Rest here ' ; but when I touch'd her, lo ! she, too,
> Fell into dust and nothing, and the house
> Became no better than a broken shed,
> And in it a dead babe ; and also this
> Fell into dust, and I was left alone.

> .   .   .   .

> " And I rode on and found a mighty hill,
> And on the top, a city wall'd : the spires
> Prick'd with incredible pinnacles into heaven.
> And by the gateway stirr'd a crowd ; and these
> Cried to me climbing, ' Welcome, Percivale !
> Thou mightiest and thou purest among men !'
> And glad was I and clomb, but found at top
> No man, nor any voice. And thence I past
> Far thro' a ruinous city, and I saw
> That man had once dwelt there ; but there I found
> Only one man of an exceeding age.
> ' Where is that goodly company,' said I,
> ' That so cried out upon me ? ' and he had
> Scarce any voice to answer, and yet gasp'd,

'Whence and what art thou ?' and even as he spoke
Fell into dust, and disappear'd, and I
Was left alone once more, *and cried in grief,*
'*Lo, if I find the Holy Grail itself*
And touch it, it will crumble into dust.'"

Such adventures as this have, and can have, no
possible connection with Map's conception of the
Quest. The unity of the Idyll would not be one
whit impaired if these adventures were blotted out
in toto. But in the romance of Walter Map, every
single adventure has a clear meaning, a distinct aim,
a well-defined connection with the spiritual life of
the individual knight, and a steady looking towards
the *finale* of the story. It is impossible to omit one
adventure without detriment to the unity of the
tale. Even when Tennyson condescends to use the
materials furnished by the romance, he invariably
contrives to eliminate their power and mystic beauty.
We may take this adventure as an instance :

"And then I chanced upon a goodly town
With one great dwelling in the middle of it ;
Thither I made, and there was I disarm'd
By maidens each as fair as any flower :
But when they led me into hall, behold,
The Princess of that castle was the one,
Brother, and that one only, who had ever
Made my heart leap ; for when I moved of old
A slender page about her father's hall,

And she a slender maiden, all my heart
Went after her with longing : yet we twain
Had never kiss'd a kiss, or vow'd a vow.
And now I came upon her once again,
And one had wedded her, and he was dead,
And all his land and wealth and state were hers.
And while I tarried, every day she set
A banquet richer than the day before
By me ; for all her longing and her will
Was toward me as of old ; till one fair morn,
I walking to and fro beside a stream
That flash'd across her orchard underneath
Her castle-walls, she stole upon my walk,
And calling me the greatest of all knights,
Embraced me, and so kiss'd me the first time,
And gave herself and all her wealth to me.
Then I remember'd Arthur's warning word,
That most of us would follow wandering fires,
And the Quest faded in my heart.

.   .   .   .   .   .

O me, my brother ! but one night my vow
Burnt me within, so that I rose and fled,
But wail'd and wept, and hated mine own self,
And ev'n the Holy Quest, and all but her."

Here, there is no temptation to sin. It is simply
a commonplace adventure, charmingly told, that
might, or might not, end in Percival's abandoning
the Quest. But in the romance, it is a weird and
terrible temptation, showing the power of the prince

of darkness, and the still mightier power of Faith, in vanquishing his wiles and producing chastity and all good works.

Or again, compare the soul-lulling expressions of Tennyson's velvet-mouthed hermit, who almost sings the penitent to sleep, with the burning words of Map's outspoken hermits. Tennyson's twelfth century confessor exclaims :

> " Oh son, thou hast not true humility,
> The highest virtue, mother of them all ;
>
> .   .   .   .
>
> Thou hast not lost thyself to save thyself
> As Galahad."

What a marked contrast is this to the stern reproof which Map's ideal hermit administers to Sir Lancelot :

" Seeke it [Holy Graal] ye may," says the hermit, " but though it were here ye shall have no power to see it, no more than a blind man should see a bright sword, and all through your sinne."

Shortly after his recovery from the effects of approaching the Saint Graal unbidden, in the castle of Carboneck, Sir Lancelot bemoans his fate as a questing knight : " ' When I sought worldly adventures and worldly desires,' he sighs . . . ' I ever achieved them . . . and never was I discomfited in no quarel . . . and now I take upon mee the adventures of holy things . . . *I see and understand that mine old sinne hindreth mee.'* . . . Then hee departed . . . into a wild forrest ; and so by prime . . . he found an hermitage, and an hermite therin which was going to masse . . . *So when masse was done sir Launcelot called the hermite to him and praied him for charitie to here his confession"* ; and when the knight had confessed, the hermit tells him : " ' For your presumption to take upon you in deadly sinne, for to bee in his presence, where his flesh and his blood was, that caused you yee might not see it [the Holy Graal] with your worldly eye. For he will not appeere where such sinners bee. . . . And there is no knight living that ought for to give unto God so great thanks as yee ; for hee hath given unto you beautie, seemelinesse and great strength, above all other knights, and therefore yee are the more beholding unto God than any other man to love and to dread him, for your strength and manhood will little availe you and God be against you . . . *Ensure mee that yee will never come in that queenes fellowship.'* . . . And then sir Launcelot promised the hermit by his faith that hee would no more come in her company. ' Looke that your heart and your mouth accord,' " said the good man. He then proceeds to tell

him " thou art more harder then any stone   .   .   .
and that is [why] the heate of the Holy Ghoost may
not enter in thee   .   .   .   bitterer then wood   .   .   .
wherefore thou art likned to an old rotten tree   .   .   .
so then, sir Launcelot, when the holy grale was
brought before thee, hee found in thee no fruite,
neither good thought nor good will, and defouled
with leachery.'   .   .   .   *Then the good man enjoyned
sir Launcelot such penance as he might doe and to
shew [follow] knighthood ;* so he assoyled sir Launcelot.   .   .   .   And then sir Launcelot repented him
greatly."

Another hermit tells Sir Gawaine : " ' It is long
time passed sith that yee were made knight and never
sith thou served thy maker and now thou art so old
a tree that in thee is neither leafe nor fruite. Where
fore bethinke thee that thou yeeld unto our Lord
the bare rinde sith the feend hath the leaves and the
fruit.' "

But we must pass on to the third section of the
Quest.

At this point all the knights, save four, grow
weary of the Quest, and return to Arthur's Court to
revel unchecked in their former sins ; and Galahad,
Percival, Bors, and Lancelot are alone left to pursue
the adventure.

Galahad is one night asleep in a lonely hermitage,

when a gentlewoman, (who proves to be Percival's saintly sister,) comes there, knocks at the door, and tells the hermit that she must see Galahad. When the knight appears, she bids him arm himself at once and follow her. "'I wil shew you,'" she explains, "'within these three dayes the hiest adventure that ever any knight saw.'" Galahad, accordingly, starts with the maiden, in the dead of night, on this mysterious journey, and they travel together, stopping only at one castle to rest, till they reach the sea-shore. Here they find a ship awaiting them, wherein are Percival and Bors, who warmly welcome their long-lost companion. No sooner are they all safely on board, than the ship moves slowly from the land and bears them away. The next morning, by dawn, they come into a narrow gulf, with high precipitous rocks on either side, and as the darkness clears away, they see another ship which gradually nears them, and at length comes alongside. At the suggestion of the holy Maid, they all leave the vessel they are on and pass to the one which has so mysteriously neared them. As they enter, they see no living being on board, but a warning inscription catches their eye, "Thou man which shall enter into this ship beware thou be in steadfast beeliefe for I am faith." On looking around they find the ship richly furnished, and standing in the midst they see a bed of curious workmanship, hung with rich silks, and on the bed a crown, and by the crown a sword half drawn from its sheath. Then, at the bidding of the maiden, Galahad takes the sword but cannot wear it, for, strange to say, it has no girdle. But the holy Maid comes to his assistance. She has a casket which she now opens, and takes therefrom a girdle of her own hair, wrought with gold threads and set with precious stones. This, she fastens to the sword and binds about the waist of Sir Galahad. This being done, they leave the ship and pass back to the one which had brought them thither.

Nothing of moment henceforth occurs, till the ship nears land and the three knights and their fair companion leave the ship. Then a strange adventure befalls them. As they pass a certain castle, they are stopped by a knight who demands their observance of a strange custom. He informs the knights, that there is a sick lady in the castle, who can be healed only by being anointed with the blood of the virgin daughter of a king; and hence, this tax of blood is demanded of every maiden who passes the castle. The demand is indignantly refused by Percival and his companions, and a fierce battle takes place in which the three Round Table knights, by their superhuman valour, overcome numerous bands of knights that successively attack them. Only when night approaches does the slaughter cease, for Galahad is determined to root out this nest of recreant barons. The next morning, however, the holy Maid, deaf to all remonstrances, resolves to give her life's blood for the healing of the sick lady, and accordingly submits to the operation. But the sacrifice proves fatal. Time and again she swoons, while being bled, and ere the wound can be staunched it is evident that death is upon her. Before she dies she assures the three knights that as soon as they be come to the city of Sarras, to achieve the Holy Graal, they will find her already there awaiting them. Then she asks for her Saviour, and when she has received Him, she dies in the arms of her brother Percival. In accordance with her dying request, she is borne to the water's edge; there laid in a barge covered with black silk, and the barge is allowed to drift away across the flood; the knights watching it in silent sorrow till it disappears from view.

Sir Lancelot, who is not present while these events are happening, now appears upon the scene. He is standing on the sea-shore, alone, when he sees a ship without sail or oar approaching him, and is told by a mysterious voice to enter the vessel, which he does, and lies down to sleep. "And when hee awoke he found there a faire bed, and thereon lying a gentle-woman dead, the which was sir Percivals sister."

For a whole month he was alone with the body in
the ship; but one night he heard the distant gallop-
ing of a horse, and knew that he must be near land.
Shortly after, he sees a knight riding towards him,
who no sooner reaches the shore than he dismounts
and enters the ship. It is Sir Galahad. Lancelot
and his son embrace one another in mutual joy, and
then, having many adventures to relate, spend the
time in the pleasures of loving intercourse. For a
full half year they remain together, serving "God
daily and nightly with all their power." It was their
last meeting; and when at length the war-beaten
knight takes a farewell of his saintly son, each one
knows that he shall not again see the other "before
the dreadful day of doome." Then at the bidding
of an unknown knight in white armour, Galahad
leaves the ship, to his father's great sorrow, and
proceeds on the Quest.

Sir Lancelot remains on the ship, and during a
month and more prays, day and night, that he may
see some tidings of the Sangraal. At length his
prayer is answered. One night, at midnight, he
arrives before a castle, and the outer gate looking
towards the sea stands open, with no warden but
only two lions to keep the entry, and "the moone
shined cleare." Then he arms himself, and leaving
the ship, walks towards the castle. At sight of the

lions he draws his sword in self-defence, but being chided for his want of faith by a voice from heaven, he returns it to its sheath. The lions make a feint as though they would tear him, but he fears them not, and passes them unhurt. As he enters the fortress, a strange sight presents itself. The castle gates stand wide open; the doors of banquet hall and armoury are open; the doors of all the chambers stand open. He ascends the grand stairway, but go where he will, the castle seems tenantless and deserted, though furnished with all the magnificence of a palace. At length he comes to a chamber, the door of which is closed. He attempts to open it, but it resists his strongest efforts. He listens, and hears a voice within singing so sweetly that it seems no earthly voice. Convinced that the Holy Graal must be there, he kneels down and in all humility prays that he may be granted a vision of the sacred Vessel. With that, the chamber door flies open, and instantly a dazzling light pervades the whole castle, "brighter than if all the torches of the world had beene there." He is about to enter, but is warned to keep aloof. He looks in, and there sees an altar of silver, and upon the altar the Sangraal *covered with red samite*. Many angels are round about it, one of whom holds a golden candlestick with a burning taper, and another a crucifix. Before the altar, stands a priest as though sacring the mass, and while so doing " it seemed unto sir Launce- lot that above the priest's hands there were three persons whereof the two put the youngest (by like- nesse) betweene the priests hands and so hee lift it up on high." Then at that moment, it seems to Sir Lancelot that the holy man, overpowered by what he holds in his hands, will fall to the earth. The knight involuntarily crosses the portal of the chamber to support the falling priest, and is about to approach the altar, when he is smitten by a fiery blast which fells him to the ground. On the morrow, the inmates of the castle find Sir Lancelot lying be- fore the chamber door, as he had fallen, and bear him, more dead than alive, to a room, and there place him on a rich bed. For twenty-four days he lies in a critical state, but at length he revives, and as he opens his eyes, ask mournfully why they have aroused him from the rapture of his trance. As soon as he is wholly recovered, he takes his leave of the lord of the castle, and, knowing well that the Quest is not for him, returns to Camelot, to King Arthur's Court, and to Guinevere, the false star of his blighted life.

In this section, the allegory is exceedingly beauti- ful ; there is the ship which receives the knights and the holy maiden, evidently an image of Holy Church, which protects her children from the perils and dangers and storms of the world. There is the ship of Faith, to which they can go when Infidelity on the one hand and Heresy on the other, like giant rocks, which impotently threaten heaven itself, menace their destruction and the shipwreck of their faith. Then there is the allegory of Martyrdom, where the world is set forth as a sick lady, for whose healing is required the blood of the martyrs. And, lastly, there is Lancelot, the image of the brave, noble, sin-stained man of the world, too weak in faith to attain to communion with the True Blood, proudly trusting in his own strength, wanting in true humility, and so failing in the heavenly Quest.

To show what Tennyson might have done, if only his poetic vision had taken in the full grandeur of this romance, we will now turn to the poet's rendering of the last scene in Lancelot's quest, of which we have just given the prose analysis :

> " . . . and then I came
> All in my folly to the naked shore,
> Wide flats, where nothing but coarse grasses grew ;
> But such a blast, my King, began to blow,
> So loud a blast along the shore and sea,
> Ye could not hear the waters for the blast,
> Tho' heapt in mounds and ridges all the sea
> Drove like a cataract, and all the sand
> Swept like a river, and the clouded heavens

Were shaken with the motion and the sound.
And blackening in the sea-foam sway'd a boat,
Half-swallow'd in it, anchor'd with a chain ;
And in my madness to myself I said,
' I will embark and I will lose myself,
And in the great sea wash away my sin.'
I burst the chain, I sprang into the boat.
Seven days I drove along the dreary deep,
And with me drove the moon and all the stars ;
And the wind fell, and on the seventh night
I heard the shingle grinding in the surge,
And felt the boat shock earth, and looking up,
Behold, the enchanted towers of Carbonek,
A castle like a rock upon a rock,
With chasm-like portals open to the sea,
And steps that met the breaker ! there was none
Stood near it but a lion on each side
That kept the entry, *and the moon was full.*
Then from the boat I leapt, and up the stairs.
There drew my sword.   With sudden-flaring manes
Those two great beasts rose upright like a man,
Each gript a shoulder, and I stood between ;
And, when I would have smitten them, heard a voice,
' Doubt not, go forward ; if thou doubt, the beasts
Will tear thee piecemeal.'   Then with violence
The sword was dash'd from out my hand, and fell.
And up into the sounding hall I past ;
But nothing in the sounding hall I saw,
No bench nor table, painting on the wall
Or shield of knight ; only the rounded moon
Thro' the tall oriel on the rolling sea.
But always in the quiet house I heard,
Clear as a lark, high o'er me as a lark,

A sweet voice singing in the topmost tower
To the eastward : up I climb'd a thousand steps
With pain : as in a dream I seem'd to climb
For ever : at the last I reach'd a door,
A light was in the crannies, and I heard,
' Glory and joy and honour to our Lord
And to the Holy Vessel of the Grail.'
Then in my madness I essay'd the door ;
It gave ; and thro' a stormy glare, a heat
As from a seventimes-heated furnace, I,
Blasted and burnt, and blinded as I was,
With such a fierceness that I swoon'd away—
O, yet methought I saw the Holy Grail,
All pall'd in crimson samite, and around
Great angels, awful shapes, and wings and eyes.
And but for all my madness and my sin,
And then my swooning, I had sworn I saw
That which I saw ; but what I saw was veil'd
And cover'd ; and this Quest was not for me."

No description could be finer than this ; and the
only, though fatal, drawback to the passage is
that it stands alone. It is exquisitely beautiful,
but in Tennyson's Idyll it is out of place. It is a
solitary gem, wrenched from its setting in a royal
diadem.

We now come to the last section.

After the departure of Sir Lancelot for the Court,
Galahad, Percival, and Bors come to the castle of
Carboneck, and, while there, have a vision of the San-

graal similar to that which was granted to Lancelot, not long before, in the selfsame castle.

We may imagine the same scene; the silver altar, the holy Vessel, and the angels. But now it is a Bishop who performs the sacred function, and as he raises the consecrated wafer, a figure in likeness of a Child, with the visage as bright as any fire, smites Himself into the bread and the bread becomes a fleshly Man. The wafer is then placed in the San-graal; *but still the holy Vessel is not revealed to them*, and the Bishop vanishes from their midst. At the same moment, *the form of a Man appears before them as though rising from the sacred Vessel, with all the signs of the passion of Jesus Christ, and reveals himself to them.* " 'My knights and my servants, and my true children, which be come out of deadly life into spiritual life, I will now no longer hide mee from you, . . . receive the hye meat which yee have so much desired.' Then tooke hee himselfe the holy vessell, and came to sir Galahad, and hee kneeled downe and there hee received his Saviour; and so after him, received all his felowes. . . . Then hee said, 'Galahad, sonne, wotest thou what I hold between my hands. . . . This is the holy dish wherein I eate the lambe. . . . *And now hast thou seene that thou desirest most to see, but yet hast thou not seene it so openly as thou shalt see it* in

the citie of Sarras, in the spirituall place. Therefore
thou must goe hence and beare with the this holy
vessell . . . goe yee three to morrow unto the
sea, where as yee shall find your ship ready . . .
and no more with you but sir Percivale and sir
Bors.' Then gave hee them his blessing and vanished away." Accordingly, on the morrow they
journey to the sea, and there find the ship, and in
the midst of it, the altar of silver and the Sangraal,
but still "covered with red samite." The voyage to
Sarras is soon accomplished. On arriving, they see
the barge which enshrines the holy maiden, Sir Percival's saintly sister. She had made good her dying
promise, and was there awaiting them. They then
take the altar and the sacred Vessel out of the ship
and bear them into the city; and the body of the
maiden they bury as richly as a king's daughter
ought to be. At the end of a year, the three
knights repair to the palace where the Sangraal had
been enthroned, a new covenant, in an ark of gold,
in an inner sanctuary. *While there, the mystery
of the Holy Graal is finally and fully revealed to
Galahad,* and in trembling accents he prays that
now he may depart in peace. Having taken an
affectionate farewell of Percival and Bors, suddenly
*his soul departs, borne by angels to Heaven, in full
view of his two companions, while a mystic hand bears*

from their sight the object of their quest, the Holy Graal.

GALAHAD HAD NOW SEEN IT, AND THE QUEST WAS ACCOMPLISHED.

Percival, as we know, becomes a hermit and soon after dies; while Bors returns to Arthur's Court, the herald of the achievement of the Quest, the ideal adventure of Arthurian Romance.

And so the legend closes, this allegory of Justification, with the Communion of Saints and Life Everlasting. And what a grand allegory it is! There is the start from Camelot; the shining light of the Graal; the straight road pointed out by the hermits; the perils and dangers of Galahad, Percival, and Bors, the Christian, Faithful, and Hopeful of this Romance; there are enchanted grounds and lands of Beulah; there is the tempestuous sea, and finally, the landing at the spiritual City of Sarras, the New Jerusalem of this mystic tale. Galahad, pure in heart, attains to full communion and sees God. Percival, faithful to his vows, attains to spiritual communion, but must still pass a probation ere he can exchange the cowl for the crown. Bors, true in his meekness of spirit, attains to holy communion, but must linger still in Arthur's Court ere a heavenly kingdom is his. Lancelot, dragged down by deadly sin, catches but a glimpse of the glorious communion of the True Blood, and relapses into lifelong remorse; while Gawaine and others soon grow weary of shrift and penance, and return to a life of self and sin.

When we remember that Walter Map was a man of exquisite, æsthetic taste, a workman of consummate genius, who, while labouring to instruct in the deepest mysteries of Christianity, still looked to the artistic finish of his romances, it is no wonder that his work is a marvel of perfection, both in unity of design and beauty of execution, or that it has lived for seven hundred years, and is to-day as deeply appreciated by every lover of true literature as it was in the twelfth century.

The epic is national property. We cannot think that the poet had the right to take any part of this ancient possession of England, which had endeared itself to the national mind by centuries of existence, and present it to the present generation in the shattered form in which he has reproduced the spiritualised romance of the *Queste del Saint Graal.*

CHAPTER IX.

King Arthur.

IN a previous chapter we traced the Arthurian epic
through the three distinctively marked versions
of the story, the Cambrian, the Breton, and the
Anglo-Norman, the last named forming, as we saw,
a continuous tale of marvellous epic power; and we
thus traversed the whole field of Arthurian Romance
from the sixth century down to the time of Sir
Thomas Malory. In presenting the Anglo-Norman
version we gave a *résumé* of the twelfth and thirteenth
century romances, with the incidents arranged, as far
as possible, in chronological order. In that study, we
necessarily touched upon the leading events in the
life of King Arthur; and all that we propose to do in
the present chapter, is to examine more closely the
only two points in his career which Tennyson reproduced in his *Idylls of the King*, viz.: the *Coming* and
the *Passing* of Arthur; and we shall then close with
a comparative study of the Arthur of the romances
and the Arthur of the Idylls; the hero of Walter
Map and the hero of Tennyson.

With the *historic* Arthur we have no concern at present. The cycle of romantic fiction simply adopts Arthur's name, and reproduces the dim traditions of his story as a skeleton to be clothed with the flesh and blood of knightly life, wearing the costume of the Plantagenet Court and adorned with the ideal graces of chivalry.

As we have already seen, the epic cyclus of Walter Map opens with the history of that mystic vessel, the Holy Graal. We first hear of it at the institution of the Holy Eucharist in the upper chamber at Jerusalem, when it is introduced in the *Roman du Saint Graal* as the cup or dish used by our Lord at the last gathering of the Apostolic fellowship previous to the Crucifixion. Shortly after, we find it in the possession of Joseph of Arimathea, and used by him as a receptacle for the sacred blood which flowed from the wounds of our Saviour during the descent from the Cross. While in the keeping of Joseph, we find it supporting miraculously that apostolic knight when cast into prison, and keeping him insensible to the pangs of hunger and thirst. Upon his release, we follow him on his journey into Britain, ever guarding that Vessel as a sacred trust. On his arrival, we see it carefully hidden away among the regalia in the treasury of the " Fisherman King." We catch sight of it, now and again, as it appears on its miraculous mission, and, like the great Healer himself, curing the sick or restoring the wounded to health. It is felt as a benign influence present among the people during those dark ages ; like the invisible presence of a mysterious power, which, even when hid from mortal eyes, is felt to be in the midst. Gradually, its manifestations become less and less frequent, till at length it is no longer seen, and only remembered as a *presence* which has passed away, but not forever. In the popular breast the feeling lingers that it will come again, and the presentiment is not groundless. A weird Prophet arises, the prophet of the gospel of the Holy Graal. He proclaims, Baptist-like, that its coming is near at hand, and predicts the approaching dawn of a bright era, during which Britain shall become the centre of an Empire, and the adventure of the Holy Graal shall be fulfilled.

Such is the background which Walter Map draws before a single line of the figure of Arthur appears upon the canvas.

Then, there looms forth the dim form of a hardy Keltic warrior, with a gold dragon-head on his helmet ; but the dust-clouds of war partially conceal him from sight, and, as we gaze upon the picture, we can distinguish only a man of colossal stature, surrounded by his clan armies, and fighting against a multitude of invaders, who bear as their ensign the head of the wild boar. The scene changes; the great Uther is dying; the nobles stand around his death-bed; Merlin on a sudden stands among them, and, regardless of Court etiquette, abruptly asks: "'Sir, shall your sonne Arthur bee king after your dayes of this realme, with all the appurtenances?'" The dying king replies with solemn brevity: "'I give him Gods blessing and mine, and bid him pray for my soule; and righteously and worshipfully that he claime the crowne upon forfeiture of my blessing.' And therewith hee yielded up the ghost." The nobles hear the stern command of their sovereign. They learn now, if they never knew it before, that the dying king has a son, and that that son is to succeed him on the throne of Britain. This accomplished, the Court prophet vanishes to put his plan into execution.

It is not enough for Merlin simply to bring the youth forward as the rightful heir and cause him to be crowned King. This might lead to anarchy and war. A mysterious sword, fast in the body of an anvil, appears one Sunday in the Cathedral church at London, and an inscription, in golden letters, tells that none save the lawful heir to the throne can draw it forth from its rest. A tournament is at once proclaimed. The chivalry of England assembles to essay the adventure, and Arthur, till then an unknown youth, becomes the hero of the hour. Every king who is present, every knight who has taken part in the adventure, sees the successful competitor. The barons may refuse obedience, but they cannot deny that Arthur alone has accomplished the feat. They were present; they saw it; they had all been challenged; they had all accepted the challenge; they had all been defeated. They may entertain murderous thoughts, so that a guard of honour has to be appointed to protect the life of the youth; but not one of them dares deny that the honour is fairly won. In sight of the assembled chiefs, the solemn coronation service of the Church is performed; the crown is placed upon Arthur's head by the hands of the holy Dubricius, the *Te Deum* is chanted, and the knightly throng disperses.

Some of the disappointed kings frown and become rebels. They vow bitter war and withdraw, wrathful and revengeful, to their own lands. But act as they may, there was not a king, nor a baron of any note in England but had seen the young King; or at least knew, from those who had seen him, that Arthur had been proclaimed by the barons and crowned by Holy Church as the rightful successor of the mighty Uther Pendragon. Accordingly the barons, in the romance, do not attempt to deny that Arthur has been duly made King of the realm; they simply refuse to recognise the beardless youth as their sovereign, or as the heir of so dreaded a warrior as Uther.

No sooner have the nobles departed to their several homes, than the treason, which had been smouldering in the breasts of some few, bursts forth into open rebellion. Six of the discontented kings gather together their forces and attack Arthur in his fortress at Caerleon. Instantly, Merlin is on the ground and confronts the rebels. They rejoice to see the great Seer and ask, " For what cause is that beardles boy Arthur made your king?" "Sirs," said Merlin, " I shall tell you the cause. For he is king Uterpendragons sonne, borne in wedlock . . . and who soever saieth nay, he shall bee king and overcome all his enemies, and or that hee die hee shall be long, king of all England, and he shall have under his obeysance Wales, Ireland, and Scotland, and many moe realmes than I wil now reherse." A parley is accordingly arranged between Arthur and his subject though rebellious kings. The youth is escorted by Merlin and the Archbishop of Canterbury and many barons, " and when they were met together there was but little meekenesse, for there was stout and hard words on both sides. But alwayes king Arthur answered them, and said he would make them to bow and he lived." In the battle which ensues the King makes good his word, for he utterly routs them and puts them to ignominous flight. Soon, however, the rebellion spreads. Eleven kings band together against the young monarch, and Merlin, to aid his master, contrives to prevail upon the kings Ban and Bors to cross the sea from France to assist his sovereign.

And now the campaign is formally opened. Arthur takes the field at the head of his forces; a series of battles is fought; the island is finally subdued, and the traitorous kings are forced to submit to his authority. These heroic deeds reach the ears of Leodegraunce, king of Cameliard, who, at this time, is hard pressed by his giant foe, king Rience of North Wales, and he accordingly sends ambassadors entreating Arthur to come to his rescue. Arthur has now vanquished all his foes; the realm is at peace; and the King sets out to assist Leodegraunce whom he loves, and finds but little difficulty in the enterprise. (Rience, he slays in single combat) the rest of the marauders are put to flight; Arthur gains the gratitude of his friend, and even the haughty Guinevere, the king's daughter, cannot restrain her love.

After the King's return to Caerleon, and as one day he is sitting in his pavilion, a young child enters and salutes him, telling him somewhat abruptly, " I know, king Arthur, what thou art, and also who was thy father and also on whom thou wert begotten;

The youth Merlin places these immediately after the coronation

king Utherpendragon was thy father and begat thee
on Igraine." The King, displeased with the intru-
sion, orders the child to leave the palace.   But a
chain of anxious thoughts arises in the King's mind,
and he sits sad and pensive.   Then there enters the
pavilion an old man of " foure score yeeres of age,"
and enquires why the King is so sad and dejected.
Arthur looks up in surprise ; but seeing an aged man
standing before him, he relates what the child had
just before said.   " Yes," said that old man, "the
child told you the truth, and more would hee have
told you and you would have suffered him."   At
these words the old man changes to Merlin, and the
Seer stands before the King in his own person.

It seems that Arthur himself, at this time, is har-
assed with doubts as to his real parentage, for no
sooner has Merlin disappeared than he inquires of
Sir Hector and Sir Ulfias what they know in refer-
ence to his lineage.   They tell him that Uther
Pendragon was his father, and queen Igraine his
mother.   Even then, not feeling thoroughly assured,
he commands Merlin to bring the queen into his
presence, adding: " If shee say so her selfe then will
I beleeve it."   In all haste the queen is brought, and
upon her arrival she asserts in the presence of Merlin,
Sir Hector, and Sir Ulfias, "Merlin knoweth well
and you, sir Ulfias, how king Uther . . . wed-

ded me, and by his commandement when the child
was borne it was delivered to Merlin, and nourished
by him ; and so I saw the child never after, nor wot
not what is his name, for I never knew him yet.
. . . Then Merlin tooke the king by the hand,
saying, ' This is your mother.' And therwith sir
Ector bare witnesse how he nourished him by king
Uthers commandement, and therewith king Arthur
tooke his mother, queene Igraine, in both his armes
and kissed her, and either wept upon other."

The report of this public acknowledgment of
Arthur, as her son, by queen Igerna, spreads far and
wide over the country, and henceforth, not a single
whisper of doubt is heard as to his being the rightful
heir to the throne,—the King *de jure* as well as *de
facto*,—and every breath of slander is henceforth
dispelled. All doubts on this head being forever
set at rest, and Arthur's sovereignty being widely
acknowledged through his brilliant victories, Merlin
is sent to Cameliard to ask the hand of Guinevere,
the beautiful daughter of Leodegraunce, in marriage.

Arthur is no longer a beardless youth ; no longer
an untried knight. His prowess has been proved in
many a hard-fought battle; he has forced his enemies to lay down their arms and do homage to him
as King; he is, moreover, the acknowledged son of

Uther; and Leodegraunce, cheerfully and unhesita-
tingly, complies.

Such, in brief, is the *Coming of Arthur* as told by
Walter Map.

It is generally understood that Tennyson's series
of Arthurian poems was completed, when he wrote
the Idyll entitled the *Coming of Arthur*, professedly as an introduction to the whole series, and
we can therefore examine his work as a finished
whole.

The first point which strikes the reader of the
Norman romances, as he opens Tennyson's poem,
is the studied silence of the Idyll on the subject
of the Holy Graal.

The minor point of the parentage of the King,
seems to be the one point in the *Coming of Arthur*
that requires to be made clear. This done, no other
introduction is needed; the King's respectability is
established in accordance with nineteenth century
notions, and he is henceforth a fit person to be
presented to socially orthodox readers. The fact of
the story being an epic, or of the Holy Graal forming the point of unity in this epic, does not seem to
have entered into the poet's conception of the story.
But this need not surprise us since, as we have
already seen, Tennyson's design was evidently to
paint a few *gems* as boudoir adornments, and not a

chef d'œuvre to be exhibited at the Academy. Of Uther Pendragon and Igerna, the Idyll gives no account that is intelligible to modern readers, and the whole story of Arthur, as a stripling, entering the old abbey and drawing forth the sword, so touchingly depicted by Map, is totally ignored. Even when the poet deigns to give his readers any part of his hero's early history, the subject is treated in a series of *on dits*, and in so summary a manner, as to leave the mind in a state of helpless bewilderment as to the truth or falsity of any of the facts. Indeed, it is only after the Norman romances have been mastered that the true beauty and relative symmetry of this, or in fact of any one of the Idylls, becomes apparent.

The poem of the *Coming of Arthur*, opens with the distress of Leodegraunce, king of Cameliard, whose territory, it seems, had been overrun with bandits and wild beasts, and in his trouble he sends to Arthur with the piteous cry :

> " Arise, and help us thou !
> For here between the man and beast we die."

This would be an intelligible statement, were it not for what immediately follows :

> And Arthur yet, had done no deed of arms.

It must seem strange, even to the casual reader, that a warrior king, like Leodegraunce, should send for

succour to an untried and almost unknown youth,
one who had " done no deed of arms." It is an inconsistency, and, like many others, due to Tennyson
alone. In the romance there is no such inconsistency. Here, Arthur has already proved himself a
mighty warrior on many a field of battle before
Leodegraunce implores his assistance. In the very
first engagement after his coronation, Map tells us,
" and alway king Arthur on horseback laid on with
a sword and did *marvelous deedes of armes*, that
many of the kings had great joy of his deedes and
hardines . . . and king Arthur was in the for-
most prees till his horse was slaine under him." The
very picture this, of a warrior knight. In the famous
battle against the eleven confederate kings, who subsequently disputed Arthur's title to the throne, the
King distinguished himself above all his peers, " and
king Arthur," says the old romancer in true Keltic
style, " was so bloody that by his shield no man
might know him, for all was blood and brains on his
sword." So long a time does the battle last, and
such terrible execution does Arthur perform with
the aid of his sword, Excalibur, that at length Merlin appears suddenly upon the scene, in true prophetic mode, and addressing the King, exclaims:
" Ye have never done? have ye not done ynough?
of three score thousand ye have left on lyve but fif-

teene thousand ; it is tyme for to saye Ho ! " Indeed, had it not been for the appearance of the sage,
Arthur would doubtless have utterly exterminated
the confederate kings and their traitorous bands.

It was shortly after the termination of this terrible
battle that the embassy arrives, bringing word "that
king Ryence of North Wales made strong warre
upon king Leodegraunce of Camelyard. For the
which thinge kinge Arthur was wrothe for hee loved
him well and hated king Ryence because hee was
always against him. . . . Then king Arthur
. . . came within six dayes into the countrie
of Camelyard, and there rescewed king Leodegraunce and slewe there much people of king Ryence unto the number of ten thousand of men and
put him to flight. . . . And there had king
Arthur the first sight of Guenever, daughter unto
king Leodegraunce and ever after he loved hir."

What are we to think, then, when Tennyson says:

> *And Arthur yet had done no deed of arms.*

We are to think that Tennyson is following a different

But there is an unfortunate consistency in Tennyson's departure from his original. Having transformed King Arthur into an unknown and untried
knight, what more natural than that Leodegraunce,
a king in his own right, should hesitate to bestow
the hand of his daughter Guinevere upon a mere

20

Chritian's scene are inconsistent with the V. Malory is inconsistent with himself and the at least Jennyson is consistent with his

306   The Arthurian Epic

potential hero? Tennyson is therefore consistent in his inconsistency, when he makes Leodegraunce ask, with true parental solicitude :

> ". . . How should I that am a king,
> However much he holp me at my need,
> Give my one daughter saving to a king.
> And a king's son?"

But in the romance, Arthur is the acknowledged lord of the land, and his sovereignty is founded more on his achievements in war than on hereditary right. But further, the account which Map gives of the reception of the ambassadors at the Court of Leodegraunce differs widely from that of the poet. According to Map, Merlin is sent to Cameliard to inform Leodegraunce of the King's desire to have his daughter Guinevere to wife. " ' That is to me,' " said King Leodegraunce, when the wily seer had delivered his courtly message, " ' the best tidings that ever I heard that so worthy a king of prowesse and of noblenesse will wed my daughter. And as for my lands I will give him, wisht I that it might please him, but he hath lands enough he needeth none, but I shal send him a gift that shal please him much more, for I shal give him the table round, the which Utherpendragon gave me.' . . . And so king Leodegraunce delivered his daughter Guinever unto Merlin and the table round with the hundred knights ; and

so they rode freshly with great royalty, what by
water and what by land, till they came that night
unto London, . . . then the Archbishop of
Canterbury was sent for and he blessed the sieges
of the table round with great roialty and devotion."

It is at once apparent, from this extract, how
widely Tennyson has diverged from the romance.
But this is not all. He has effected this divergence
at the sacrifice of unity, consistency, and beauty.
Having adopted so unkingly a view of Arthur, and
having made a petty king of Cornwall hesitate,
whether or not to give his daughter in marriage
to a "doubtful king," it became necessary to introduce a string of new incidents to account for the
final marriage of Arthur and Guinevere. Accordingly, Bedivere is represented in the Idyll, in the
grotesque character of a kingly ambassador urging
his master's suit by repeating the slanders and
tainted gossip of envious foes ; and, what is more,
as actually blackening the King's character with his

"Sir, there be many rumours on this head,"

and (with an unctious deprecation of what he knows
to be untrue) actually repeating the untruth (with
embellishments of his own.

At this juncture, while Leodegraunce is debating
within himself

whether there were truth in anything

said by this knight, there comes to Cameliard, Lot's wife of Orkney, Bellicent, although nothing in the context calls for it, and although her appearance, in its very unnaturalness, shows to what straits Tennyson was reduced by his departure from the romance. However, her visit affords the king a fine opportunity to make further enquiries, which Bellicent answers to his gratification, but so long a tale does she tell, that she thoroughly wearies out the aged monarch, and at length, in defiance of all the laws of knighthood, he actually goes to sleep in her presence! *It never occurred to me that Bellu still in the room while Leodegran mused*

> She spake and King Leodegran rejoiced,
> But musing, shall I answer yea or nay
> *Doubted and drowsed, nodded and slept.*

His drowse, nod and sleep seem, however, to have had a most beneficial effect upon his spirits, for as soon as he awakes his perplexing doubts no longer disturb him.

> And Leodegran awoke, and sent
> Ulfias, and Brastias and Bedivere,
> Back to the court of Arthur answering yea.

To crown all these inconsistencies, Tennyson places the twelve great battles, by which Arthur established his sovereignty in Britain, after the arrival

of the Roman embassy. In other words, he makes
Arthur the *Emperor* of the civilised world before he
is so much as *King* of Britain. So much, then, for
Tennyson's introductory Idyll, the *Coming of
Arthur*.

The events which comprise what we have styled
the second section of the legend, viz. : from the
arrival of the Roman embassy to the beginning of
the Quest of the Holy Graal, find no place whatever
in the *Idylls of the King*, although they are related
both in the Armorican version, as translated by
Geoffrey of Monmouth, and in the Anglo-Norman
version of Walter Map. This section, therefore, requires no further examination.

The third section, containing the Quest of the
Holy Graal, we considered in the preceding chapter,
and have nothing left, therefore, but to pass on at
once to the last scenes in the life of the King, the
final battle of Camlan, and his translation to the isle
of Avalon, which is the subject of Tennyson's concluding Idyll, the *Passing of Arthur*.

In order to paint these scenes more vividly to the
mind, we must keep in view the circumstance, stated
in every version of the story, that Modred was
Arthur's natural son by his half sister; and that in
consequence of the disclosure of the King's near
relationship with Morgause, he makes a weak and

cruel effort to avert the meed of his sin, predicted by
Merlin, (that he who should destroy the King should
be born on May-day,) by the massacre of all noble
children born on that particular day, Modred escap-
ing to become, as we have seen, his father's curse ;
that, failing to accomplish his object, he afterwards
reposes in him the utmost confidence, and actually
leaves his kingdom and wife in Modred's charge
while he attempts to chastise Lancelot.

Modred, thus left as ruler of all England, causes letters to be written, as though they came from beyond
the sea, stating that King Arthur had been slain in
battle against Lancelot, and having summoned a Par-
liament, he causes himself to be elected and crowned
king.   He then endeavours to force queen Guinevere
to wed him, thinking in this way to assure the position which he has usurped.   But the Queen is too
shrewd to fall into the trap.   "Shee durst not discover her heart," says the old romancer, " but speake
faire, and agreed to sir Modreds will.   Then she desired of sir Modred for to goe to London for to bye
all maner thing that belonged unto the wedding ;
and because of her faire speech, sir Modred trusted
her well enough, and gave her leave to goe. And
when shee came to London she toke the toure of
London, and sodeinly in all hast possible she stuffed
it with all manner of vittaile, and well garnished it

with men and so kept it." Modred, enraged at
being thus thwarted, besieges the Tower of London,
but though "he made many great assaults thereat
and threw many great engines unto them, and shot
great gunnes," yet is unable to capture the place.
The Archbishop of Canterbury, hearing of the attack
upon the Queen, presents himself before Modred,
and threatens to curse him "with booke, bell and
candell" unless he at once ceases his unknightly
war. Modred, however, defies the prelate, and chal-
lenges him to do his worst, and the Archbishop forthwith "did the cursse in the most orguloust wise that
might be done."

Arthur no sooner learns of the events that are
transpiring at home, than he immediately raises the
siege of Joyous Gard and returns to England. Modred hastens to Dover to oppose his landing, accompanied by many knights and barons, who have been
beguiled by the promises of the traitor to desert
their King. A terrible battle ensues, but the rebels are
defeated ; Arthur effects a landing ; routs Modred's
forces ; pursues him as he flies inland ; drives him
from city to city, till at length the two armies meet
at Camlan, and the final battle takes place which the
romancer thus describes :

"And never was there seene a more dolefuller battaile in no christian land, for there was but rashing

and riding, foyning and stricking, and many a grim
word was there spoken, either to other, and many
a deadly stroke.   But alway king Arthur roade
throughout the battaile . . . and did there
right nobly as a noble king should doe, and at all
times he never fainted. . . . *And thus they fought
all the long day*, and never stinted till the noble
knights were laid to the cold ground ; and ever they
fought still, till it was nigh night, and by that time,
was there an hundred thousand laid dead upon the
doune.   Then was king Arthur wroth out of measure
when he saw his people so slaine from him.   Then
the king looked about him, and then was hee warre
that of all his hoost and of al his good knights, were
left no moe alive but two knights, that was sir Lucan
and sir Bedivere, his brother, and they were right
sore wounded.   'Jesu mercy!' said king Arthur,
'where are all my noble knights become ? Alas ! that
ever I should see this dolefull day . . .   would to
God that I wist were that traitour sir Modred is,
which hath caused all this mischiefe.' *Then was king
Arthur ware where sir Modred leaned upon his sword
among a great heepe of dead men.* 'Now give mee
my speare,' said king Arthur to sir Lucan, 'for yonder I have espied the traitour which hath wrought
all this woe.' 'Sir, let him be !' said sir Lucan . . .
'and if yee passe this unhappy day yee shall bee right

well revenged upon him. . . .' 'Betide me death, betide me life,' said the king, ' now I see him yonder alone hee shall never escape my hands.' Then king Arthur gate his speare in both his hands and ranne toward sir Modred crying 'Traitour, now is thy death day come.' And when sir Modred heard king Arthur, hee ran unto him with his sword drawen in his hand, and there king Arthur smote sir Modred under the shield with a foine of his speare throughout the body more than a fadom. And when sir Modred felt that hee had his death wound, he thrust himselfe with all the might that hee had up to the end of king Arthurs speare, and right so, he smote his father Arthur with his sword that hee held in both his hands on the side of the head, that the sword perced the helmet and the brain-pan. And therwith sir Modred fel downe starke dead to the earth, and the noble king Arthur fell in a sowne to the earth, and there hee sowned oftentimes. And sir Lucan and sir Bedivere oftentimes heaved him up, *and so weakly they lad him betweene them both unto a little chappell not farre from the sea side.''*

Next to the Idyll of *Lancelot and Elaine*, that of the *Passing of Arthur* is, without doubt, the finest of the series. In this Idyll, Tennyson has kept closely to his original, both in his choice of incident and in the wording of many passages in the poem.

But in addition to this, he seems to have caught, for the time being, the spirit of weirdness which is a marked feature in the whole of Keltic literature. We do not refer to the naked weirdness of the old bards and annalists, but to that idealised weirdness, the result of the christianised chivalry of the age which produced it, and which throws around the simplicity of the story a charm unique in itself. In all of Map's productions this weird element is retained, and it is wonderful to notice with what consummate skill he has worked it in with his own Norman notions of knighthood, blending the two in such a delicate manner, that the weird gives pungency to the chivalric and the chivalric lends grace to the weird. It is the absence of this ethereal weirdness in his other Idylls which renders so much of Tennyson's descriptive poetry tame and insipid. His graphic description, however, of the last great battle of Camlan presents a picture of desolation most impressive :

> Nor ever yet had Arthur fought a fight
> Like this last, dim, weird battle of the west.
> A deathwhite mist slept over sand and sea :
> Whereof the chill, to him who breathed it, drew
> Down with his blood, till all his heart was cold
> With formless fear ; and ev'n on Arthur fell
> Confusion, since he saw not whom he fought.
> For friend and foe were shadows in the mist,

And friend slew friend not knowing whom he slew ;
And some had visions out of golden youth,
And some beheld the faces of old ghosts
Look in upon the battle ; and in the mist
Was many a noble deed, many a base,

. . . .

And ever and anon with host to host
Shocks, and the splintering spear, the hard mail hewn,
Shield-breakings, and the clash of brands, the crash
Of battleaxes on shatter'd helms, and shrieks
After the Christ, of those who falling down
Look'd up for heaven, and only saw the mist ;
And shouts of heathen and the traitor knights,
Oaths, insult, filth, and monstrous blasphemies,
Sweat, writhings, anguish, labouring of the lungs
In that close mist, and cryings for the light,
Moans of the dying, and voices of the dead.

Last, as by some one deathbed after wail
Of suffering, silence follows, or thro' death
Or deathlike swoon, thus over all that shore,
Save for some whisper of the seething seas,
A dead hush fell ; but when the dolorous day
Grew drearier toward twilight falling, came
A bitter wind, clear from the North, and blew
The mist aside, and with that wind the tide
Rose, and the pale King glanced across the field
Of battle : but no man was moving there ;
Nor any cry of Christian heard thereon,
Nor yet of heathen ; only the wan wave
Brake in among dead faces, to and fro
Swaying the helpless hands, and up and down

Tumbling the hollow helmets of the fallen,
And shiver'd brands that once had fought with Rome,
And rolling far along the gloomy shores
The voice of days of old and days to be.

The spectral land in which the battle is fought, the spectral shapes about it, the darkness, the confusion, the fear,—these things so graphically portrayed in the Idyll—are immediately potent with those who have experienced them, who understand what a terrible conflict is intended by the poet; and they make a chord vibrate even in the hearts of those who feel but have never experienced a battle.

A comparison of Malory's rendering of the account of the removal of the wounded King from the field of battle, and the return of Excalibur to the Lady of the Lake, will show, in a very clear light, the strong points in Tennyson's version of the story.

So all day long the noise of battle roll'd
Among the mountains by the winter sea ;
Until King Arthur's Table, man by man,
Had fall'n in Lyonnesse about their lord,
King Arthur.   Then, because his wound was deep,
The bold Sir Bedivere uplifted him,
And bore him to a chapel nigh the field,
A broken chancel with a broken cross,
That stood on a dark strait of barren land :
On one side lay the Ocean, and on one
Lay a great water, and the moon was full.

Then, as the King feels that death is upon him, he
says to Sir Bedivere (for Sir Lucan meantime had
died of his wounds), "'My time hieth fast, therfore
take thou Excalibur, my good sword, and goe with it
unto yonder water side, and when thou commest
there I charge thee throw my sword into that water,
and come againe and tell me what thou shalt see
there.' 'My lord,' said Sir Bedivere, 'your com-
mande shall be done, and lightly bring you word
again.'"

Then spake King Arthur to Sir Bedivere :

.   .   .   .

"I am so deeply smitten thro' the helm
That without help I cannot last till morn.
Thou therefore take my brand Excalibur,
Which was my pride : for thou rememberest how
In those old days, one summer noon, an arm
Rose up from out the bosom of the lake,
Clothed in white samite, mystic, wonderful,
Holding the sword—and how I row'd across
And took it, and have worn it, like a king ;
And, wheresoever I am sung or told
In aftertime, this also shall be known :
But now delay not : take Excalibur,
And fling him far into the middle mere :
Watch what thou seëst, and lightly bring me word."

Speaking a few kind words, Sir Bedivere departed :
" And by the way he beheld that noble sword where
the pummell and the haft were all of precious stones,

and then hee said to himselfe : 'If I throw this rich
sword into the water, therof shall never come good,
but harme and losse.' And then sir Bedivere hid
Excalibur under a tree, and as soone as hee might
he came againe unto king Arthur and said, 'hee
had beene at the water, and had throwen the sword
into the water.' ' What sawest thou there,' said the
king. ' Sir,' said he, ' I saw nothing but waves and
wind.' "

So saying, from the ruin'd shrine he stept,
And in the moon athwart the place of tombs,
Where lay the mighty bones of ancient men,
Old knights, and over them the sea-wind sang
Shrill, chill, with flakes of foam. He, stepping down
By zigzag paths, and juts of pointed rock,
Came on the shining levels of the lake.

There drew he forth the brand Excalibur,
And o'er him, drawing it, the winter moon,
Brightening the skirts of a long cloud, ran forth
And sparkled keen with frost against the hilt :
For all the haft twinkled with diamond sparks,
Myriads of topaz-lights, and jacinth-work
Of subtlest jewellery. He gazed so long
That both his eyes were dazzled as he stood,
This way and that dividing the swift mind,
In act to throw : but at the last it seem'd
Better to leave Excalibur conceal'd
There in the many-knotted waterflags,
That whistled stiff and dry about the marge.
So strode he back slow to the wounded King.

Then spake King Arthur to Sir Bedivere :
" Hast thou perform'd my mission which I gave ?
What is it thou hast seen ? or what hast heard ?"

And answer made the bold Sir Bedivere :
" *I heard the ripple washing in the reeds,*
And the wild water lapping on the crag."

Arthur then accuses the knight of having been
false to him, and commands him to return and spare
not, but throw the sword into the lake. " Then
sir Bedivere returned againe, and tooke the sword
in his hand; and then him thought it sinne and
shame to throw away that noble sword. And so eft
[again] hee hid it, and returned againe and told
to the king that hee had beene at the water and
done his command. ' What saw yee there?' said the
king. ' Sir,' said he, ' I saw nothing but the water
wap [pale] and the waives waune.' ' Ah, traitour untrue!' said king Arthur, ' now hast thou betraied me
two times. Who would have wend [thought] that
thou that hast beene unto me so selfe and deere, and
thou art named a noble knight, and wouldest betray mee for the rich sword! But now goe againe
lightly, for thy long tarying putteth me in great
jeopardie of my life, for I have taken cold ; and but
if thou doe as I commaund thee, and if ever I may
see thee, I shall sley thee with my owne hands, for
thou wouldst for my rich sword see mee dead.' "

How exquisitely this scene is described in Tennyson:

> Then went Sir Bedivere the second time
> Across the ridge, and paced beside the mere,
> Counting the dewy pebbles, fix'd in thought;
> But when he saw the wonder of the hilt,
> How curiously and strangely chased, he smote
> His palms together, and he cried aloud:
>
> " And if indeed I cast the brand away,
> Surely a precious thing, one worthy note,
> Should thus be lost for ever from the earth,
> Which might have pleased the eyes of many men.
> What good should follow this, if this were done?
> What harm, undone? "
>
> .   .   .   .
>
> So spake he, clouded with his own conceit,
> And hid Excalibur the second time,
> And so strode back slow to the wounded King.
>
> Then spoke King Arthur, breathing heavily:
> "What is it thou hast seen? or what hast heard?"
>
> And answer made the bold Sir Bedivere:
> " I heard the water lapping on the crag,
> And the long ripple washing in the reeds."
>
> To whom replied King Arthur, much in wrath:
> " Ah, miserable and unkind, untrue,
> Unknightly, traitor-hearted!   Woe is me!
> Authority forgets a dying king.
>
> .   .   .   .

I see thee what thou art,
For thou, the latest-left of all my knights,
In whom should meet the offices of all,
Thou wouldst betray me for the precious hilt :

.   .   .   .

Get thee hence :
But, if thou spare to fling Excalibur,
I will arise and slay thee with my hands."

Then Sir Bedivere went the third time, his heart
being melted by the touching appeal of the dying
King, "for thy long tarying," said Arthur, " putteth
me in great jeopardie of my life." So " sir Bedivere
departed, and went to the sword, and lightly tooke
it up, and went to the waters side ; and there hee
bound the girdell about the hilts, and then hee threw
the sword into the water as farre as hee might ; and
there came an arme and an hand above the water,
and met it and caught it, and so shooke it thrise and
brandished. And then the hand vanished away with
the sword in the water. So sir Bedivere came againe
to the king and told him what he had seene."

Then quickly rose Sir Bedivere, and ran,
And, leaping down the ridges lightly, plunged
Among the bulrush beds, and clutch'd the sword,
And strongly wheel'd and threw it. The great brand
Made lightnings in the splendour of the moon,
And flashing round and round, and whirl'd in an arch,
Shot like a streamer of the northern morn,
21

Seen where the moving isles of winter shock
By night, with noises of the Northern Sea.
So flash'd and fell the brand Excalibur :
But ere he dipt the surface, rose an arm
Clothed in white samite, mystic, wonderful,
And caught him by the hilt, and brandish'd him
Three times, and drew him under in the mere.
And lightly went the other to the King.

 Then spoke King Arthur, drawing thicker breath :
" Now see I by thine eyes that this is done.
Speak out : what is it thou has heard, or seen ? "

 And answer made the bold Sir Bedivere :
" Sir King, I closed mine eyelids, lest the gems
Should blind my purpose, for I never saw,
Nor shall see, here or elsewhere, till I die,
Not tho' I live three lives of mortal men,
So great a miracle as yonder hilt.
Then with both hands I flung him, wheeling him ;
But when I look'd again, behold an arm,
Clothed in white samite, mystic, wonderful,
That caught him by the hilt, and brandish'd him
Three times, and drew him under in the mere."

 " ' Alas ! ' said the king, ' helpe me from hence, for
I dread me I have taried over long.'   Then sir Bedivere took king Arthur upon his backe and so went
with him to the waters side.   And when they were
at the waters side, even fast by the banke hoved a
little barge with many faire ladies in it, and among
them all was a queene, and all they had blacke

hoods and they wept and shriked when they saw king Arthur. ' Now, put mee into the barge,' said the king, and so hee did softly ; and there received him three queenes with great mourning, and so these three queenes set them downe, and in one of their laps king Arthur laide his head. And then that queene said, ' Ah, deer brother, why have ye taried so long from me ? ' . . . And so then they rowed from the land, and sir Bediver beheld al those ladies goe from him ; then sir Bedivere cried, ' Ah, my lord Arthur, what shall become of mee now ye goe from me, and leave me here alone among mine enemies ? ' ' Comfort thy selfe,' said king Arthur, ' and do as well as thou maiest, for in mee is no trust for to trust in ; for I wil into the vale of Avilion for to heale me of my greivous wound, and if thou never heere more of mee, pray for my soule.' But evermore the queenes and the ladies wept and shriked, that it was pittie for to heare them. And as soone as sir Bedivere had lost the sight of the barge, hee wept and wailed and so tooke the forrest ; and so he went all the night."

Here is the stricken King's farewell in the poet's rich verse :

> And answer made King Arthur, breathing hard :
> " My end draws nigh ; 't is time that I were gone.
> Make broad thy shoulders to receive my weight,

And bear me to the margin ; yet I fear
My wound hath taken cold, and I shall die."

So saying, from the pavement he half rose,
Slowly, with pain, reclining on his arm,
And looking wistfully with wide blue eyes
As in a picture.   Him sir Bedivere

. . . . . .

Then took with care, and kneeling on one knee,
O'er both his shoulders drew the languid hands,
And rising bore him through the place of tombs.

But, as he walk'd, King Arthur panted hard,

. . . . . .

Muttering and murmuring at his ear, " Quick, quick !
I fear it is too late, and I shall die."
But the other swiftly strode from ridge to ridge,

. . . . . .

And on a sudden, lo ! the level lake,
And the long glories of the winter moon.

Then saw they how there hove a dusky barge,
Dark as a funeral scarf from stem to stern,
Beneath them ; and descending they were ware
That all the decks were dense with stately forms,
Black-stoled, black-hooded, like a dream—by these
Three Queens with crowns of gold : and from them rose
A cry that shiver'd to the tingling stars,
And, as it were one voice, an agony
Of lamentation.

. . . . . .

Then murmur'd Arthur, " Place me in the barge."
So to the barge they came.   There those three Queens
Put forth their hands, and took the King, and wept.
But she, that rose the tallest of them all
And fairest, laid his head upon her lap,
And loosed the shatter'd casque, and chafed his hands,
And call'd him by his name, complaining loud,
And dropping bitter tears against a brow
Striped with dark blood : for all his face was white
And colourless, and like the wither'd moon
Smote by the fresh beam of the springing east ;

     .   .   .   .

So like a shatter'd column lay the King ;
Not like that Arthur who, with lance in rest,
From spur to plume a star of tournament,
Shot thro' the lists at Camelot, and charged
Before the eyes of ladies and of kings.

    Then loudly cried the bold Sir Bedivere :
" Ah ! my Lord Arthur, whither shall I go ?
Where shall I hide my forehead and my eyes ?

     .   .   .   .

But now the whole Round Table is dissolved
Which was an image of the mighty world,
And I, the last, go forth companionless.

As we have said elsewhere, it is not our object to
enter into the merits of Tennyson except as the narrator of an epic which is national property.   We are
willing to grant that the early writer's style does not
gratify the ear, as does the rich music of Tennyson's

verse ; still the palm for consistency, unity, and simplicity rests with the older writer, and his work carries us back, as Tennyson's seldom does, to knightly days.

This is especially noticeable in the delineation of the character of the King himself.

The portrait of King Arthur as it came from the hands of Walter Map is a masterpiece. The grouping of each picture in which it stands, with it accessories of regal or imperial pomp, is unapproachable. These pictures are drawn by no unskilful or unpractised hand, and nowhere do they evince the crude touches of the tyro. You may examine the portrait of the King by itself, and it is a perfect work of art. You may take it as one figure in the group of Round Table knights, and still it is in just proportion to the surrounding figures and harmonises strictly with its setting.   From the delivery, to Merlin, of Arthur, as a babe wrapped in a cloth of gold at the postern gate of the castle, until his disappearance in the sable barge together with the three queens, there are no inconsistencies or breaks in the continuity of the character.   His birth takes place in the palace of a king ; his public advent is attended by miracle ; his coronation is performed by the Archbishop ; his prowess on the field of battle is unsurpassed · his Court of Round Table knights is

celebrated in every castle of Christendom; he goes
on from conquest to conquest, step by step, in a
logical succession of events, (till at length he estab-
lishes a universal Empire and is crowned Emperor
at the Pope's own hands.) *in Malory only*

But even this is not sufficient for the fervid imagination of the Norman trouvère. The culminating
point of his reign is attained, only when the highest
adventure of human aspiration is finally achieved,
viz.: the Quest of the Holy Graal. Even the descent from Empire to desolation is clothed with
appalling grandeur. The death of the monarch is
kingly and his translation to Avalon is a no less
regal termination to the entire legend. Whether
viewed as a character portrait or as a panoramic
picture of knightly life, Map's production is perfect.

As we approach the comparative study of the
Arthur of the romances and the Arthur of the Idylls,
we naturally recall to mind the course which Tennyson pursued with respect to other personages in these
tales. We remember that Merlin is degraded from
the grand and often Elijah-like being of Map to the
level of the mediæval magician and necromancer;
that the pure and affectionate nymph of the Lake
is painted by Tennyson as a "harlot"; we cannot
forget that Gawaine, the pet of the old tales, becomes
the shallow fool of the Idylls; that Percival, the

*de Malory Sawai is only a murderer who kills
King Pellinore here to one and Sir Samorak 4to one
In the Vulgate Version he kills 11 knights of the
Round Table in the Quest of the Graal*

Christian knight, whose humility shines forth pre-
eminently, is transformed into an (egotist whose
vanity and conceit must be distasteful to any one of
refined tastes;) that the character of Pelleas is, to say
the least, open to grave suspicions; and that Galahad himself, the heavenly knight, and God's knight,
becomes a (mere day-dreamer,) who follows "wandering fires" and who "loses himself to save himself."

It would not be surprising, therefore, if even the
noble, warlike, knightly hero, King Arthur himself,
should share a similar fate at the hands of the poet;
and this we find to be the case. Under Tennyson,
Arthur becomes a mere statue; a lifeless figurehead;
at times enshrined in a sphinx-like mystery, brusque
even to his knights, peevish to his Court, discourteous
to his fallen Queen, and finishing his career with a
discourse which must doubtless have been deeply interesting to the queens who were soothing his pedan-
tic brow.

We have said that the portrait of King Arthur as
it came from the hands of Walter Map is a masterpiece. Can we prove it? We also maintain that the
portrait of King Arthur, as it appears in Tennyson's
Idylls, is, by comparison, crude and inartistic. Can
we make good our position?

In order to form a true estimate of the subject, we
must never lose sight of the fact that the Anglo-

Norman romancers set themselves the task of drawing, not simply a series of separate tales, but a connected epic cyclus. Consistency and unity were to
them, therefore, the very soul of their labours. What
Arthur was as a simple squire in Sir Hector's Cornish
castle, that must he be as the dying hero of Camlan,
modified only by such changes of character as the
circumstances of his life would naturally bring about.
He must be drawn in accordance with twelfth century notions, idealised, as matter of necessity, since
he was the hero of a romance, but, nevertheless, a
being with all the passions and failings of humanity
clinging to him. He must not, in word, thought, or
deed, contradict the majestic movement of the story,
whether with respect to the Graal Quest or the working out of the tragic curse. He must be true King,
true knight, true warrior, true husband, true man ;
and yet, withal, true to the honest failings as well as
to the noblest aspirations of poor, frail humanity. If
Lancelot is the ideal of earthly knighthood, Galahad
of earthly purity, Merlin of worldly wisdom, Elaine
and Vivienne of human love ; so Arthur must be the
ideal *King*, surpassing neither Lancelot in knighthood, Galahad in purity, Elaine in love, nor Merlin
in wisdom ; but surpassing all his knights in kingly
character. And we hold that this delicate balance
has been maintained in the narrative of the Norman

trouvères. In the Anglo-Norman version of the epic
there is a curse that dogs the whole life of King
Arthur, and which stands out as one of the grand
projections of the picture; an idea too vast to have
had its birth in the imagination of one man; a
dark, overhanging shadow, doubtless cast by some
national tradition of a terrible disaster. This tragic
element was seized upon by the Norman romancer
and worked into the legend. Following older traditions, Map had to bring about the fall of the King,
in a final battle, the utter ruin and desolation of
which required the richest imagination to scheme
and the broadest genius to depict. It was to be the
finale of a knightly epoch; the closing scene of a
curse; the death of King and knights at the hands
of an abandoned and traitorous wretch. How could
the Norman romancer heighten the colouring of
the picture more effectively than by adopting the
story already in existence, and depicting the wretch
whose hands were to be stained with the blood of his
sovereign, as the natural offspring of the monarch?
And if, in addition, this miscreant should be painted
not only as a natural son, but as the result of a terrible sin, an incest, on the part of the King himself,
what could possibly be wanting to render the ending,
in the highest degree, tragic? But the deadly sin of
incest must be unwittingly committed, else the King

would be a villain. And all this is duly carried out
by the Norman romancer. To draw Arthur as
Tennyson does,

> blameless King and stainless man,

or

> selfless man and stainless gentleman,

is to eliminate the curse, the tragic element from the *[handwritten marginalia]*
romance, and destroy the most appalling, and at the
same time the most telling part of the narrative. A
" blameless " king, whether of the sixth, twelfth or
nineteenth century, is unthinkable. Even Tennyson
himself tells us:

> He is all fault who is no fault at all.

To make Arthur " blameless " and " stainless " is to
confound two distinct personages, Galahad and
Arthur, and by so doing, to destroy the perfection
of the epic. *[handwritten: O Tenny]*

But not only is the tragic element in the epic destroyed by the introduction of a "blameless King,"
but Arthur himself retains in Tennyson, few if any
of the characteristics of the *warrior* king. In Map's
romance, when the Roman embassy arrives, the
twelve ancient men present the following manifesto
from the Roman Emperor:

" The high and mighty emperour Lucius sendeth

[handwritten: Tennyson draws Arthur in a Platonic philosopher king with warrior king as only one of his many facets]

unto thee, king of Brittaine, greeting, commanding
thee to knowledge him for thy lord, and to send
him the truage due of this realme unto the empire,
which thy father and other tofore thy predecessors
have payed as it is of record, and thou as a rebell not
knowing him as thy soveraigne withholdest and re-
tainest, contrary to the statutes and decrees made by
the noble Julius Cesar, conquerour of this realme and
first emperour of Rome.   And if thou refuse his demand and commandement, know thou for a certaine
that he shal make strong warre against thee and thy
realmes and lands, and shal chastise thee and thy
subjects, that it shall bee an ensample perpetuall unto all kings and princes for to denie their truage
unto that noble empire which dominereth upon the
universall world."

A council of state is then held, at which are present the mightiest kings, princes, and barons of the
realm, each pledging himself to bring into the field
a vast number of men.

" And when king Arthur understood their courage
and good will, he thanked them heartily, and after
he let cal the embassadours that they should heare
their answer.   And in presence of all his noble lords
and knights he said to them in this wise: 'I will
that yee returne unto your lord and procurour for
the common weale for the Romaines, and say to him,

of his demand and commandement I set nothing, and that I know of no truage ne tribute that I owe to him ne to none earthly creature nor prince, christian nor heathen, but I pretend to have and occupie the soveraintie of the empire, wherein I am entituled by the right of my predecessours, sometime kings of this land. And say to him that I am delivered and fully concluded to goe with mine army with strength and power to Rome, by the grace of God to take possession in the empire, and subdue them that bee rebells; wherefore I command him and al them of Rome that incontinent they make to me their homage, and to knowledge me for their emperour and governour upon paine that shal ensue.' "

In this extract, not only does the romancer *call* Arthur a King, but, in addition to this, he gives us thoughts and words and acts which are kingly. And this is what Tennyson does not do. He certainly tells us of Arthur's "simple words of great authority," and "large, divine and comfortable words," but what we miss is the proof; what was the mode of speech by which Arthur so affected men as Tennyson reports that he did? so that:

Some
Were pale as at the passing of a ghost
Some flush'd, and others dazed, as one who wakes
Half-blinded at the coming of a light.

Arthur, as drawn by the romancers, is, on the contrary, kingly in every thought and word and act, from the haughty defiance which he thunders forth in the face of the six rebel kings who dispute his title to the throne, down to the last command, his dying one, to Sir Bedivere. Indeed, if there is any fault to be found, it is not that Arthur is deficient in the kingly character, but that he is drawn too much in accordance with notions which were current during the reign of Henry II., when a mere hint from the sovereign stained the altar-steps of Canterbury Cathedral with a Cardinal's blood. In the Romance, the kingly character of Arthur is stamped upon every page.

Nor is this all. In the Romance, Arthur is presented not only as a King, but as a *knightly* king; staunch in his loyalty; pre-eminent in his courtesy, and grand in his munificence.

At the interview between the King and the " twelve ancient men," who came as ambassadors from Rome, some of the knights of the Round Table would have summarily resented what they considered an insult to their King and country: " Then some of the young knights, hearing their (the embassadours') message, would have set upon them for to have slaine them, saying that it was a rebuke unto al the knights there being present to

suffer them to say so to the king. Anon the king
commanded that none of them upon paine of death
to missay them, ne doe to them any harme, and
commanded a knight to bring them to their lodging,
'and see that they have all that is necessary and
requisite for them with the best cheere ; and that
no daintie be spared ; for the Romaines beene great
lords and, though their message please me not, nor
my court, yet I must remember mine honour.'"

Moreover, after the King had formally notified the
ambassadors of his reply, "he commanded his treas-
urer to give them great and large gifts, and to pay
all their expenses, and assigned sir Cador to convey
them out of the land."

Subsequently, after the famous battle in which the
Roman Emperor Lucius was slain, "the king rode
straight to the place where the emperour Lucius lay
dead, and with him hee found slaine . . . two noble kings with seventeene other kings of divers . . .
regions, and also threescore senatours of Rome all
noble men, whom the noble king Arthur did em-
baulme and gumme with many good aromatike
gummes, and after hee did ceere them in threescore
fold of ceered cloth of sendale, and then laid them
in chests of lead, because they should not chauffe
nor savour ; and upon all these bodyes were set their
shields with their armes and banners, to the end they

should bee known of what countrey they were."
And thus escorted by three senators, he commanded
that the bodies should be borne in state to Rome.

When, on one occasion, the King is overthrown in
a joust by one of his own knights, who, for good
reason, fails to recognise him, his assailant exclaims,
" And but thou yeeld thee as overcome and recreaunt
thou shalt die," (the customary form of demanding
surrender in single combat,) the King instantly replies, forgetful of his royalty, " as for death, welcome
bee it when it commeth, but as to yeeld mee to thee
as recreaunt, I had lever die than to be so shamed."

At another time, when one of the knights of his
Court had slain a lady under the excitement of strong
provocation, the King exclaims, " For shame, sir
knight, why have yee done so ? ye have shamed me
and all my court ; for this was a lady that came hither
under my safe conduct . . . therefore withdraw
you oute of my court in all haste that ye may."

But, perhaps, the noblest instance of his loyalty to
the spirit of chivalry is seen in King Arthur's staunch
and heroic devotion to his Queen, little though she
may have deserved it.

When Sir Modred, with the true instinct of the
villain, endeavours to excite the King against Sir
Lancelot by insinuating that the latter is a traitor to
his person in the matter of queen Guinevere, "' Wit

yee well,' replies the King . . . 'but I would
be loth to begin such a thing [suspicion of an in-
trigue between the Queen and Lancelot] but if I
might have prooves upon it, for I tell you sir Launcelot is an hardy knight and all yee know hee is the
best knight among us all.' . . . For king Arthur
was loth therto that any noise should bee upon sir
Launcelot and his queene, for the king had a deem-
ing, but he would not here of it for sir Launcelot
had done so much for him and for his queene so many
times that wit ye well king Arthur loved him passing
well." Even when Lancelot's guilt had been so fully
proved, that the King was compelled in honour to
resent the treachery of his knight, still it was with re-
luctance that he besieged the castle of Joyous Gard ;
and when later, he was dying from the death wound
of the wretch who had been foremost in stirring up
hostilities, the King bemoans " Ah sir Launcelot this
same day have I sore missed thee. Alas ! that ever
I was against thee." Sir Lancelot had assured the
King of Guinevere's innocence and the noble-minded,
courteous monarch, too late, deplores his over-hasti-
ness in having listened to what he now believes to be
a cowardly lie, invented and worked out by Modred
for his own selfish ends. Moreover, in the romance,
it may be remembered, King Arthur does not see
the Queen after her retirement to the convent, and

22

even if he had, he would have been the last man in the world to have embittered her own unhappy thoughts by so burning a reproof as Tennyson places in the mouth of her husband. Cynics may call the King a fool, but true men must admire the loyalty with which, in the romance, he clung to Guinevere to the very last, since her guilt had not been proved except by her enemies. True men must admire a love which was as staunch when he fell mortally wounded on the field of battle, as it was when, years before, he had wedded her, a pure, and loving princess in the old Cathedral church.

We look in vain through all these many hundred lines of Tennyson's for any portrait of a knightly King. In the introductory lines the poet dedicates his Idylls to the memory of the Prince Albert

> Since he held them dear,
> Perchance as finding there unconsciously
> Some image of himself;

and the poet adds:

> Indeed He seems to me
> Scarce other than my king's ideal knight.

In other words, King Arthur is painted to the poet's own mind in accordance with nineteenth century notions, as a "selfless gentleman" and not in accord-

ance with twelfth century ideas, as a true knight and
true king.

Indeed, in reading Tennyson's *Idylls*, the thought
forces itself upon the mind that King Arthur, on
more than one occasion, is scarcely what is generally
understood by the term " selfless gentleman."*
According to Tennyson's version of the story of the
Holy Grail, Percivale tells the monk, that at the
King's own desire he related all that had befallen
him during the Quest, and he adds :

> " So when I told him all thyself hast heard,
>   .   .   .   and my fresh but fixt resolve
> To pass away into the quiet life,
> *He answer'd not, but, sharply turning, ask'd*
> *Of Gawain, ' Gawain, was this Quest for thee ?'*

Why the King should have turned away so sharply
from Sir Percival, who had been recounting his adventures with great courtesy, and who might have
looked for some notice in return, is not evident ; all
that could be implied by this gesture, is rudeness or
impatience in Arthur, a feeling foreign to one of
gentle birth.

In the romance, so far as King Arthur is concerned, the tale closes with a few simple words, such
as the dying monarch might fitly address to Sir Bedi-

* *Vide* Note T.

vere in answer to his heart-rending appeal " Ah ! my
lord Arthur, what shall become of mee now ye
goe from me, and leave me here alone among my
enemies ? "

"Comfort thy selfe," said King Arthur, " and do as
well as thou maiest, for in mee is no trust for to trust
in ; for I wil into the vale of Avilion for to heale me
of my grevious wound ; and if thou never heere
more of mee, pray for my soule."

It is needless to give in full, Tennyson's elaborate farewell to Sir Bedivere. The following extract
will be sufficient :

" Comfort thyself : what comfort is in me ?
I have lived my life, and that which I have done
May He within himself make pure ! but thou,
If thou shouldst never see my face again,
Pray for my soul. More things are wrought by prayer
Than this world dreams of. Wherefore, let thy voice
Rise like a fountain for me night and day.
For what are men better than sheep or goats
That nourish a blind life within the brain,
If, knowing God, they lift not hands of prayer
Both for themselves and those who call them friend ?
For so the whole round earth is every way
Bound by gold chains about the feet of God.
But now farewell. I am going a long way
With these thou seëst—if indeed I go
(For all my mind is clouded with a doubt)—
To the island-valley of Avilion ;
Where falls not hail, or rain, or any snow,

Nor ever wind blows loudly ; but it lies
Deep-meadow'd, happy, fair with orchard-lawns
And bowery hollows crown'd with summer sea,
Where I will heal me of my grievous wound."
So said he, and the barge with oar and sail
Moved from the brink, like some full-breasted swan.

     .   .   .   .

       Long stood Sir Bedivere
Revolving many memories, till the hull
Look'd one black dot against the verge of dawn,
And on the mere the wailing died away.

We prefer the simple, tender expressions in the romance to this elaborate sermonising, excellent though the sentiments may be, since the former is far more natural as coming from a dying monarch. The sermon is noble in its way; but the way is the way of the poet, and not of the warrior King.

Arthur is not in Tennyson mere warrior King

CHAPTER X.

Geraint and Enid.

IN order to make the analysis which we have given of the Arthurian Epic as complete as possible, we propose, in the present chapter, to gather up some of the loose threads which we have left in our brief survey, such for example as the romance of *Geraint and Enid*, the Round Table legend, and one or two minor points of interest.

Before passing on to these subjects, however, it may be advisable to recapitulate, in brief, the points which we have hitherto endeavoured to establish.

We have shown that the series of Anglo-Norman tales which relate to Arthur and his knights formed, at the time when Tennyson took the subject in hand, an epic cyclus. They do not form what is usually understood by the term *epic*, as they are not cast in the shape of a continuous narrative ; nor do they exist as a continuous and complete poem. At the same time, the *story itself* is complete. There is the introductory romance of the Holy Graal, the story of Uther

Pendragon; the advent of the Hero; the British
wars which end in Arthur's undisputed sovereignty as
King; the continental wars which result in his coronation as Emperor; the Quest of the Holy Graal;
the fall of Guinevere; the siege of Lancelot's Castle
of Joyous Gard; the treason of Modred; the last
great battle of Camlan; the passing of Arthur; the
dissolution of the Round Table; and, finally, the
deaths of the Queen and Lancelot.   These, together,
form a perfect and complete story.   There is nothing wanting to make it an organic whole.   What is
wanting to complete the character of an epic is the
form; the unbroken narration of events, instead of
a series of separate romances.   Apart from this one
defect, they constitute a true epic.

Indeed, they possess the chief essentials of the
classic epic; there is a point of unity, viz.: the Graal,
around which all the romances cluster; but whereas
in the classic epic, the plot opens up in a chronological sequence, the incidents in this tale are presented
in clusters, each cluster gravitating, so to speak,
around some one individual hero, and these clusters
again, gravitating around the central point of all, the
Holy Graal.   It is as if the writer of the *Iliad,* instead of presenting us with a continuous narrative,
had left a connected series of tales, each one having
as its central figure some one of the Homeric heroes,

and then, had made the entire series to revolve around
its point of unity, the rape of Helen.

Nor is the tragic element, another essential of the
classic epic, wanting in this Arthurian cyclus.   Underlying the whole story, there is the existence and
working out of a curse, a Kymric Ate, set in motion
by the King himself, and hanging equally over the
monarch, the Queen, and the knights, from the highest to the lowest; a curse which pervades every romance and is seen to be working itself out as each
individual knight, by his own misdoing, hastens on
the final catastrophe.

Finally, the characters introduced are perfectly
finished portraits; they are drawn by a master-hand,
and there is not one but is worthy to fill a niche in
the Arthurian Epic.

To these points we have hitherto steadily confined
our attention, for they form the criterion by which
to judge of Tennyson's metrical version.   With regard to Tennyson, we have seen that, in his *Idylls
of the King*, he lost sight of the fact that these tales
existed as an epic cyclus, and, accordingly, he has
left us simply a few fragments of the epic; omitting
at times large portions of the tales, and at others
adding an incident, or series of incidents, from the
storehouse of his own fancy.   In other words, he has
not reproduced the epic as a whole.

He has omitted the Graal romance, the point of
unity of the epic; the British wars and the Roman
wars; the tragic ending which follows the death of
the King; and, by his wish to make Arthur stand
well with the respectabilities of the world, he has
eliminated the sin of the monarch, and therefore the
tragic curse.

Moreover, he has made important additions to
the story. He has added the visit of Arthur to the
Queen after her retirement to the convent, besides
other minor incidents. He has remodelled the *Coming of Arthur*; the attachment of *Merlin and Vivienne*; and the *Quest of the Holy Graal*; and finally
he has given a different complexion to the characters
of all but one of the Round Table knights.

In addition to all this, the chaste fantasy of Tennyson has often taken a crude idea from the trouvères, and has infused into it a subtle, poetic charm;
or, he has rendered it more radiant by the fire of his
genius, as in the scene where Elaine enters the cell
in which Sir Lancelot is lying sick; or as in the fine
description of the battle of Camlan.

At the same time, he now and again has marred
the beauty of a passage by the introduction of his
own fancies, as when he places the letter in Elaine's
left hand so as to leave the right hand free for his
own conceit of the lily; or he has destroyed the

force of a passage and even of a tale, as in the case
of the Quest, by making Galahad boast that he had
seen the sacred Vessel before ever the Quest had
begun. Such, briefly stated, are the results of our
inquiry thus far.

The reader has doubtless remarked that, hitherto,
we have made no mention whatsoever of the story of
Gareth and Liones or of *Pelleas and Etarre* or of *Tristan and Isoude*, and perhaps he has already anticipated
the reason of this omission. The fact is, these ro-
mances do not form an essential part of the epic.
They are simply episodes, beautiful in themselves,
and intimately connected with the epic, but still,
strictly speaking, not organic parts of the tale. They
do not stand on the same level as the story of *Elaine
la Blaunch*, which is one of those bright lights in the
picture which bring out in bolder relief, the dark
tragic shadows of the work, and is therefore essential to the perfection of the epic. Even if we were
to supplement the preceding studies with an analysis
of Tennyson's version of these tales, the result would
simply substantiate more fully the conclusions at
which we have already arrived. It would present
only additional instances of the strong and weak
points in Tennyson's method. At times, we should
see the brilliant imagination of the poet casting an
imperishable radiance over the scenes which he re-

produces; at others, we should find him retouching
and resetting the grand masterpieces of mediæval
romance till he had rendered them well-nigh impossible of recognition.

All the romances which we have hitherto examined
or mentioned, have been connected with the epic
cyclus of the Anglo-Norman trouvères. While, however, Archdeacon Walter Map was at work on the
Arthurian Romance in his study at Oxford, and
Luces de Gast in his castle near Salisbury, *le bon
père Chrêstien* was busy in his cell at Troyes in Brittany, writing the tale of Erec, and his wandering
with the faithful Enid, and thus gathering up the
crumbs which the plethoric Normans were allow-
ing to fall to the ground. It was a tale already in
existence. It was a favourite fireside story of the
Kymry, and at the time when Chrêstien wrote, had already been reduced to writing. It figures among the
Mabinogion, or Kymric tales which Lady Charlotte
Guest translated from a tenth century manuscript
preserved in the library of Jesus, the Welsh college
at Oxford, and, as this tale did not appear in the
French scrolls from which Sir Thomas Malory compiled his *Mort Darthur*, it forms, naturally enough,
no part of his famous work. Indeed, the very names
of Geraint and Enid find no mention there; nor is
there any separate English version which relates the

adventures of this knight, similar to those of Merlin, Lancelot, etc. In other words, the story of Geraint and Enid never seems to have found favour with the Norman writers, and hence never found its way into the castles of Norman England. It was the offspring of Wales ; it was developed in Wales ; and had it not been for Chréstien, it might never have been heard of beyond the borders of the land which produced it. We must therefore now bid adieu to the Plantagenet Court and the trouvères who have been entertaining us hitherto ; we must take our leave of Malory and honest William Caxton and make an excursion into Wales and Brittany.

In that noble and spirited poem by Llywarch Hên (parts of which we have quoted in previous chapters) viz.: the Elegy on the death of *Geraint-ab-Erbin*, we have direct, genuine, and contemporary evidence to the fact that Geraint actually lived, and was a noted warrior, at the time when the Britons were engaged in their fierce struggle with the Saxons for the possession of their ancestral lands.

When Geraint was born, the portals of heaven opened ;
The Christ granted the prayers of men :
Prosperity and glory to Britain.

Geraint, blood-stained, is celebrated by all,—
The warrior-chief,—and I too sing of Geraint,
The foe of the Saxons, the friend of the Saints.

Before Geraint, the terror of the foe,
I saw steeds fall in the toil of battle ;
And after the shout of war, a dreadful onset.

.   .   .   .

Before Geraint the scourge of the enemy,
I saw steeds white with foam ;
And after the shout of battle, a furious torrent.

.   .   .   .

At Longport I saw the raging of slaughter,
And myriads of the dead ;
Warriors, blood-stained, from the assault of Geraint.

.   .   .   .

At Longport was Geraint slain,
The valiant chief of the woodlands of Devon,
Slaying the enemy in his fall.*

In the Welsh Triads, Geraint appears as one of
the three great naval commanders, with twice threescore ships under his orders, and each ship manned
by twice threescore seamen.

In the life of St. Teiliaw, second Bishop of Llan-
daff, given in the *Lives of the Welsh Saints*, we find
a quaint, mediæval legend respecting our hero. The
Bishop, upon the breaking out of a pestilence in
Wales, fled to Armorica, and on his journey was entertained by Geraint, king of Cornwall, from whom
he received the highest marks of distinction. When
about to depart, the saint promised that the king
should not die until he had received the Holy Sacrament at the Bishop's own hands. Many years after

* *Vide* Note U.

this, Geraint was taken with a mortal illness, and the Bishop, warned miraculously of the fact, took ship immediately for Cornwall. The sailors, unable to carry on board a huge sarcophagus which the saint wished to take with him as a tribute to the memory of his former friend, he performed a miracle and the stone coffin floated at the ship's prow, and arrived safely at its destination. On his arrival, the Bishop finds the king *in extremis*, administers the last rites of the Church, and thus fulfills his previous promise.

Subsequently, a still higher honour awaited him. In a history of Hereford, of the last century, there is an account of one of the churches there, of which the records prove that it was originally dedicated to Geraint as its patron saint. Moreover, in a list of Welsh saints, published by Mr. Ritson, are the names of two sons of Geraint, Jestin ap Geraint ap Erbin and Silwen verch Geraint ap Erbin.

In the Cambrian bards of the Middle Ages, Geraint appears as the husband of Enid, daughter of Ynywl. This heroine of the Welsh is honoured in the Triads as one of the three fairest ladies of Arthur's Court, in beauty the peer of the Queen herself, and as remarkable for her gentleness as was Guinevere for her haughty disposition.

But the first connected account which we possess of the courtship and subsequent history of Geraint

and Enid is in the *Llyfr Coch O Hergest* or *Red Book
of Hergest*, where the romance is entitled *Geraint
ab Erbin*.

According to this story, King Arthur was seated
at table one day during Pentecost, when a tall youth,
with masses of auburn hair, dressed in diapered satin,
and wearing a rich sword with a gold hilt, enters the
banquet hall, advances towards the King and salutes
him. "Lord," said he, "in the forest I saw a stag,
the like of which beheld I never yet. . . . He is
of pure white, Lord, and he does not herd with any
other animal, through stateliness and pride, so royal
is his bearing." In consequence of this information,
the King commands his heralds to proclaim a grand
hunt for the morrow, and even Gwenhwyvar and the
ladies of the Court crave, and obtain permission to
take part in the adventure. At Gawaine's suggestion,
Arthur ordains that the huntsman who shall be for-
tunate enough to run the stag to the ground, be he
knight or commoner, shall have the stag's head as
his prize, and shall be allowed to present it to any
one he may please, be she queen or peasant. The
next morning, at daybreak, the King arises, the horns
are sounded, the huntsmen assemble, and the chase
begins. Gwenhwyvar, however, awakens too late to
take part in the start and, accompanied by a single
maid of honour, follows the track of the field.

As they are cantering along the road, they hear the clatter of hoofs behind them, and, on looking around, see a young knight, mounted on a horse of mighty size, and hastening to overtake them. The rider is a fair-haired youth of princely mien, a golden-hilted sword dangles at his side, he wears a robe of satin, and across his shoulders is a scarf of blue purple, ornamented at either end with a golden apple. The knight salutes the Queen, " And why didst thou not go with thy lord to hunt?" enquires Queen Gwenhwyvar. But Geraint, like the Queen, had slept late, and was hastening to overtake the Court. Unwilling, however, to leave his royal mistress, he rides on at her side, chatting pleasantly till they come to the outskirts of the forest. "From this place," exclaimed the Queen, "we shall hear when the dogs are let loose." Scarcely has she done speaking when a sound of approaching horsemen breaks upon the air, and the next moment, they see a dwarf mounted on a foaming horse, strong and spirited, and holding in his hand a hunting whip. Following close behind, is a lady clothed in a garment of gold brocade, seated upon a white palfry, while at her side is a knight armed and riding his war horse. The Queen asks Geraint whether he knows the strange knight, but he does not. "Go, maiden," said Gwenhwyvar to her lady in waiting, "and ask the dwarf who that knight is." The dwarf refuses to divulge the name of his master, and upon the lady's advancing to ask it in person, the villain strikes her across the face with his whip, so that the blood streams down her cheek. Geraint, seeing this cowardly attack, this insult to his Queen, puts spurs to his horse, rides up to the dwarf and renews the demand. But the churl repeats the insult, and now strikes Sir Gawaine across the face, drawing the blood and staining his scarf. It was not allowable for a knight to battle with any but one of his own order, nor could he, being unarmed, battle with the strange knight. He accordingly rides back to the Queen and exclaims : " Lady, I will follow him yet, with thy permission; and at last he will come to some inhabited place, where I may have arms . . . so that I may encounter the knight." The Queen grants him permission, and Geraint dashes into the forest and is soon out of sight.

Keeping the knight and his companions in sight, Geraint follows them till they come to a town at the extremity of which stands a fortress and a castle, where knight, lady, and dwarf enter amid the rejoicings of the people. Geraint watches for a while to see whether the knight will remain in the castle, and when he is certain that he will do so, he looks around him, and at a little distance from the town, he sees

23

" an old palace in ruins." As he comes near the palace he sees " a hoary-headed man," upon whom are tattered garments, and by him he is heartily welcomed to the humble cheer of the place. Here Geraint learns that the object of his pursuit is a powerful (bandit) knight who lives near-by, and who will appear the next day in a tournament which is held yearly, and at which, without exception, he has hitherto carried off the hawk, the prize of the conqueror. Each combatant in this tournament, however, has to appear accompanied by his lady, who is required to place her hand upon the bird, and then the champions fight for it. Geraint has no lady for whom to do battle, but at that palace he meets the beautiful Enid, daughter of his host, and with her, when the time arrives, he enters the lists. In the single combat which ensues, Geraint finally overpowers his antagonist, and compels him to swear, on pain of instant death, to present himself at Court and beg pardon of the Queen for the insult offered to her attendant. Subsequently, having married Enid, Geraint conducts her to Caerleon where the Queen robes her in one of her royal dresses, and the King, at Guinevere's request, presents her with the head of the white stag, which he has meantime won in the hunt. "Let it be given to Enid, the daughter of Ynywl, the most illustrious maiden," said the Queen, " and

I do not believe that any will begrudge it her, for between her and everyone here there exists nothing but love and friendship." At length the newly wedded knight obtains the King's permission to return, together with his wife, to the kingdom of his father, Erbin, who was waxing " heavy and feeble and advancing in years," and so he bids adieu to Queen and Court.

But while at home in his own kingdom, ease and luxury take possession of him; his barons begin to murmur at his want of knightly ambition, and even Enid weeps when she thinks of the derisive rumours in dispraise of her husband, which continually reach her ears. Gentle is her nature, she has not the heart to tell her husband of all the scorn and bitter contempt which, now and again, express themselves in the looks, the words, and the acts of his warlike barons. But her countenance betrays her grief, and Geraint, in the littleness of a jealous nature, imagines that she is pining for the love of some absent knight. He resolves to leave his kingdom, to snatch her from the imaginary danger, and to seek, amid the hardships of knightly adventure, to make her forget this fictitious lover. Adventures follow thick and fast, but Geraint is ever victorious; now he leaves his assailant dead on the field; now he is himself wounded and in peril of death; but through-

out all their romantic journey the heart of Enid ever
yearns towards him, and in spite of his harsh reproofs, in spite of his morose conduct, she shows
herself a true wife, till even Geraint is won back by
her tender loyalty. Thoroughly assured of her love
for him alone, he returns to his kingdom, a warrior
prince as of old; his barons return to their allegiance; the sorrow vanishes from Enid's countenance, and so the romance ends.

Such then, is the outline of the story of *Geraint-
ab-Erbin* as told by the nameless writer of this Welsh
Mabinogi. At what date this tale was written we
have no means of judging. We may safely assert,
however, that it was committed to writing at least
a hundred years before Walter Map's time, since the
manuscript which contains the romance is conclu-
sively proved to belong to the eleventh century.
But doubtless, like the other tales or Mabinogion, in
the *Red Book of Hergest*, the one in question, had
existed for centuries as an oral tradition, related by
bards in the castles of the nobles, and by humbler
story-tellers at cottage firesides, till at length it was
committed to writing by some unknown lover of his
early native literature. No sooner had this plaintive Welsh tale made its appearance, than it was
seized upon by the minstrels of Brittany, and
during the twelfth century was translated into

French by *le bon père Chréstien* whom we before mentioned.

It will not be necessary to analyse the French romance, since the leading incidents are the same as in the Kymric tale; but there are certain points of difference between the two versions both in matters of fact and motives of action, as well as interesting additions introduced by the trouvère, which we shall glance at in passing.

In the Welsh story, Arthur holds his Court at Caerleon on Usk, (Monmouth,) just as he does in the Anglo-Norman romances. He is now represented as an Emperor as well as King, and what more natural than to make his capital the City of Legions in imitation of that northern Caerleon where real Roman Emperors had dwelt, from which they had issued their imperial decrees, and which, even in after times, showed by the remains of palaces, amphitheatres, and temples, the grandeur to which it had once attained. But Chréstien states that the King held his Court at Cardigan and not at Caerleon. The point is curious, for although Chréstien's motive in making the change is not apparent, yet before the time of Geoffrey, we do not find that Caerleon holds the distinguished position which it afterwards did. In the oldest traditions of Arthur, we find that his permanent residence, his chief palace, was at Kelliweg in Devonshire; and this

perfectly accords with the oldest accounts which state
him to have been a petty prince of Cornwall, and not
a Welsh Emperor.   In the Triads, however, we are
told that Arthur had three chief palaces, his favourite one being at Kelliweg, the second at Caerleon, and
the third at Penryhn in the North.   That Caerleon,
even in early times, had become the favourite royal
city with writers on this subject, is clear from the
fact that, in a later triad, one of the three great festivals of Britain is said to be that which Arthur annu-
ally held at Caerleon.   It is not then surprising that
Chréstien should have changed the site of the King's
palace, but that he should have done so without any
assignable reason.

With the French trouvère, Arthur is King not Emperor; but whereas the Welsh writer simply says in
plain unvarnished prose that "he held his Court,"
the Frenchman makes him a most mighty monarch,
whose Court eclipsed in splendour anything that the
world had ever known, and as its highest glory, he
draws the fellowship of Round Table knights as they
are depicted in the Anglo-Norman romances.

And here we are met by a second curious fact.
Arthur being a Kymric hero, we should naturally
expect to find, either in the writings of the Welsh
bards, or in those of the Bretons, the first mention
of this celebrated order of the Round Table.   But

in this we are disappointed. The Kymric poems, the Triads, and the Kymric prose tales do not so much as refer to the subject. The bardic remains of the Breton refugees of Armorica are also silent upon the matter of the Round Table. Geoffrey of Monmouth seems to have been as ignorant of its existence as any of his predecessors. It is in the *Roman de Brut* of Wace that we hear of the Round Table for the first time, and he dismisses the subject abruptly in two lines:

> Fist Arthur la roonde table
> Dont Britons dient mainte fable.

Layamon, coming close upon the heels of Wace, expands this simple statement and gives the story of the carpenter coming to the King and proposing to make a table at which the high should be even with the low, and so rivalries and bloodshed be henceforth prevented. This origin of the Round Table, if known to the author of the *Roman de Merlin* and of the *Roman du Saint Graal*, was not compatible with his christianised treatment of the subject, and accordingly, he connected it with the legend of the Holy Graal, and represented it as the Table used by our Saviour at the Last Supper. One fact is deserving of notice. · The Anglo-Norman Wace states that the Britons of his day knew of the Round Table, and had

people of Brittany, and Wales

many stories about it ; the Welsh Layamon repeats the statement ; the French Chréstien, avowedly copy-ing from a Breton original, has the legend in its most fully developed form, though without the spirituali-sation of Walter Map, whereas no extant Welsh tale seems to know so much as the bare existence of the Round Table.

In the Kymric tale, moreover, our hero is called simply " Geraint son of Erbin," thus agreeing with the genuine and ancient accounts of his genealogy ; but Chréstien calls him Erec, son of a king, the pow-erful Lac, and not content with this, he unblushingly makes Geraint say,.

" Ainsi m'apèlent li Breton."

According to this account, he becomes in time, a knight of the Round Table, is most highly esteemed and most dearly beloved by King and Court; he is handsome, brave, graceful, and generous ; although but twenty-five years of age, yet, in the wide world, there were few knights to be found his equal, whether on the field of battle or in the tournament.

The gentle Enid, as we have already seen, is cele-brated in the Triads as one of the three most beauti-ful women at Arthur's Court ; the later Welsh ro-mancer calls her the most beautiful in Britain ; the Frenchman, not to be outdone, introduces her as the most beautiful that ever lived. "She was," he says, "perfectly beautiful as nature can testify, no fairer has ever been seen in the world." Moreover, he makes Queen Guinevere, (the highest judge of female beauty), adorn Enid with her own hands, whereas the Welsh writer simply says "and the choicest of all Gwenhwyvar's apparel was given to the maiden."

Throughout the French version, we find all the rough lines of the Kymric picture softened down, all that is weird transformed and polished, and nothing allowed to remain that might, in the slightest degree, grate upon the polite ears of French chivalry. The dwarf no longer carries in his hand a rude hunting whip, but a delicate switch, and when the Queen's attendant attempts to near the knight, the dwarf, bursting with rage, *aims a blow at her face*, but she, raising her arm, wards off the blow and so he strikes her across the bare hand. There is no whip, no brutal stroke across the face, no spurting forth of the blood.

So, in the Welsh romance, the prize at the chase of the white stag is the bleeding head of the animal. Geraint says to the Emperor, "Permit that into whose hunt soever the stag shall come, that one, be he a knight or one on foot, may cut off his head, and give it to whom he pleases, whether to his own

lady-love or to the lady of his friend," and so it was
granted.   But in the French romance, Geraint's request is changed ; here he asks the King: " Sire, we
understand that there is an ancient custom at the
chase of a white stag, that he who kills the stag, shall
have the right to kiss the fairest lady of your Court,"
and accordingly, after the hunt, and when Geraint
has brought his fair wife Enid to the Court, Guinevere tells her husband the King, who has meantime
won the prize, " Sire, you may kiss Enid as the most
beautiful lady of the Court, for she is the fairest of
the world."   Thus permitted, Arthur replies, " She
shall have the prize of the white stag, for no one
shall ever accuse me of not maintaining the ancient
customs of my realm."   Then turning to Enid he
adds : " Sweet friend, I give you my love," and em-
braces her.   The prize of the bleeding head was too
primitive, too rude, too weird for Chréstien to adopt.
In his eyes, the ladies of Arthur's Court required
one more delicate, more refined, more gallant, in a
word more French, and hence the bleeding head is
transformed into a kiss.

But by far the most important of these refining
touches of the trouvère, appears in the motive
which he attributes to Erec for abandoning his life
of ease and luxury.   The Welsh story-teller makes
Geraint to have been actuated by jealousy of some

imaginary rival, from whose fascinating power he is determined to snatch his wife. But, *le bon père Chréstien* could not, for one moment, allow his hero to be moved by so earth-born a passion ; to do so, would be to endorse indirectly, that which his Church condemned, and accordingly, in the French romance, Erec is prompted to seek adventures from a high sense of duty ; a motive far less natural than that of jealousy, and one which was all but unknown to the ancient Kymry.

Chréstien made, moreover, one important addition to the ending of the legend. While the Welsh romancer concludes with the somewhat trite remark that Geraint "went towards his own dominions and thenceforth reigned prosperously," the trouvère states that, upon his return to Arthur's Court, he found ten barons awaiting him with the intelligence that his father, king Lac, was dead, and that, having done homage to the King for his estates, he obtained permission to depart and receive the fealty of his vassals.

To say that Tennyson's Idylls of *The Marriage of Geraint* and *Geraint and Enid* contain nothing that is especially original in incident, is simply to say that the poet has followed faithfully the leading incidents of the Welsh story. It is a very graphic and very pathetic tale ; and, as embodying a leading episode in the life of one of the most distinguished knights of the Round Table, is of interest in such a review of the Arthurian Epic as we are now taking. At the same time, our object in introducing this tale, which has no organic connection with the cyclus, is chiefly to show the picturesque weirdness of a Welsh Mabinogi or romance, and the refined and delicate manner in which the poet has reset the tale.

The romance of *Geraint-ab-Erbin* opens, as we have just seen, with the proclamation by the King's heralds of the chase of the white stag, and the permission granted to Gwenhwyvar to be present, on the morrow, at the hunt. After narrating these incidents the Welsh romancer proceeds to give a description of the start of Arthur and the Court for the Forest of Dean, and Gwenhwyvar's late appearance on the ground : " And after Arthur had gone forth from the palace, Gwenhwyvar awoke, and called to her maidens, and apparelled herself. ' Maidens,' said she, ' I had leave last night to go and see the hunt. Go one of you to the stable, and order hither horses.' . . . And Gwenhwyvar and one of her maidens mounted them, and went through the Usk, and followed the track of the men and the horses. And as they rode thus, they heard a loud and rushing sound ; and they looked behind them, and beheld

a knight upon a hunter foal of mighty size ; and the
rider was a fair-haired youth . . . of princely
mien, and a golden-hilted sword was at his side, and
a robe and a surcoat of satin were upon him, . . .
and around him was a scarf of blue purple, at each
corner of which was a golden apple. And his horse
stepped stately, and swift, and proud ; and he overtook Gwenhwyvar, and saluted her. ' Heaven pros-
per thee, Geraint,' said she ; ' I knew thee when first
I saw thee just now. And the welcome of heaven be
unto thee. And why didst thou not go with thy lord
to hunt ? ' ' Because I knew not when he went,' said
he. . . . ' I too was asleep, and knew not when he
went,' [said Gwenhwyvar] . . . ' it may be that
I shall be more amused with the hunting than they ;
for we shall hear the horns when they sound, and
we shall hear the dogs when they are let loose and
begin to cry.' So they went to the edge of the Forest, and there they stood. ' From this place,' said
she, ' we shall hear when the dogs are let loose.' And
thereupon, they heard a loud noise, . . . and
they beheld a dwarf riding upon a horse. . . .
And in the hand of the dwarf was a whip. And near
the dwarf they saw a lady upon a beautiful white
horse, . . . and she was clothed in a garment
of gold brocade. And near her was a knight upon
a warhorse of large size, with heavy and bright

armour both upon himself and upon his horse. And truly they never before saw a knight, or a horse, or armour, of such remarkable size. . . . 'Geraint,' said Gwenhwyvar, 'knowest thou the name of that tall knight yonder?' 'I know him not,' said he, 'and the strange armour that he wears prevents my either seeing his face or his features.' 'Go, maiden,' said Gwenhwyvar, 'and ask the dwarf who that knight is.' Then the maiden went up to the dwarf; . . . and inquired of the dwarf who the knight was. 'I will not tell thee,' he answered. 'Since thou art so churlish as not to tell me,' said she, 'I will ask him himself.' 'Thou shalt not ask him, by my faith,' said he. 'Wherefore?' said she. 'Because thou art not of honour sufficient to befit thee to speak to my lord.' Then the maiden turned her horse's head towards the knight, upon which *the dwarf struck her with the whip that was in his hand across the face and the eyes, until the blood flowed forth.* And the maiden, . . . returned to Gwenhwyvar, complaining of the pain. 'Very rudely has the dwarf treated thee,' said Geraint. 'I will go myself to know who the knight is.' 'Go,' said Gwenhwyvar. And Geraint went up to the dwarf. 'Who is yonder knight?' said Geraint. 'I will not tell thee,' said the dwarf. 'Then will I ask him himself,' said he. 'That wilt thou not, by my faith,' said the dwarf;

'thou art not honourable enough to speak with my lord.' . . . [And Geraint] turned his horse's head towards the knight; but the dwarf overtook him, and struck him as he had done the maiden, *so that the blood coloured the scarf* that Geraint wore. Then Geraint put his hand upon the hilt of his sword, but he . . . considered that it would be no vengeance for him to slay the dwarf, . . . so he returned to where Gwenhwyvar was. . . . 'Lady,' said he, 'I will follow him yet, with thy permission; . . . so that I may encounter the knight.' 'Go,' said she, . . . 'I shall be very anxious concerning thee, until I hear tidings of thee.' 'If I am alive,' said he, 'thou shalt hear tidings of me by tomorrow afternoon'; and with that he departed."

This scene, as reproduced by Tennyson, has lost none of the refined simplicity of the original tale.

> But Guinevere lay late into the morn,
> . . . forgetful of the hunt;
> But rose at last, a single maiden with her,
> Took horse, and forded Usk, and gain'd the wood;
> There, on a little knoll beside it, stay'd
> Waiting to hear the hounds; but heard instead
> A sudden sound of hoofs, for Prince Geraint,
> Late also, wearing neither hunting-dress
> Nor weapon, save a golden-hilted brand,
> Came quickly flashing thro' the shallow ford
> Behind them, and so gallop'd up the knoll.

A purple scarf, at either end whereof
There swung an apple of the purest gold,
Sway'd round about him, as he galloped up
To join them, glancing like a dragon fly
In summer suit and silks of holiday.
Low bow'd the tributary Prince, and she,
Sweetly and statelily, and with all grace
Of womanhood and queenhood, answer'd him :
"Late, late, Sir Prince," she said, " later than we ! "
" Yea, noble Queen," he answer'd, "and so late
That I but come like you to see the hunt,
Not join it."   " Therefore wait with me," she said ;
" For on this little knoll, if anywhere,
There is good chance that we shall hear the hounds ;
Here often they break covert at our feet."

And while they listen'd for the distant hunt,
And chiefly for the baying of Cavall,
King Arthur's hound of deepest mouth, there rode
Full slowly by a knight, lady, and dwarf :
Whereof the dwarf lagg'd latest, and the knight
Had vizor up, and show'd a youthful face,
Imperious, and of haughtiest lineaments.
And Guinevere, not mindful of his face
In the King's hall, desired his name, and sent
Her maiden to demand it of the dwarf ;
Who being vicious, old and irritable,
And doubling all his master's vice of pride,
Made answer sharply that she should not know.
" Then will I ask it of himself," she said.
" Nay, by my faith, thou shalt not," cried the dwarf ;
" Thou art not worthy ev'n to speak of him ; "

And when she put her horse toward the knight,
Struck at her with his whip, and she return'd
Indignant to the Queen ; whereat Geraint
Exclaiming, "Surely I will learn the name,"
Made sharply to the dwarf, and ask'd it of him,
Who answer'd as before ; and when the Prince
Had put his horse in motion toward the knight,
Struck at him with his whip, and cut his cheek.
The Prince's blood spirted upon the scarf,
Dyeing it ; and his quick, instinctive hand
Caught at the hilt, as to abolish him :
But he, *from his exceeding manfulness*
And pure nobility of temperament,
Wroth to be wroth at such a worm, refrain'd
From ev'n a word, and so returning said :
" I will avenge this insult, noble Queen,
Done in your maiden's person to yourself :
And I will track this vermin to their earths :
For tho' I ride unarm'd, I do not doubt
To find, at some place I shall come at, arms
On loan, or else for pledge ; and, being found
Then will I fight him, and will break his pride,
And on the third day will again be here,
So that I be not fall'n in fight.   Farewell."

In one point in the above extract it will be seen
that Tennyson has followed the French romance
rather than the Welsh story, for he tells us that the
dwarf,

Struck at her with his whip.

24

The maiden was indignant, as was natural, but she does not appear to have been otherwise hurt, nor is there any mention of the spirting forth of blood.

In order to punish the insult offered to his Queen, as well as to himself, by the dwarf who accompanied the bandit knight, Geraint followed him the livelong day till at length he came to a town where the knight had his castle.

"At a little distance from the town," says the romancer, "he saw an old palace in ruins, wherein was a hall that was falling to decay. And as he knew not anyone in the town, he went towards the old palace; and when he came near to the palace, he saw but one chamber, and a bridge of marble-stone leading to it. And upon the bridge he saw sitting a hoary-headed man, upon whom were tattered garments. And Geraint gazed steadfastly upon him for a long time. Then the hoary-headed man spoke to him. 'Young man,' he said, 'wherefore art thou thoughtful?' 'I am thoughtful,' said he, 'because I know not where to go to-night.' 'Wilt thou come forward this way, chieftain?' said he, 'and thou shalt have of the best that can be procured for thee.' So Geraint went forward. And the hoary-headed man preceded him into the hall. And in the hall he dismounted, and he left there his horse. Then he went on to the upper chamber with the hoary-headed

man.   And in the chamber he beheld an old decrepit
woman, sitting on a cushion, with old, tattered garments of satin upon her; and it seemed to him that
he had never seen a woman fairer than she must
have been, when in the fulness of youth.   And beside
her was a maiden, upon whom were a vest and a
veil, that were old, and beginning to be worn out.
And truly, he never saw a maiden more full of come-
liness, and grace, and beauty, than she.   And the
hoary-headed man said to the maiden, 'There is no
attendant for the horse of this youth but thyself.'
'I will render the best service I am able,' said she,
'both to him and to his horse.' "

How gracefully does Tennyson draw this picture
of by-gone days.

> Then rode Geraint, a little spleenful yet,
> Across the bridge that spann'd the dry ravine.
> There musing sat the hoary-headed Earl,
> (His dress a suit of fray'd magnificence,
> Once fit for feasts of ceremony) and said :
> "Whither, fair son?" to whom Geraint replied,
> "O friend, I seek a harborage for the night."
> Then Yniol, "Enter therefore and partake
> The slender entertainment of a house
> Once rich, now poor, but ever open-door'd."

> .   .   .   .

> Then rode Geraint into the castle court,
> His charger trampling many a prickly star

Of sprouted thistle on the broken stones.
He look'd and saw that all was ruinous.
Here stood a shatter'd archway plumed with fern ;
And here had fall'n a great part of a tower,
Whole, like a crag that tumbles from the cliff,
·And like a crag was gay with wilding flowers :
And high above a piece of turret stair,
Worn by the feet that now were silent, wound
Bare to the sun, and monstrous ivy-stems
Claspt the gray walls with hairy-fibred arms,
And suck'd the joining of the stones, and look'd
A knot, beneath, of snakes, aloft, a grove.

  . . . .

        Entering then,
Right o'er a mount of newly fallen stones,
The dusky-rafter'd many-cobweb'd hall,
He found an ancient dame in dim brocade ;
And near her, like a blossom vermeil-white,
That lightly breaks a faded flower-sheath,
Moved the fair Enid, all in faded silk,
Her daughter. In a moment thought Geraint,
" Here by God's rood is the one maid for me."
But none spake word except the hoary Earl :
" Enid, the good knight's horse stands in the court ;
Take him to stall, and give him corn, and then
Go to the town and buy us flesh and wine ;
And we will make us merry as we may.
Our hoard is little, but our hearts are great."

Geraint and Earl Ynywl, after the frugal banquet,
spend the evening hours talking of the old palace
wherein they sat, its history and of by-gone days, and
of the castle on the hill, the town, and of the knight

of the Sparrow-Hawk, and of the tournament on the morrow; and then Geraint recounts his adventure and the insult he had received. "Sir," said Geraint, "what is thy counsel to me concerning this knight, on account of the insult which I received from the dwarf, and that which was received by the maiden of Gwenhwyvar, the wife of Arthur?" And Geraint told the hoary-headed man, what the insult was that he had received. "'It is not easy to counsel thee, inasmuch as thou hast neither dame nor maiden belonging to thee, for whom thou canst joust.' . . . 'Ah! Sir,' said he, . . . 'And if, when the appointed time shall come to-morrow, thou wilt permit me, Sir, to challenge for yonder maiden that is thy daughter, I will engage, if I escape from the tournament, to love the maiden as long as I live.' . . . 'Gladly will I permit thee,' said the hoary-headed man; . . . and thus it was settled. And at night, lo! they went to sleep."

In the Idyll of the *Marriage of Geraint* these incidents are portrayed with remarkable fidelity. Here, the hoary-headed Earl, after he had heard Geraint's vow to avenge the Queen, tells him,

"But in this tournament can no man tilt,
Except the lady he loves best be there.

  .   .   .   .

But thou, that hast no lady, canst not fight."

Then

> Geraint with eyes all bright replied,
> Leaning a little toward him, "Thy leave!
> Let *me* lay lance in rest, O noble host,
> *For this dear child* . . .
>   . . . if I live,
> So aid me Heaven when at mine uttermost,
> As I will make her truly my true wife."

After the joust and overthrow of the Sparrow-Hawk, Geraint and his friends return to the ruined palace, and after the knight had come from the anointing of his wounds, "'where,' said Geraint, 'is the Earl Ynywl, and his wife, and his daughter?' 'They are in the chamber yonder,' said the Earl's chamberlain, 'arraying themselves.' . . . 'Let not the damsel array herself,' said he, 'except in her vest and her veil, until she come to the Court of Arthur, to be clad by Gwenhwyvar, in such garments as she may choose.' So the maiden did not array herself. . . . Then spoke Earl Ynywl to Geraint. 'Chieftain,' said he, 'behold the maiden for whom thou didst challenge at the tournament; I bestow her upon thee.' 'She shall go with me,' said Geraint, 'to the Court of Arthur; and Arthur and Gwenhwyvar they shall dispose of her as they will.' And the next day they proceeded to Arthur's Court . . . and there was a watch set on the ramparts

by Gwenhwyvar, lest he [Geraint] should arrive una-
wares. And one of the watch came to the place where
Gwenhwyvar was. 'Lady,' said he, 'methinks that
I see Geraint, and the maiden with him. He is on
horseback, . . . and the maiden appears to be
in white, seeming to be clad in a garment of linen.'
. . . And Gwenhwyvar went to meet Geraint and
the maiden. And when Geraint came to the place
where Gwenhwyvar was, he saluted her. . . .
'Heaven reward thee [said she], that thou hast so
proudly caused me to have retribution.' 'Lady,'
said he, 'I earnestly desired to obtain thee satisfaction according to thy will; and, behold, here is the
maiden through whom thou hadst thy revenge.'
'Verily,' said Gwenhwyvar, 'the welcome of Heaven
be unto her; and it is fitting that we should receive
her joyfully.' Then they went in and dismounted.
And Geraint came to where Arthur was and saluted
him. 'Heaven protect thee,' said Arthur, 'and the
welcome of Heaven be unto thee.' . . . 'Now,'
said Arthur, 'where is the maiden for whom I heard
thou didst give challenge?' 'She is gone with
Gwenhwyvar to her chamber,' said the knight. Then
went Arthur to see the maiden. And Arthur, and
all his companions, and his whole Court, were glad
concerning the maiden. And certain were they all,
that had her array been suitable to her beauty, they

had never seen a maid fairer than she.   And Arthur
gave away the maiden to Geraint . . . and the
choicest of all Gwenhwyvar's apparel was given to
the maiden."

In the Idyll, while Enid is arraying herself for the
journey to Arthur's Court, Geraint

> Woke where he slept in the high hall, and call'd
> For Enid, and when Yniol made report
> Of that good mother making Enid gay
> In such apparel as might well beseem
> His princess, or indeed the stately Queen,
> He answer'd : " Earl, entreat her by my love,
>
> .   .   .   .   .   .
>
> That she ride with me in her faded silk."
> Yniol with that hard message went ; it fell
> Like flaws in summer laying lusty corn :
> For Enid, all abash'd she knew not why,
> Dared not to glance at her good mother's face,
> But silently, in all obedience,
> Her mother silent too, nor helping her,
> Laid from her limbs the costly-broider'd gift,
> And robed them in her ancient suit again,
> And so descended.

Geraint

> Then seeing cloud upon the mother's brow,
> Her by both hands he caught and sweetly said,
>
> .   .   .   .   .   .
>
> " When late I left Caerleon, our great Queen,
>
> .   .   .   .   .   .
>
> Made promise, that whatever bride I brought,

Herself would clothe her like the sun in Heaven.
Thereafter, when I reached this ruin'd hall,
Beholding one so bright in dark estate,
I vow'd that could I gain her, our fair Queen,
No hand but hers, should make your Enid burst
Sunlike from cloud."

And so they bid adieu to the ruined palace and start for Caerleon and the Court.

Now thrice that morning Guinevere had climb'd
The giant tower, from whose high crest, they say,
Men saw the goodly hills of Somerset,
And white sails flying on the yellow sea ;
But not to goodly hill or yellow sea
Look'd the fair Queen, but up the vale of Usk,
By the flat meadow, till she saw them come ;
And then descending met them at the gates,
Embraced her with all welcome as a friend,
And did her honour as the Prince's bride,
And clothed her for her bridals like the sun ;
    .   .   .   .

But Enid ever kept the faded silk,
Remembering how first he came on her,
Drest in that dress, and how he loved her in it,
And all her foolish fears about the dress,
And all his journey toward her, as himself
Had told her, and their coming to the court.

We cannot refrain from noticing one incident, among many, in the Idyll of the *Marriage of Geraint*, where the poet's fancy has added a tender touch to the Welsh story, viz.: where the mother discloses to an artless child the fact that she is beloved by Geraint-ab-Erbin, prince of Devon.

The Earl, after Enid has gone to her chamber for the night, speaking to his wife

> And fondling all her hand in his he said,
> " Mother, a maiden is a tender thing,
> And best by her that bore her understood.
> Go thou to rest, but ere thou go to rest
> Tell her, and prove her heart toward the Prince."
>
> So spake the kindly-hearted Earl, and she
> With frequent smile and nod departing found,
> Half disarray'd as to her rest, the girl ;
> Whom first she kiss'd on either cheek, and then
> On either shining shoulder laid a hand,
> And kept her off and gazed upon her face,
> And told her all their converse in the hall,
> Proving her heart : but never light and shade
> Coursed one another more on open ground
> Beneath a troubled heaven, than red and pale
> Across the face of Enid hearing her ;
> While slowly falling as a scale that falls,
> When weight is added only grain by grain,
> Sank her sweet head upon her gentle breast ;
> Nor did she lift an eye nor speak a word,
> Rapt in the fear and in the wonder of it.

These are the pictures in which Tennyson excels: scenes, in which the chasteness and purity of his genius can find expression. But in the single combats with recreant knights and bandit earls, he falls far below both Welsh and French narrator. The Kymric weirdness in the description of wanderings and of conflicts is gone ; and the vividness and reality which characterise this part of the French version are lost. Indeed the poet seems to have belonged too intimately to the nineteenth century, and to have been too deeply imbued with its spirit of refinement, courtesy, and self-abnegation, to be able to depict the rougher aspects of twelfth century life.

It will not be necessary to examine, in detail, the latter part of the Welsh story, descriptive of the wanderings of Geraint-ab-Erbin and Ynywl's lovely daughter, which Tennyson reset as a separate poem in his Idyll of *Geraint and Enid*. We shall compare only the two most striking passages in this part of the tale, viz.: the events which led to the estrangement between the knight and his devoted wife, and the death of the " brute " Earl which led to their full and final reconciliation.

The knight, says the narrator of the tale, " began to love ease and pleasure, for there was no one who was worth his opposing. And he loved his wife, and liked to continue in the palace, with minstrelsy and diversions. And for a long time he abode at home. And after that, he began to shut himself up in the chamber of his wife, and he took no delight in anything besides, in so much that he gave up the friendship of his nobles, together with his hunting and his amusements, and lost the hearts of all the host in his court ; and there was murmuring and scoffing concerning him among the inhabitants of the palace, on account of his relinquishing so completely their companionship for the love of his wife. And these tidings came to Erbin. And when Erbin had heard these things, he spoke unto Enid, and enquired of her whether it was she that had caused Geraint to act thus, and to forsake his people and his hosts. 'Not I, by my confession unto Heaven,' said she ; 'there is nothing more hateful to me than this.' And she knew not what she should do, for although it was hard for her to own this to Geraint, yet was it not more easy for her to listen to what she heard, without warning Geraint concerning it. And she was very sorrowful.

"And one morning in the summer time, they were upon their couch, and Geraint lay upon the edge of it. And Enid was without sleep in the apartment which had windows of glass. And the sun shone upon the couch. And the clothes had slipped from off his arms and his breast, and he was asleep. Then she gazed upon the marvellous beauty of his appearance, and she said : 'Alas, and am I the cause that these arms and this breast have lost their glory and the warlike fame which they once so richly enjoyed?'

And as she said this, the tears dropped from her eyes,
and they fell upon his breast. And the tears she shed,
and the words she had spoken, awoke him; and another thing contributed to awaken him, and that was
the idea that it was not in thinking of him that she
spoke thus, but that it was because she loved some
other man more than him, and that she wished for
other society, and thereupon Geraint was troubled
in his mind."

How finely is this told by the poet! Geraint and
Enid,

> . . . past to their own land ;
> Where, thinking, that if ever yet was wife
> True to her lord, mine shall be so to me,
> He compass'd her with sweet observances
> And worship, never leaving her, and grew
> Forgetful of his promise to the King,
> Forgetful of the falcon and the hunt,
> Forgetful of the tilt and tournament,
> Forgetful of his glory and his name,
> Forgetful of his princedom and its cares.
> And this forgetfulness was hateful to her.
> And by and by the people, when they met
> In twos and threes, or fuller companies,
> Began to scoff and jeer and babble of him
> As of a prince whose manhood was all gone,
> And molten down in mere uxoriousness.
>
> .   .   .   .   .   .
>
> And day by day she thought to tell Geraint,
> But could not out of bashful delicacy ;

While he that watch'd her sadden, was the more
Suspicious that her nature had a taint.

At last, it chanced that on a summer morn
(They sleeping each by either) the new sun
Beat thro' the blindless casement of the room,
And heated the strong warrior in his dreams ;
Who, moving, cast the coverlet aside,
And bared the knotted column of his throat,
The massive square of his heroic breast,
And arms on which the standing muscle sloped,
As slopes a wild brook o'er a little stone,
Running too vehemently to break upon it.
And Enid woke and sat beside the couch,
Admiring him, and thought within herself,
Was ever man so grandly made as he ?
Then, like a shadow, past the people's talk
And accusation of uxoriousness
Across her mind, and bowing over him,
Low to her own heart piteously she said :

" O noble breast and all-puissant arms,
Am I the cause, I the poor cause that men
Reproach you, saying all your force is gone ?
I *am* the cause, because I dare not speak
And tell him what I think and what they say.
And yet I hate that he should linger here ;
I cannot love my lord and not his name.
Far liefer had I gird his harness on him,
And ride with him to battle and stand by,
And watch his mightful hand striking great blows
At caitiffs and at wrongers of the world.
Far better were I laid in the dark earth,

Not hearing any more his noble voice,
Not to be folded more in these dear arms,
And darken'd from the high light in his eyes,
Than that my lord thro' me should suffer shame.
Am I so bold, and could I so stand by,
And see my dear lord wounded in the strife,
Or maybe pierced to death before mine eyes,
And yet not dare to tell him what I think,
And how men slur him, saying all his force
Is melted into mere effeminacy?
O me, I fear that I am no true wife."

Half inwardly, half audibly she spoke,
And the strong passion in her made her weep
True tears upon his broad and naked breast,
And these awoke him, and by great mischance
He heard but fragments of her later words,
And that she fear'd she was not a true wife.
And then he thought, " In spite of all my care,
For all my pains, poor man, for all my pains,
She is not faithful to me, and I see her
Weeping for some gay knight in Arthur's hall."
Then tho' he loved and reverenced her too much
To dream she could be guilty of foul act,
Right thro' his manful breast darted the pang
That makes a man, in the sweet face of her
Whom he loves most, lonely and miserable.

The last incident that we shall compare, viz.: the
death of the " brute Earl " and consequent renewal
of Geraint's love, is perhaps the strongest, most tragic
scene in the romance. In a terrible encounter,

Geraint, though victorious, is left on the field dangerously wounded and in a swoon.

"Piercing and loud and thrilling was the cry that Enid uttered. And she came and stood over him [Geraint] where he had fallen. And at the sound of her cries came the Earl of Limours, and the host that journeyed with him, whom her lamentations brought out of their road. And the Earl said to Enid, 'Alas, Lady, what hath befallen thee?' 'Ah! good Sir,' said she, 'the only man I have loved, or ever shall love, is slain.' . . . The Earl thought that there still remained some life in Geraint; and to see if he yet would live, he had him carried with him in the hollow of his shield, and upon a bier." And when they arrived at the court, "Geraint was placed upon a litter-couch in front of the table that was in the hall. Then they all took off their travelling gear, and the Earl besought Enid to do the same, and to clothe herself in other garments. 'I will not, by Heaven,' said she. 'Ah! Lady,' said he, ' be not so sorrowful for this matter.' 'It were hard to persuade me to be otherwise,' said she. 'I will act towards thee,' said the Earl, 'in such wise, that thou needest not be sorrowful, whether yonder knight live or die. Behold, a good Earldom, together with myself, will I bestow on thee; be, therefore, happy and joyful.' 'I declare to Heaven', said she, ' that henceforth I shall

never be joyful while I live.' 'Come then,' said he,
'and eat.' 'No, by Heaven, I will not,' she answered. 'But, by Heaven, thou shalt,' said he. So
he took her with him to the table against her will,
and many times desired her to eat. 'I call Heaven
to witness,' said she, 'that I will not eat until the
man that is upon yonder bier shall eat likewise.'
'Thou canst not fulfil that,' said the Earl, 'yonder
man is dead already.' 'I will prove that I can,'
said she. Then he offered her a goblet of liquor.
'Drink this goblet' he said, 'and it will cause thee
to change thy mind.' 'Evil betide me,' she answered, 'if I drink aught until he drink also.'
'Truly,' said the Earl, 'it is of no more avail for me
to be gentle with thee than ungentle.' And he
gave her a box in the ear. Thereupon she raised a
loud and piercing shriek, and her lamentations were
much greater than they had been before, for she
considered in her mind that had Geraint been alive,
he durst not have struck her thus. But, behold, at
the sound of her cry, Geraint revived from his swoon,
and he sat up on the bier, and finding his sword in
the hollow of his shield, he rushed to the place where
the Earl was, and struck him a fiercely-wounding,
severely-venomous, and sternly-smiting blow upon
the crown of his head, so that he clove him in twain,
until his sword was stayed by the table. Then all

25

left the board and fled away. And this was not so
much through fear of the living as through the dread
they felt at seeing the dead man rise up to slay
them."

In the Idyll, how faithfully has Tennyson portrayed the brutal character and disposition of the
Earl ; the tender heroic love of Enid and the almost
superhuman strength that the assurance of her love
imparts to Geraint :

But at the point of noon the huge Earl Doorm,
Broad-faced with under-fringe of russet beard,
Bound on a foray, rolling eyes of prey,
Came riding with a hundred lances up ;
But ere he came, like one that hails a ship,
Cried out with a big voice, " What, is he dead ? "
" No, no, not dead ! " she answer'd in all haste.
" Would some of your kind people take him up,
And bear him hence out of this cruel sun ?
Most sure am I, quite sure, he is not dead."
Then said Earl Doorm : " Well, if he be not dead,
Why wail ye for him thus ? ye seem a child.
And be he dead, I count you for a fool ;
Your wailing will not quicken him : dead or not,
Ye mar a comely face with idiot tears.
Yet, since the face *is* comely—some of you,
Here, take him up, and bear him to our hall :
An if he live, we will have him of our band ;
And if he die, why earth has earth enough
To hide him.   See ye take the charger too,
A noble one."

After their arrival at the castle, and

When Earl Doorm had eaten all he would,
He roll'd his eyes about the hall, and found
A damsel drooping in a corner of it.
Then he remember'd her, and how she wept ;
And out of her there came a power upon him ;
And rising on the sudden he said, " Eat !
I never yet beheld a thing so pale.
God's curse, it makes me mad to see you weep.
Eat ! Look yourself.   Good luck had your good
    man,
For were I dead who is it would weep for me ?
Sweet lady, never since I first drew breath ·
Have I beheld a lily like yourself.
And so there lived some color in your cheek,
There is not one among my gentlewomen
Were fit to wear your slipper for a glove.
But listen to me, and by me be ruled,
And I will do the thing I have not done,
For ye shall share my earldom with me, girl,
And we will live like two birds in one nest."

      ·   ·   ·   ·   ·   ·   ·

But like a mighty patron, satisfied
With what himself had done so graciously,
Assumed that she had thank'd him, adding, " Yea,
Eat and be glad, for I account you mine."

    She answer'd meekly, " How should I be glad
Henceforth in all the world at anything,
Until my lord arise and look upon me ? "

    Here the huge Earl cried out upon her talk,
As all but empty heart and weariness

And sickly nothing ; suddenly seized on her,
And bare her by main violence to the board,
And thrust the dish before her, crying, " Eat."

" No, no," said Enid, vext, " I will not eat
Till yonder man upon the bier arise,
And eat with me." " Drink, then," he answer'd.
   " Here ! "
(And fill'd a horn with wine and held it to her,)
" Lo ! I, myself, when flush'd with fight, or hot,
God's curse, with anger—often I myself,
Before I well have drunken, scarce can eat :
Drink therefore and the wine will change your will."

" Not so," she cried, " by Heaven, I will not drink
Till my dear lord arise and bid me do it,
And drink with me ; and if he rise no more,
I will not look at wine until I die."

   .   .   .   .

Then strode the brute Earl up and down his hall,
And took his russet beard between his teeth ;
Last, coming up quite close, and in his mood
Crying, " I count it of no more avail,
Dame, to be gentle than ungentle with you ;
Take my salute," unknightly with flat hand,
However lightly, smote her on the cheek.

Then Enid, in her utter helplessness,
And since she thought, " He had not dared to do it,
Except he surely knew my lord was dead,"
Sent forth a sudden sharp and bitter cry,

As of a wild thing taken in the trap,
Which sees the trapper coming thro' the wood.

This heard Geraint, and grasping at his sword
(It lay beside him in the hollow shield),
Made but a single bound, and with a sweep of it
Shore thro' the swarthy neck, and like a ball
The russet-bearded head roll'd on the floor.
So died Earl Doorm by him he counted dead.
And all the men and women in the hall
Rose when they saw the dead man rise, and fled
Yelling as from a spectre, and the two
Were left alone together.

The romance of *Geraint-ab-Erbin*, as we before
said, does not form part of the Anglo-Norman Epic.
It belongs to a grander cyclus than even that of
Walter Map. It belongs to the European cyclus of
which Map's romances form the heart, the core, the
soul. In the days when the second Henry sat on
the English throne; when Frederick Barbarossa was
in the maturity of his power as Emperor; when the
first two Crusades had aroused the slumbering minds
of men to the possibility of heroes, and had made a
camp romance of Religion itself, a new and soul-stir-
ring literature burst forth in every European country. While England and France were breaking away
from the strict scholasticism of the cloister, and pant-
ing for the rise of a wider range of literary thought,
Germany too was aroused, and as, in the one case, the

national mind poured itself out in heroic legends
of Arthur and other native heroes, so in Germany, old
floating traditions of Sigfried and Chriemhilde's revenge were knit together and worked into the *Niebe-
lungenlied*. We cannot stay to speak of the Spanish
Poem of the Cid or of the seed time of Italian literature.
The movement was general. The Dark Ages were
past and gone. The first half of the Middle Ages
had glided away with its wholesome monastic discipline and necessary priestly supervision. The second half of that period had begun, and Europe had
arrived at adolescence when this sudden blossoming
forth of true literature commenced.

So far as the Arthurian romances are concerned, it
was not in England alone that they seized upon the
imagination. The chord struck by Walter Map vibrated throughout France, Germany, and Flanders.
It penetrated even to Spain and Italy. It raised an
echo in its old Welsh home, and a faint response
came even from Constantinople. It was in France,
however, that we find these Arthurian legends taking
the firmest hold and receiving the fullest *foreign*
development. But this is only natural. That land
seems marked out by nature as the meeting point of
the various streams of tradition and song. In the
north, the Franks brought the old traditions of their
German fatherland ; the Northmen, the wild sagas

of Scandinavia; old Keltic stories of kings and enchanters flowed in from Brittany. In the south, the Troubadours met their brethren of Italy, who cultivated Provençal; Moorish and Arabic tales passed over the Pyrenees; there were Greek colonists at Marseilles, and Latin stories were diffused, partly through the learned clerks, partly through the traditions of the Province. The Crusaders, too, brought back from the East new store of wonders, and the whole of society was coloured and animated by a chivalrous spirit and a love of adventure. Songs of knightly prowess passed from hall to hall and from hamlet to hamlet; the demand stimulated the trouvères to ever fresh invention, and the minstrel, whose business was song, was found in every hall of the land. Pre-eminent among the French compeers of Walter Map stands Chréstien, the translator of *Geraint-ab-Erbin*. It was he who wrote *Percival le Gallois*, which reproduces the Graal story; *Le Roman de la Charette* an episode of Lancelot; *Le Chevalier au Lion*; the *Romance of Fregus*, which has a Scotchman for its hero; a *Romance of Tristan*, now lost; and other romances in which the creations of either the English or Welsh romancers were reproduced, reset, or remodelled, to suit his own fancy or that of his readers. In Germany, Hartmann von Aue, Wolfram von Eschenbach, and others, sang of Erec and Ywaine and

Percival. The Holy Graal romance became tinged with the gentle mysticism of the age, and the hero of the Kymry found a place even in the hearts of the race whose compatriots he had fought and conquered.

In Flanders, the Count Philip, in his enthusiasm for Arthurian Romance, kept in his pay, poets of Artois and others, to translate into Flemish the Anglo-Norman romances of chivalry. In this manner the fame of the Round Table, the loves of Lancelot and Guinevere, the prowess of Tristan, the achievements of Galahad, the magnificence of Arthur were recited or sung in every castle of Christendom, eclipsing more pretentious works and overshadowing even native productions. It is difficult at this day to form any adequate idea of the hold which these romances took upon the imagination of Europe. They formed the chief recreation of barons in their castles, yeomen in the cities, and peasants in their cottages. Even after the introduction of printing, the presses both of France and England teemed with these romances. Poets seized with avidity upon the chaste creations of the Anglo-Norman trouvère. Painters transferred chivalric legends to their canvas. Sculptors busied themselves with Arthurian heroes or heroines. It was an age of strong ideality when knight-errantry was a reality, when real kings could be captured and ransomed, when heroes lived and

dared, and when the rights of women consisted in
being protected, loved, and worshipped. Throughout the thirteenth, fourteenth, fifteenth, sixteenth,
and seventeenth centuries, these romances retained
their hold upon the affections of men. It was
not till 1634 that the last black-letter edition of
Malory was issued in England. But with the in-
coming of the eighteenth century they disappeared.
The fact is instructive. Sidney's *Arcadia* was full of
ideality. Bunyan's *Pilgrim's Progress* marked at
once its culmination and eclipse. It was the absence
of this ideality in the eighteenth century, which
sounded the death-knell of Arthurian Romance.
Men settled down to the everyday romance of real
life with its hard prosaic incidents. From 1688, the
year of the English revolution, to about 1789, the
year of the French revolution, both in Britain and
over the civilised world was a century bereft of those
high qualities of heroism, poetry, and faith which we
discern in the mind of previous periods. This century was distinguished by a critical and mocking
spirit in literature, a superficial and wide-ranging
levity in speculation, and an absence of ideality in
everything. Take Defoe as an instance. When the
ghost of Mrs. Veal appears to Mrs. Bargrave at
Canterbury, it is " in a scoured silk, newly made up,"
and the apparition is seen " in the street in the face of

the beast market on a Saturday, being market day at
Canterbury at three quarters after one in the afternoon." No wonder that Arthurian Romance was unread when such prosaic details could find favour not
only with threadbare apprentices, but even with my
lord Chatham! No wonder that Arthurian Romance
was unread when Richardson's sickly morality kept
noble ladies from church, and drew tears from their
eyes which even the sight of a starving Magdalene
could not excite! But the change came at last. A
hero arose, and the world vibrated at the touch of
Napoleon. Sleepy priests, dull-witted statesmen,
and the ignorant masses were frightened out of their
fictitious wits. Napoleon revived the truth that
life is a journey of forced marches, that men are
more than systems, a *beau sabreur* than an *idéalogue*.
Dukes once more became *leaders*, and again was
seen in the world a Round Table at which each guest
ranked by his achievements. The Iron Duke stood
forth. England rubbed her eyes, shook off her leth-
argy, and awoke to the fact that true chivalry was
not antiquated. Great deeds followed; and with
the national awakening returned the old ideality of
England. The first demand after the battle of
Waterloo was for the long-neglected *Mort Darthur*,
not for Swift, not for Defoe, not for Fielding, Richardson or Smollett, but for Malory. No longer

did the deeds related in these ancient legends seem
idle fables; no longer was heroism sneered at as impossible or chivalry as utopian.   Napoleon seemed
like a modern Arthur, Wellington like another Lancelot, Waterloo like a modern Camlan; and the legends
revived.   Another half century passed.   Colonel In-
glis at Lucknow, Mr. Strattford in the infected hos-
pitals of Scutari, Havelock fighting against Eastern
miscreants, showed that neither chivalry nor knight-
errantry nor knighthood was dead.   Was it chance
or was it the free action of the national mind which
gave birth at this time to Tennyson's poems of
chivalry ?   We prefer to think that they are popular
now as they were in the twelfth century, and sung
by poets now as by minstrels of the old time, because they teach us eternal lessons and imperishable
truths.   The ideal knight of the twelfth century was
the image of the Christian warrior, and the romance
but painted in living colours the soul's aspiration
after ideal perfection.   It taught the world's incapacity to fulfil its highest longings, its noblest
tendencies, unless they are hallowed by faith and
sanctified through the True Blood.   They show,
under knightly guise, the Christian paradox that
the noblest victory is gained by humility, the highest happiness by self-denial.   Now, as in the dawn
of the Plantagenet era, when the race of life seems

crowded with competitors, and the world stands ready to crown the victor of whatever rank, these grand old legends teach us that it is by obedience men are made more than kings, and that faith is the substance, the very present possession, of things hoped for.

No wonder then, that at times when Christian knights can be found ready to do and to die, who would liefer sacrifice life itself than be recreant to the vows of Christian chivalry, these noble legends of ideal bravery, ideal purity, and ideal love should have regained their hold upon the national heart and once again be read at the fireside of palace, hall, and cottage.

NOTES.

Francesca, daughter of Guido da Polenta, lord of Ravenna, was given by her father in marriage to Lanciotto, son of Malatesta, lord of Rimini, a man of extraordinary courage but deformed in his person. His brother Paolo, who unhappily possessed those graces which the husband of Francesca wanted, engaged her affections ; and being taken in adultery, they were both put to death by the enraged Lanciotto. Troya relates that they were buried together, and that three centuries after, the bodies were found at Rimini, whither they had been removed from Pesaro, with the silken garments yet fresh.

This incident was seized upon by the powerful imagination of Dante, and, being interwoven with the story of the fatal love between Guinevere and Lancelot, forms one of the most pathetic touches in the *Inferno*.

Vide Dante's *Inferno*, ll. 69–135, translated by the Rev. H. F. Cary, M. A.

This passage is alluded to by Petrarch in his *Triumph of Love*, c., iii.

> " Ecco quei che le carte empion di sogni
> Lancilotto Tristano e gli altri erranti :
> Onde convien che 'l vulgo errante agogni ;
> Vedi Ginevra, Isotta e l'altre amanti ;
> E la coppia d'Arimino che cusieme
> Vanno facendo dolorosi pianti."

Leigh Hunt, in his poem entitled the *Story of Rimini*, has expanded this episode with the force and charm of true poetic genius.

NOTE B.

From his Latin poem to Manso, written at Naples just before his return to England, and from his *Epitaphium Damonis*, written immediately after his return (1641), it is proved beyond dispute that while in Italy, Milton had conceived the notion of an English epic poem on the subject of the legendary history of Britain, including the romances relating to Arthur and his knights of the Round Table, and that for some time, at least, after his return, this idea still fascinated him.

In his *Mansus* he writes :

> " O mihi si mea sors talem concedat amicum,
> Phœbæos decorâsse viros qui tam bene nôrit,
> Siquando indigenas revocabo in carmina reges,
> Arturumque etiam sub terris bella moventem,
> Aut dicam invictæ sociali fœdere mensæ
> Magnanimos Heroas, et (O modò spiritus adsit)
> Frangam Saxonicas Britonum sub Marte phalanges ! "

Vide Milton's *Works*, Masson's edition, vol. iii., p. 86, ll. 78–84,
In the *Epitaphium Damonis* he writes :

> " Ipse etiam—nam nescio quid mihi grande sonabat
> Fistula—ab undecimâ jam lux est altera nocte—
> Et tum fortè novis admôram labra cicutis :
> Dissiluere tamen, ruptâ compage, nec ultra
> Ferre graves potuere sonos : dubito quoque ne sim
> Turgidulus ; tamen et referam ; vos cedite, sylvæ.

> " Ite domum impasti ; domino jam non vocat, agni.
> Ipse ego Dardanias Rutupina per æquora puppes
> Dicam, et Pandrasidos regnum vetus Inogeniæ,
> Brennumque Arviragumque duces, priscumque Belinum,
> Et tandem Armoricos Britonum sub lege colonos ;
> Tum gravidam Arturo fatali fraude Iögernen ;
> Mendaces vultus, assumptaque Gorlöis arma,
> Merlini dolus.   O, mihi tum si vita supersit,
> Tu procul annosâ pendebis, fistula, pinu
> Multùm oblita mihi, aut patriis mutata Camœnis

Brittonicum strides ! Quid enim ? omnia non licet uni,
Non sperâsse uni licet omnia ; mî satis ampla
Merces, et mihi grande decus (sim ignotus in ævum
Tum licet, externo penitùsque inglorius orbi),
Si me flava comas legat Usa, et potor Alauni,
Vorticibusque frequens Abra, et nemus omne Treantæ,
Et Thamesis meus ante omnes, et fusca metallis
Tamara, et extremis me discant Orcades undis."

Vide Milton's *Works*, Masson's edition, vol. iii., p. 92, ll. 155–178.

NOTE C.

"The eldest of the three is named *Mater Lachrymarum*, Our Lady of Tears. She it is that night and day raves and moans, calling for vanished faces. She stood in Rama, when a voice was heard of lamentation,—Rachel weeping for her children, and refusing to be comforted. She it was that stood in Bethlehem on the night when Herod's sword swept its nurseries of Innocents, and the little feet were stiffened forever. . . .

"Her eyes are sweet and subtle, wild and sleepy by turns ; oftentimes rising to the clouds ; oftentimes challenging the heavens. She wears a diadem round her head. And I knew by childish memories that she could go abroad upon the winds, when she heard the sobbing of litanies or the thundering of organs, and when she beheld the mustering of summer clouds. This sister, the elder, it is that carries keys more than Papal at her girdle, which open every cottage and every palace. . . . By the power of her keys it is that our Lady of Tears glides a ghostly intruder into the chambers of sleepless men, sleepless women, sleepless children, from Ganges to the Nile, from Nile to Mississipi. And her, because she is the first-born of her house, and has the widest empire, let us honour with the title of *Madonna*.

"The second sister is called *Mater Suspiriorum*—Our Lady of Sighs. She never scales the clouds, nor walks abroad upon the winds. She wears no diadem. And her eyes, if they were ever seen, would be neither sweet nor subtle ; no man could read their story ; they would be found filled with perishing dreams, and with wrecks of forgotten delirium. But she raises not her eyes ; her head . . . droops forever, forever fastens on the dust. She weeps not. She groans not. But she sighs inaudibly at intervals. Her sister, Madonna, is oftentimes stormy and frantic, raging in the highest against heaven, and demanding back her darlings. But Our Lady of Sighs never clamours, never defies, dreams not of rebellious aspirations. . . . Murmur she may, but it is in her sleep. Whisper she may, but it is to herself in the twilight. Mutter she does at times, but it is in solitary places that are desolate as she is desolate, in ruined cities, and when the sun has gone down to his rest. . . . She also carries a key ; but she needs it little. For her kingdom is chiefly amongst the tents of Shem, and the houseless vagrant of every clime. Yet in the very highest walks of man she finds chapels of her own ; and even in glorious England there are some that, to the world, carry their heads as proudly as the reindeer, who yet secretly have received her mark upon their foreheads.

" But the third sister, who is also the youngest——— ! Hush, whisper whilst we talk of *her !* Her kingdom is not large, or else no flesh should live ; but within that kingdom all power is hers. Her head, turreted like that of Cybele, rises almost beyond the reach of sight. She droops not ; and her eyes rising so high *might* be hidden by distance, but, being what they are, they cannot be hidden ; through the treble veil of crape which she wears, the fierce light of a blazing misery, that rests not for matins or for vespers, for noon of day or noon of night, for ebbing or for flowing tide, may be read from the very ground. She is the defier of God. She is also the mother of lunacies, and the suggestress of suicides. Deep lie the roots of her power ; but narrow is the nation that she rules. For she can approach only those in whom a profound nature has been upheaved by central convulsions ; in whom the heart trembles, and the brain rocks under conspiracies of tempest from without and tempest from within. Madonna moves with uncertain steps, fast or slow, but still with tragic grace. Our Lady of Sighs creeps timidly and stealthily. But this youngest sister moves with incalculable motions, bounding, and with tiger's leaps. She carries no key ; for, though coming rarely amongst men, she storms all doors at which she is permitted to enter at all. And *her* name is *Mater Tenebrarum*—Our Lady of Darkness."

NOTE D.

In Anglo-Saxon, *cedpian* signifies to barter, to cheapen, to buy ; and *cedp* means price or bargain. Hence our ancestors spoke of good *cheap*—a good bargain (*bon marché*), and bad *cheap*—a bad bargain. *Chapman* was the merchant, the man who bargained, etc. *Chap-side* or *Cheapside* was the merchants' quarter in London, and the modern slang English word " *Chap* " is an abbreviation of chapman and in olden times signified a peddler, or travelling merchant. To " *chap* and *change* " is simply to bargain and exchange. The *chap-book* was an inexpensive book of popular tales, sold by an itinerant dealer, hawker, or peddler

NOTE E.

Nearly every nation which has produced verse literature of the Imagination has applied to the writers of such literature a title signifying *maker*, *finder*, or *inventor*. The Greek ποιητής, the Latin *poeta*, the English *poet*, can all be traced back to a common origin in the Greek ποιέω, " I make." The Norman French *trouvère* is the finder, the inventor, French *trouver*, "to find." The Provençal *Troubadour* has the same signification, and comes from the Old French of the South of France *trouber* = *trouver* "to find."

In Anglo-Saxon, the poet or gleeman was called the *Scóp*, " the maker," from *scapan*, " to form," " to create."

Minstrel, is the modernised form of an Old French word, *menestrel*, a workman (*cf.* English *artist*, root AR, plough, toil). *Gestour* is the *narrator* of facts, Latin *gestum*, a thing done, a history, a merry history, and hence a jest in the modern sense of the word (*cf. Chansons de Geste, Gesta Romanorum*, etc.). *Jongleur*, is the *prattler*, Old French *jongler*, " to prattle," and was the news-gatherer and reporter before the newspaper had an existence.

NOTE F.

In the dedication of the first edition of the *Mabinogion* to her children Ivor and Merthyr, Lady Guest says : " I cannot dedicate more fitly than to you, these memorable relics of ancient lore, and I

26

do so in the hope of inciting you to cultivate the literature of ' Gwyllt Walia' in whose beautiful language you are being initiated, and amongst whose free mountains you were born.

" May you become early imbued with the chivalric and exalted sense of honour, and the fervent patriotism for which its sons have ever been celebrated."

NOTE G.

William of Newburgh's most complimentary epithets in speaking of Geoffrey are, " fabulator ille " or " homo ille." Geoffrey's work he compliments as follows : " Præterea, in libro suo, quem Britonum historiam vocat, quam petulanter et quam impudenter fere per omne mentiatur, nemo nisi veterum historiarum ignarus, cum in librum illum inciderit, ambigere sinitur."

And again : ". . . cuncta, quæ homo ille de Arturo et ejus successoribus scribere curavit, partim ab ipso, partim et ab aliis constat esse conficta ; sive effrœnata mentiendi libidine ; sive etiam gratia placendi Britonibus, quorum plurimi tam bruti esse feruntur, ut adhuc Arturum tanquam venturum expectare dicantur, eumque mortuum, nec audire patiantur. . . . De successoribus vero Arturi pari impudentia mentitur."

Vide Proœmium to William of Newburgh's *Historia Rerum Anglicarum.*

NOTE H.

The manuscript which contains the Norman-French *Roman du Saint Graal,* has attached to it the name of Robert de Borron ; but M. Paulin Paris, one of the most accomplished and learned critics of France, (where the oldest manuscript of this romance is preserved), believes, and doubtless correctly, that the original author was not de Borron but Map. In his opinion it was not a knight or a *jongleur* who was so well read in the apocryphal gospels, the legends of the first Christian centuries, rabbinical fancies and old Greek mythology ; and there is all this in the *Roman du Saint Graal.* They came from an ecclesiastic and a man of genius. But if so, why should we refuse credit to the assertion, repeated in every manuscript, that it was first written in Latin? and why refuse to accord the authorship to Map, the only *littérateur* of the age whom we know to have been equal to the task. The same argument, *cæteris paribus*, applies to the *Roman de Merlin*.

NOTE I.

The conclusions here stated are fully confirmed by scholars of the deepest research and erudition. Mr. Sharon Turner, in his *Vindication of the Genuineness of the Ancient British Poems*, contends that " the Welsh bards of the sixth century commemorate Arthur, though not with that excelling glory with which he has been surrounded by subsequent traditions." And he adds: "Llywarch the aged, who lived through the whole period of slaughter and had been one of the guests and counsellors of Arthur, yet displays him not in transcendent majesty."

The Abbé de la Rue in his *Recherches sur les Ouvrages des Bardes Armoricaines*, gives it as his opinion that " although Arthur was known in Wales as the valiant opponent of Cerdic, yet he was but one of the many kings and warriors who fought, though in vain, against the Saxons."

Mr. Thomas Stephens, whose essay on the *Literature of the Kymry* was crowned by the Prince of Wales, at the Abergavenny Eisteddvod, 1849, states, as the result of his researches, that " in the early poetry of Wales there is no trace of the *hero* " in the delineation of Arthur. He fully recognises, however, the historic reality of Arthur the warrior.

M. de la Villemarqué in his introduction to the poem *Maronad Gerent Mab Erbin*, in *Les Bardes Bretons*, says : " A la bataille de Longport s'il faut en croire Liwarc'h Henn, les chefs des petites souverainetés indépendantes du sud l'île de Bretagne auraient été confédérés sous les ordres du fameux Arthur, dont la renommée fabuleuse obscurcit plus tard la gloire historique ; mais l'une ne devait commencer qu'à la mort du prince breton, et l'autre, à ce qu'il semble, malgré sa longue et mémorable résistance à Kerdic, méritait moins à cette époque l'admiration que l'estime des ses contemporains, car Liwarc'h Henn donne plus d'éloges aux guerriers du général-en-chef, et particulièrement à Ghérent qu'au généralissime lui-même."

Lady Charlotte Guest, in a note to her translation of *Geraint-ab-Erbin*, expresses the opinion that "he [Geraint] was a Prince of Dyvnaint [Devon] and fell fighting valiantly against the Saxons *under Arthur's banner* in the battle of Llongborth."

NOTE J.

Alanus de Iusulis, writing in the twelfth century, informs us, that if any one was heard, in Bretagne, to deny the fact that Arthur lived, the people would have stoned him. His words are most significant, as he was neither a Cambrian nor a Breton ; and they show, in spite of the hyperbole of the passage, that early in the twelfth century a real, historic Arthur was generally believed to have existed. He writes :

" What place is there within the bounds of the empire of Christianity, to which has not extended the winged praise of the Arthur of the Britons? who is there, I ask, who does not speak of Brittanic Arthur, who is but little less known to the people of Asia than to the Britons, as we are informed by our pilgrims who return from the countries of the East? The Easterns speak of him, as also do the Westerns, though the breadth of the whole earth lies between them. . . . Rome the Queen of cities, sings his deeds, and his wars are not unknown in her former competitor, Carthage. His exploits are praised in Antioch, Armenia and Palestine. He will be celebrated in the mouths of the people, and his acts shall be food to those who relate them."

NOTE K.

Words, like the precious metals, become tarnished with use, lose their pristine brilliancy, and need to have the incrustations of modern thought scaled off, if we would see their true beauty and poetic force. An etymology, perhaps accidentally stumbled upon in some old author, will often cast a perfectly electric light upon many a passage in modern literature, causing the author's meaning to stand out in bold relief, whereas before, we failed to detect in it anything especially striking. The words " baffle " and " recreant " may be taken as good examples of our meaning.

In Shakespeare's *Richard II.*, Mowbray, Duke of Norfolk, accused of high treason, exclaims in the presence of the King:

> " I am disgraced, impeach'd and *baffled* here ;
> Pierced to the soul with slander's venom'd spear."

But few readers, perhaps, appreciate the full force of this passage. In the age of chivalry, however, the word *baffle* was suggestive of the deepest social infamy. In an old poem relating to the death of Turpin we read :

> "And after all for greater infamie,
> He by the heels him hung upon a tree,
> And *baffled* so that all which passèd by
> The picture of his infamie might see."

This passage gives a clue to the nature of the disgrace of baffling ; but if we turn to the customs of chivalry as described by Holingshed, we shall get a clearer insight yet. " Baffulling," says this writer, " is a great disgrace, the punishment of perjured knights ; and when a knight is openly purjured, they make of him an image painted, reversed, with his heels upwards, with his name, wondering, crying and blowing out of him with horns in the most despiteful manner they can, in token that he is to be exiled the company of all good creatures."

So, in the *Faerie Queene*, book v., canto 3, where the poet describes the punishment of Talus, we read :

> " First he his beard did shave and foully shent,
> Then from him reft his shield and it rénverst,
> And blotted out his arms with falsehood blent,
> And himself *baffuld* and his arms unherst,
> And broke his sword in twain and all his armour sperst."

We can now see the force of this word " baffle " which Shakespeare puts into the mouth of the Duke of Norfolk as he stood disgraced and dishonoured before his King.

The term *recreant* is another of the words which have, imbedded within them, a fossilised relic of chivalry. We call a coward a *craven ;* but how did these two words, originally and etymologically distinct, arrive at this oneness of meaning ?

In one of Ford's plays, the dramatist makes one of his characters say : " Come, Sir, stand to your tackling ; if you prove *craven* I 'll make you run quickly." So, in Shakespeare's *Cymbeline*, when Imogen hands her husband's servant the dagger with which to strike her dead, she says :

> " Against self slaughter
> There is a prohibition so divine
> That *cravens* my weak hand."

This word "craven" comes from an old French verb signifying "to be worsted" or "beaten," and is not a derivative of the Anglo-Saxen *crafian* (Eng. crave) which means simply "to ask."

In the romance of *Ywaine and Gawaine* (an English rendering of the *Chevalier au Lion*) the full meaning which attached to the word in the customs of chivalry is distinctly apparent.

> " Thai say, sir Knight, thou must nede
> Do the lioun out of this place
> Or yelde the to us als *cravant*."

This word was a cry which the cowardly knight, when overcome, was forced to utter unless he was willing to forfeit his life to his vanquisher ; the signal that he acknowledged his defeat and begged for his life—an act unworthy of one of gentle birth and noble blood.

The modern word *recreant* is but another form of this same cry. The ancient oath taken by the knight before single combat ran thus : " Je suis prest de le prouver de mon corps contre le sien, et le rendre mort ou *recreant* . . . et véez çy mon gage."

In a combat of this kind, when the vanquished knight begged for his life, Sir Gawaine says :

> " I graunt it the,
> If that thou wil thi selven say
> That thou art overcomen this day.—
> He said, I graunt withouten fail
> I am overcomen in batail
> For pur ataynt and *recreant*."

Thus the word became a term of the utmost disgrace and of far deeper significance than coward.

Another instance of the full force of this word will be found on page 336 of this work, when King Arthur was overcome in single combat by Sir Pellinore, and spurned the idea of saving his life at the expense of his knighthood.

NOTE L.

The Peace and the Truce of God (La paix et la trève de Dieu), which took its rise late in the tenth or early in the eleventh century, was an institution that had its origin in the Church. In those turbulent times, the licence of private baronial warfare and the absence of any sufficiently centralised, restraining power, exposed the persons and property even of non-combatants to injury and loss. Moreover, the Church herself, at times, was no inconsiderable sufferer from the lawlessness of the age, and partly to protect herself, though more especially as the guardian of justice and preserver of moral order, she established a system which for more than two centuries exercised a beneficent influence over the rude manners and customs of the age.

Technically speaking, the *Truce of God* was an agreement between the ecclesiastical authorities of a diocese on the one hand, and on the other, the barons, nobles, and warrior class generally, that the latter would bind themselves, under oath, to conform to the terms of the decrees on this subject which had been formulated and sanctioned by Holy Church.

According to this agreement, the barons and warrior class were required, in the event of private warfare, to suspend hostilities from the hour of noon on Saturday in each week until the hour of prime (daybreak) on the Monday following; also on certain Festivals and Saints' Days; and during the seasons of Advent and Lent.

They were furthermore pledged, during times of warfare, to extend full protection to women, priests, pilgrims, monks, travellers, merchants, and agriculturalists; to abstain from the destruction or injury of farm implements, the burning of crops, and the killing of the live stock of the peasants; in other words, they were pledged to respect permanently all the rights and liberties of those who followed purely peaceful pursuits.

In all cases where an appeal to arbitration between combatants, whether on questions of indemnity or other disputed points, might become necessary, it was agreed that such appeal should be to the ecclesiastical authorities of the diocese, and that their decision should be final.

The penalties for contumacy, or breach of the Truce, comprised money fines, bafflings, banishment, and excommunication.

This wise, far-seeing system took its rise in the South of France. At a Synod held at Tuluges in the Comté de Roussillon (1027) it was decreed :

" Personne n'attaquerait son ennemi, depuis l'heure de none du Samedi jusqu'au Lundi à l'heure de prime, pour rendre au Dimanche l'honneur convenable ; que personne n'attaquerait, en quelque manière que ce fut, un moine, un clerc marchant sans armes, ni un homme allant à l'église, ou qui en revenait, ou qui marchait avec des femmes ; que personne n'attaquerait une église, ni les maisons d'alentour à trente pas : les contrevenants étaient frappés d'excommunication."

This was probably the first formal recognition by the Church, in convention, of the *Truce of God* as already established and in force in various dioceses ; but from this time forward, the benefits of the system became so apparent that within fourteen years from the Synod of Tuluges, the institution of *la paix et la trève* had been adopted throughout the whole of France, and thence spread rapidly into Germany, Italy, Spain, and England. At length, and after the provisions of the *Truce of God*, in their fully developed form, had been confirmed by several local Councils, it received the solemn approval of the Council of Clermont (1095) when Pope Urban II. proclaimed its universal extension throughout Christendom.

With the gradual consolidation of the kingly or imperial power during the twelfth and thirteenth centuries, all over Europe, the Crown by degrees assumed many of the protective functions which the Church had hitherto performed. In this way *la paix et la trève de Dieu* was replaced by an institution analogous in its objects, in its name, and in its effects ; but which emanated from the King and not from the Church. This system, called *the Peace and Truce of the King (La paix et la trève du Roi)*, in the place of the old familiar name, was simply Royalty imitating the good works of the clergy and appropriating their ideas and method. But the system underwent certain changes in order to make it conform to the altered conditions of the times. Whenever one of the warrior class decided to have recourse to private warfare for the redress of his wrongs, real or supposed, he was required to declare his intention forty days before the beginning of hostilities, so as to allow time for arbitration and an amicable settlement of disputes. The protection of the persons and property of non-combatants was provided for as strictly as under the Church system, and the penalties for breach of the conditions of the Truce were equally stringent and severe.

The more strictly secular colouring of the *Peace of the King* appeared especially, in the provisions for the termination of hostilities between the parties to a private warfare. If at any time during hostilities, either of the combatants desired peace, he was required to make a formal request to the *haut-justicier* to secure such peace on his behalf ; and it was the duty of the latter to compel the other party to the war to desist from further hostilities, whether by accepting a stated settlement or indemnification, or by consenting to an *acte d'assurement, i. e.,* to an agreement that he would suspend hostilities pending the arrangement of a settlement. When hostilities were temporarily discontinued under an *assurement,* the petitioner begged for a judgment or sentence, and by so doing had the right to demand the protection of his feudal lord should his enemy break the *assurement* and recommence the war. By the mutual agreement to this *assurement* the parties to the warfare were said to enter into the *Peace of the King (la paix du Roi).* To be guilty of a breach of this solemn pledge was tantamount to making war on the King himself. The baron or feudal lord who failed to protect his feudatory who had placed himself under the *Peace of the King*, was liable to fine and other penalties of a more or less severe character.

Next to the crime of *lèse majesté* or high treason, the one most severely punished was the violation *des traités de paix* and *des assurements.* The party to either of these engagements, who was guilty of a violation of the Truce, rendered himself liable to degradation and the confiscation of his estates.

Vide, La Paix et la Trève de Dieu (Semichon, Paris, 1857) where the rise of the modern municipality or commune is traced to the associations or confréries of *la Paix.*

NOTE M.

The following is Malory's account of the death and burial of Gawaine in the *Mort Darthur :*

"And then sir Gawaine wept and also king Arthur ; and then they sowned both. And when they awaked both, the king made sir Gawaine to receive his Saviour. *And then sir Gawaine prayed the king to send for sir Launcelot and to cherish him above all other knights.* And so at the houre of noone sir Gawaine betooke his soule into the hands of our Lord God. And then the king let bury him in a chappell within the castle of Dover ; and there yet unto this day all men may see the skull of sir Gawaine and the same wound is seene that sir Launcelot gave him in battaile."

Leland (*Collectanea,* vol. iii., p. 56) tells us that the bones of Sir Gawaine were shown to him when he visited Dover ; but they have since disappeared. "The chapel alluded to was, no doubt," says Mr. Wright, "the very ancient building attached to the Roman *pharos* in Dover castle."

According to the narrative in Map's *Mort Artus,* Gawaine's body was taken to Camelot to be buried by the side of his brother Gaheret. Other versions of the romance give very different accounts both of the place of Gawaine's death and that of his burial.

NOTE N.

"In the year 1189, when romance had begun to magnify his [Arthur's] fame, his body was diligently sought for in the Abbey of Glastonbury. The circumstances attending this search, give us the first clear and historical certainty about this celebrated man, and are therefore worth detailing. They have been transmitted to us by Giraldus Cambrensis, who saw both the bones and the inscription, as well as by a monk of the abbey ; and the same facts are alluded to by William of Malmesbury, a contemporary, and by others.

"The substance of the account of Giraldus is this. Henry the Second, who twice visited Wales, had heard from a British bard that Arthur was interred at Glastonbury, and that some pyramids marked the place. The King communicated this to the Abbot and monks of the monastery, with the additional information, that the body had been buried very deep, to keep it from the Saxons ; and that it would be found not in a stone tomb but in a hollowed oak. There were two pyramids or pillars at that time standing in the cemetery of the abbey. They dug between these, till they came to a leaden cross lying under a stone, which had this inscription, and which Giraldus says he saw and handled :

> " ' Hic jacet sepultus inclytus Rex
> Arthurus in insula Avallonia. '

Below this, at the depth of sixteen feet from the surface, a coffin of hollowed oak was found, containing bones of an unusual size. The leg bone was three fingers longer than that of the tallest man then present. This man was pointed out to Giraldus. The skull was large, and showed the marks of ten wounds. Nine of these had concreted into the bony mass, but one had a cleft in it, and the opening still remained ; apparently the mortal blow.

" Giraldus says, in another place, that the bones of Arthur's wife were found there with his, but distinct, at the lower end. Her yellow hair lay apparently perfect in substance and colour, but on a monk's eagerly grasping and raising it up, it fell to dust.

" The bones were removed into the great church at Glastonbury, and deposited in a magnificent shrine, which was afterwards placed, in obedience to the order of Edward I., before the high altar. He visited Glastonbury with his Queen in 1276, and had the shrine of Arthur opened to contemplate his remains. They were both so interested by the sight that the King folded the bones of Arthur in a rich shroud, and the Queen those of his wife ; and replaced them reverentially in their tomb.

" The pyramids or obelisks that are stated to have marked the place of Arthur's interment, long remained at Glastonbury." [1]—SHARON TURNER, *History of the Anglo-Saxons*, vol. i., pp. 294-6. Fifth edition, London, 1828.

In the *Annales Marganenses* we find the following account of the discovery of Arthur's tomb :

" Inventa sunt ossa famosissimi Arthuri quondam regis majoris Brittaniæ, in quodam vetustissimo sarcophago recondita, circa quod

---

[1] On the cover of this volume, may be seen a fac-simile of the upper part of one of these pyramids or obelisks, taken from a drawing in Camden's *Britannia*, edited by Richard Gough, Vol. i., p. 93.

duæ pyramides stabant erectæ, in quibus literæ quædam exaratæ
sunt, sed ob nimiam barbariem et deformitatem legi non poterant:
inventa sunt antem hac occasione dum inter prædictas pyramides
terram quidam effoderant, ut quendam monachum sepelirent, qui ut
ibi sepeliretur à conventu pretio impetraverat ; reperierunt quoddam
sarcophagum in quo quasi ossa muliebria cum capillitio adhuc incorrupto
cernebantur ; quo amoto reperierunt et aliud priori substratum, in
quo ossa virilia continebantur, quod etiam amoventes invenerunt et
tertium duobus primis subterpositum ; cui crux plumbea superposita
erat, in qua exaratum fuerat.

    " ' Hic jacet inclytus Rex Arthurus sepultus in insula Avellana.'

    " Locus enim ille paludibus inclusus insula Avallonis vocatus est,
i. e., insula pomorum, nam, *aval*, Brittanice pomum dicitur. Deinde
idem sarcophagum aperientes invenerunt prædicti principis ossa
robusta nimis et longa, quod cum decente honore et magno apparatu
in marmoreo mausoleo intra ecclesiam suam [Glaston] monachi collo-
caverunt. Primum tumulum dicunt fuisse Gwenhaveræ Reginæ
uxoris ejusdem Arthuri ; secundum Modredi nepotis ejusdem ; tertium
prædicti principis."—Thomas Gale's *Historiæ Anglicanæ Scriptores*,
vol. ii., pp. 10 and 9.

Translation.

    The bones of the renowned Arthur, formerly King of Britain, were
discovered in a very ancient sarcophagus, near which stood two pyramids, on which were inscribed some letters ; but which, on account
of their barbarous and uncouth form, could not be read. The occasion of their being found was this. Whilst some persons were digging
the earth between the aforesaid pyramids, in order to bury a certain
monk, who had purchased permission to be buried there, they found
a sarcophagus, in which they observed what appeared to be the bones
of a woman, with the hair still undecayed ; which being removed,
they found another, laid beneath, in which were the bones of a man ;
and having removed that also, they found a third below the other two,
upon which was placed a leaden cross, on which was inscribed,

    " ' Here lies buried the renowned King Arthur in the Island of
Avallon.' "

    For that place, being surrounded by marshes, is called the Island
of Avallon, that is, the island of apples, because an apple is called in
British *aval*. Then opening this sarcophagus, they found the bones of

the aforesaid prince, very large and long, which the monks placed with due honours in a marble tomb within their church [of Glastonbury]. The first grave is said to have been that of Queen Guinevere, the wife of the said Arthur ; the second that of Modred his nephew ; and the third that of Arthur himself.

Matthew of Paris, under date of 1191 and reign of Richard I., makes a similar statement :

"Eodem anno, inventa sunt ossa famiosissimi Regis Britanniæ Arthuri in quodam vetustissimo recondita sarcophago, circa quod duæ antiquissimæ pyramides stabant erectæ in quibus literæ erant exaratæ; sed ob nimian barbariem et deformitatem, legi minimè potuerunt. Inventa sunt autem hâc occasione. Dum enim ibidem effoderent, ut monachum quemdam sepelirent, qui hunc locum sepulturæ, vehementi desiderio in vita sua præoptaverat ; quoddam reperiunt sarcophagum, cui crux plumbea superposita fuerat, in qua exaratum erat.

"'Hic jacet inclytus Britonum Rex Arthurus in insula à Avolonis sepultus.'"

Johannis Fordun has the following note to the same effect:

"Nota, quod anno Domini 542 Arthurus, in bello lethaliter vulneratus, abiit ad sananda vulnera in insulam Avallonis ; non legimus, quo fine pausavit, sed quia in ecclesia monasteriali de Glasmbery dicitur esse tumulatus, cum hujusmodi epitaphio, sic eum ad præsens ibidem credimus, unde versus.

"'Hic jacet Arthurus, Rex quondam, Rexque futurus.'

"Credunt enim quidam de genere Britonum, eum futurum vivere, et de servitute ad libertatem eosque reducere."—THOMAS GALE'S *Historiæ Anglicanæ Scriptores*, vol. iii., p. 637.

Translation.

Note, that in the year 542, Arthur being mortally wounded in battle, went to be healed of his wounds to the Island of Avallon. We do not know how he died ; but as he is said to have been buried in the Abbey church of Glastonbury with an epitaph in this manner, so we believe him to remain there still, whence the line :

"Here lies Arthur a King that was, and a King to be,"

for some of the race of the Britons believe that he will live again and restore them from a state of servitude to liberty.

NOTE O.

A careful examination of the names of the various persons and places introduced into the Arthurian Epic by Walter Map, will show, beyond reasonable doubt, that the clever Chaplain to Henry II. followed a few very simple rules in his French rendering of Keltic proper names, whether Cambrian or Breton. His invariable practice appears to have been either (1) to take the Keltic form of the word with scarcely any change whatever, provided it was sufficiently euphonious, and not likely to grate on French ears, as for example the name of the King, *Arthur ;* or (2) to make some slight change by the transliteration of Keltic letters or sounds into their equivalents in French, as Bedwyr into *Bedivere ;* or (3) not only to transliterate, but to clothe the name in French garb, so as to make it both appear and sound like a native French word, as Gwenhwyvar into *Guinevere*, and Vivlian into *Vivienne.* In no case that we can recall, does Map *translate* a Cambrian or Breton name into its French equivalent.

But, besides this *à priori* reason for rejecting the theory of M. de la Villemarqué, there seems to be an insuperable difficulty in deriving the name *Lancelot*, from the old French *ancelle* through the Latin *ancilla.*

The Latin *ancilla* is not only a feminine form, but is a natural feminine, like the Latin *regina*, queen, and has no corresponding masculine form. Nor can we recall a single instance in which *ancel*, the supposed masculine form of *ancelle*, is used by any of the old French writers.

In the English translation of the *Magnificat*, the sentence
   " For He hath regarded the lowliness of His *handmaiden*,"
is an admirable rendering of the Latin,
   " Quia respexit humilitatem ancillæ suæ."
The old French poets use the word *ancelle* just as the Latin writers do *ancilla*, to designate a female servant. " Nos anciens poètes semblent avoir pris plaisir à retracer par ce mot, l'idée pieuse de l'humble résignation avec laquelle la Sainte Vièrge consentit, à devinir mère :
   "' Fille, de Dieu mère et *ancelle*.' "

Many other derivations of Lancelot's name, like that of *Paladrddellt* (splintered spear), have been proposed, but we shall not stay to discuss them here.

In default of any proof to the contrary, we feel inclined to think that the surface etymology of the name of Map's famous knight is not only admissable, but extremely likely to be the true one, and that Map invented or coined the name of his "knight peerless" in tournament, from the *lance* or tournament spear (French, *lance*) which was the knight's distinguishing weapon in combat, and that he intended to express by the diminutive or endearing termination, "a darling lance" or "a favourite of the tournament."

There is, doubtless, a philological difficulty in this derivation of the name viz.: the introduction of the "1" in Lance(l)ot; but if Map did coin the name in the manner suggested, as is more than likely, philology would have had little, if anything, to do with the matter.

Note P.

It is not easy to see why Tennyson should have changed the imagery in the old romance, and have placed the letter in Elaine's *left* hand, reserving the right hand for his own conceit of the lily. Surely, when the poet himself makes Elaine say of the letter,

"But I myself must bear it"

the right hand would have been the more appropriate one.

So again, according to Tennyson,

Arthur spied the letter in her hand

whereas the old romancer tells us, "then the *queen* espied the letter in the right hand and told the king thereof"; a far more natural situation than that which the poet's imagination suggested. The King would naturally be too much occupied with the "faire corpse," to see so trifling a thing as a letter in the hand. It would take a woman's keen perception in such matters (as the old romancer well knew) to detect this.

These points, in themselves, are scarcely worth noticing, and yet they show how dangerous it is to alter even the most minute touches in Map's finished work.

Note Q.

This episode of Elaine, according to the chronology of the Epic, is supposed to have occurred some time *after the achievement* of the

Quest of the Saint Graal. This being the case, it is difficult to see
how either Percival or Galahad could have been present when the
corpse of the maid of Astolat reached the royal landing, as Percival
had already retired to a monastery and Galahad had been translated
to heaven.

NOTE R.

We have seen already, that Tennyson has widely departed from all
Anglo-Norman versions of the story (1) in making Queen Guinevere
retire to a convent *before the death of the King ;* and (2) in depicting
Arthur as visiting the convent and hurling a withering rebuke at his
fallen Queen. Far more touching and natural, is the romancer's
description of the flight of the Queen to the convent, *after hearing
of her husband's death,* and the portrayal of her repentant interview
with Lancelot. The scene in the Idyll of Guinevere presents the
King as anything but a " gentleman " while the corresponding scene
in the romance, shows Lancelot to be, every inch, a courtly and
gentle knight.

Mr. F. J. Furnivall, in the Preface to his *Queste del Saint Graal*
edited for the *Roxburghe Club,* expresses very frankly his literary
affection for the late Poet Laureate when he says : " Tennyson   .   .   .
is to me personally more than all the other English poets put together,
save alone Chaucer " ; and yet on this question of Tennyson's picture
of King Arthur as a " stainless gentleman," he is bound to acknowledge :

" To any one knowing his Maleore,—knowing that Arthur's own
sin was the cause of the breaking up of the Round Table, and Guinevere's, the means only through which that cause worked itself out,—
having felt Arthur's almost purposed refusal to see what was going
on under his own eyes between his queen and Lancelot, so as to save
a quarrel with his best knight, till it was forced on him ; having
watched with what a sense of relief, as it were, Arthur waited for his
wife to be burnt on her second accusal,—then for one so primed to
come on Mr. Tennyson's representation of the King, in perfect words,
with tenderest pathos, rehearsing to his prostrate queen his own noble-
ness and her disgrace ; the revulsion of feeling was too great ; one
was forced to say to the Flower of Kings, ' if you really did this, you
were the Pecksniff of the period.' "

NOTE S.

The similarity of sound between the words Sangraal and Sangréel has been the occasion of a great deal of confusion of thought among writers on this subject both of former and modern times. The Saint Graal or Sangraal was the sacred dish or cup which held a relic of Sangréel or True Blood, *i. e.*, the blood of our Saviour. It was the Sangraal or cup which was the object of the Quest and not the Sangréel which the Sangraal enshrined. All that the questing knights hoped to *see* was the Sangraal, the human or material part, and not the Sangréel or the divine and inner part. The Incarnation idea of the divine and human in one Person which underlies the whole of the dogmatic and sacramental teaching of the Catholic Church is here shadowed forth under the image of the Saint Graal.

NOTE T.

It seems probable that in later years even the poet himself entertained a suspicion that King Arthur, as he had depicted him in the Idylls, was not altogether the "selfless man," "stainless gentleman" and "ideal knight" that he would have his readers imagine him to have been. In the early editions of *Merlin and Vivien* Tennyson tell us

> For once, when Arthur, walking all alone,
> *Vext at a rumour rife about the Queen,*
> Had met her, Vivien, etc.

But in later editions these lines are altered and read :

> For once, when Arthur walking all alone,
> *Vext at a rumour issued from herself,*
> *Of some corruption crept among his knights,*
> Had met her, Vivien, etc.

This correction is significant. The passage was doubtless altered in order to shield the character of the King. It is evident that the alteration was not made for the purpose of darkening Vivienne's character, as Tennyson had not left her any character to darken. It could scarcely have been changed to shield the Queen, because at the time when the episode of Merlin's attachment to Vivienne is supposed to have occurred, *i. e.*, very early in the story, no "rumours" are related by the romancer as having been "rife about the Queen." The more

27

probable supposition is, that Tennyson expunged the original passage from the Idyll and substituted that which now takes its place, from a desire to efface the slightest shadow of a spot upon the character of the hero of his Idylls, so that he might appear to approach as nearly as possible the " blameless King " which he is said to have been.   It has always seemed rather incongruous that a " blameless King " and "stainless gentleman " should be represented as being " vext " at " rumours " rife about his wife.   The true " gentleman," though not " blameless " or " selfless," would scarcely allow himself to be vexed at mere rumours ; or even if he should so far allow himself to be an-noyed, would he vent his irritation on a coquette who made eyes at him, by gazing at her blankly and passing by.   In the dedication of these Idylls to the memory of a noble Prince, among his many vir-tues which the poet so justly celebrates, is one which above all others is the especial mark of those of gentle blood ; the Prince,

> Spake no slander, *no, nor listen'd to it.*

In the Idyll of Guinevere we meet with another instance of a change made in the later editions of the *Idylls of the King*, and curiously enough the verse or line here inserted also relates to Vivienne.   In the early editions of the Idyll we read that the Queen and Sir Lance-lot

> .   .   .   Were agreed upon a night
> (When the good King should not be there) to meet
> And part forever.   Passion-pale they met, etc.

In later editions this passage reads :

> And then they were agreed upon a night
> (When the good king should not be there) to meet
> And part for ever.   *Vivien, lurking, heard,*
> *She told Sir Modred.*   Passion-pale they met, etc.

It will be seen that not only do both of these alterations have refer-ence to Vivienne, but more than this, the extra line in each case pre-sents Vivienne in the despicable light of an eavesdropper and carrier of foul rumour.   It is difficult to see what the poets' object could have been in making this second alteration.   In the early editions of the *Idylls* he had already dealt a mortal blow at Vivienne's woman-hood, and surely any further stab could only be like an attempt at " slaughtering the slain."

Note U.

The Welsh original of this elegy, to which frequent reference has been made in this volume, may be seen in the *Myvyrian Archaiology of Wales*, vol. i., p. 101. As it may be matter of interest to some readers, we give below the translation of the last seventeen stanzas of this poem by the Vicomte Hersart de la Villemarqué, in his *Bardes Bretons*, Paris, 1860.

The first part of this elegy refers to the heroic deeds of the warriors, especially Geraint, at the famous battle of Longport; the second part (which we have not given), relates chiefly to the war horses and their bearing in the battle.

CHANT DE MORT DE GHÉRENT, FILS D'ERBIN.

Quand Ghérent naquit, les portes du ciel s'ouvrirent ; le Christ accorda ce qu'on lui demanda : temps heureux, gloire à la Bretagne.

Que chacun célèbre le rouge Ghérent, le chef d'armée ; je célèbre moi-même Ghérent, l'ennemi des Saxons, l'ami des Saints.

Devant Ghérent, impitoyable envers l'ennemi, j'ai vu les chevaux [menacés] d'un commun désastre par la battaille, et, après le cri de guerre, un rude effort.

Devant Ghérent, effroi de l'ennemi, j'ai vu les chevaux sous [le coup d'un] commun désastre, et, après le cri de guerre, une furieuse résistance.

Devant Ghérent, fléau de l'ennemi, j'ai vu les chevaux blancs d'écume, et, après le cri de guerre, un furieux torrent [de guerriers].

A Longport, j'ai vu du tumulte, et des cadavres, [nageant] dans le sang, et des hommes rouges [de sang] devant l'assaut ennemi.

A Longport, j'ai vu le carnage, et des cadavres en grand nombre, et des hommes rouges [de sang] devant l'assaut de Ghérent.

A Longport, j'ai vu le sang couler, et des cadavres devant les armes, et des hommes rouges [de sang] devant l'assaut de la Mort.

A Longport, j'ai vu les éperons d'hommes qui ne reculaient point devant la peur des lances, et qui avaient bu du vin dans des verres brillants.

A Longport, j'ai vu [s'élever] une épaisse vapeur, et des hommes endurant des privations et le manque après l'abondance.

A Longport, j'ai vu [briller] les armes des guerriers, et [couler] le sang dans les vallées, et, après le cri de guerre, une terrible conflagration.

A Longport, j'ai vu l'engagement, des hommes en émoi et du sang sur la joue, devant Ghérent, l'illustre fils de son père.

A Longport, j'ai vu du tumulte ; sur les rochers les corbeaux faisant festin ; et, sur le sourcil du général en chef, une tache rouge.

A Longport, j'ai vu une presse roulante d'hommes réunis, et du sang aux pieds : "Que ceux qui sont les guerriers de Ghérent se pressent."

A Longport, j'ai vu un conflit tumultueux d'hommes réunis, du sang jusqu' aux deux genoux, devant l'assaut du grand fils d'Erbin.

A Longport, a été tué Ghérent, le vaillant guerrier du pays boisé de la Domnonée, les tuant, ceux-là qui le tuèrent.

A Longport, furent tués à Arthur de vaillants soldats qui tranchaient avec l'acier ; [à Arthur] le généralissime, le conducteur des travaux [de la guerre].

INDEX.

Arthurian Epic—*Continued*

structure of, 15 ; an epic cyclus, 16, 80, 205 ; its point of unity, 75, 76 ; various elements, *viz.:* historical, 47, 48, mythological, 49–51, ecclesiastical, 51, biblical, 52, classical, 52, 53, Christianity, 54, tragic, 54, generalised ideas, 54, spiritualisation, 74, 75, 78, 79 ; knight-errantry and chivalry, 103

——, synopsis of (1) Bard's, 91–104 ; (2) Chroniclers, 105–111 ; (3) Romancers, 136–160

——, according to Romancers the Epic falls into five sections, *vide* Diagram, 149. 1st Section : Uther attacks Gorlois, 136 ; captures castle, 136 ; marries Igerna, 136 ; Arthur born, 136 ; given to Merlin, 136 ; Arthur baptised, 137 ; delivered to Hector's wife, 137 ; Uther's death, 137 ; leaves crown to Arthur, 137 ; Arthur draws sword out of anvil, 137 ; crowned King, 138 ; battles for sovereignty, 139 ; helped by kings Ban and Bors, 139 ; conquers eleven confederate kings, 139 ; arrival of Morgause, 142 ; Arthur's incest, 142 ; succours Leodegraunce, 139 ; sees Guinevere for first time, 139 ; obtains Excalibur, 139 ; marries Guinevere, 141 ; institutes Round Table, 141 ; imprisonment of

Merlin by Vivienne, 143. 2d Section : Arrival of Roman embassy, 143 ; Round Table council, 143 ; war determined upon, 143 ; battle between Arthur and Lucius, 143, 144 ; Lucius slain, 144 ; Arthur crosses Alps, 144 ; enters Rome, 144 ; crowned Emperor, 145 ; returns to Britain, 145. 3d Section : Lancelot visits king Pelles, 150 ; has vision of Holy Graal, 150 ; Galahad born, 150 ; famous knights admitted to Round Table, 150 ; Tristan, 151 ; Percival, 152 ; Galahad knighted, 153 ; goes to Court, 153 ; is seated in the " siege perillous," 153 ; appearance of Sangraal, 153 ; the Quest begun, 153 ; all but Lancelot, Bors, Percival, and Galahad abandon Quest, 154 ; Quest achieved, 154 ; episode of Elaine of Astolat, 155 ; the Queen sentenced to death, 155 ; carried off by Lancelot, 155 ; Joyous Gard besieged by Arthur, 156 ; leaves kingdom and wife in Modred's charge, 156. 4th Section : Revolt of Modred, 156 ; return of Arthur, 157 ; death of Gawaine, 157 ; battle of Camlan, 159 ; death of King, 159. 5th section : Finale of the Epic, 160

——, Map's object in writing it, 4, 244–246 ; received as authentic history, 132 ; spread

Furnivall, Frederick J., extract from Preface to *La Queste del Saint Graal*. Note R

G

Galahad, son of Lancelot by daughter of king Pelles, 216; educated by nuns, 246; knighted by Lancelot, 247; brought to Court, 248; adventure of the sword, 248, 249; his first tournament, 249; wins his spurs, 249; fulfils the "siege perillous," 248; takes the avow, 250; starts on the Quest, 251; presented with miraculous shield, 264; first adventure, 264, 265; recognised as *the* knight, 255; vanquishes Tristan and Lancelot in single combat, 266; the fight at the castle of Maidens, 265; meets Lancelot in the ship, 283; has vision of Sangraal at castle of Carboneck, 289; goes to Sarras, 290; Saint Graal fully revealed, 290; Quest accomplished, 291; translated to Heaven in sight of Bors and Percival, 290; image of purity, 241, 329

Galiot, king, makes war on Arthur, 213, 214

Gareth and Liones, romance of, 346

Gast, Luces de, not cleric, 14; his romances, 81

Gawaine, Sir, his avow, 250; at confession, 279; at Astolat,

222, 223; break with Lancelot, 235; wounded by Lancelot before Joyous Gard, 235; his letter to Lancelot, 157, 158; his death, 108, Note M

Geoffrey of Monmouth, cleric, 13, 69; receives Breton manuscript from Walter Calenius, 68; with request to translate it, 105; translates it into Latin under title of *Historia*, 69; sharply criticised, 70, Note G; nicknamed " Arturus," 13

——, *Historia*, synopsis of, 105–109; falls into three sections (1) from birth of Arthur to arrival of Roman embassy, 105–107; (2) from arrival of Roman embassy to revolt of Modred, 107, 108; and (3) from revolt of Modred to battle of Camlan and death of the King, 108, 109; Diagram of the tale according to Geoffrey's *Historia*, 134; criticism of Geoffrey's work, 112, 113; received as veritable history, 132; the fountain-head of English romantic fiction, 70; chivalry and knight-errantry introduced by Geoffrey, 110

Geraint, lived sixth century, 48; celebrated by Llywarch Hên, 48, 348, 349; in Welsh triads, 349; in life of St. Teiliaw, 349; church in Hereford dedicated to him, 350; commemorated by Cambrian bards of the Middle Ages, 350; called Ger-

Index

429

Graal, Saint, Romance of the Quest of, synopsis of, 246–291. (α) events immediately preceding the Quest, 246–253 ; comparative study, 253–261. (β) the Quest itself, by all of the Round Table knights, 262–272 ; comparative study, 272–279. (γ) the achievement of the Quest, 279–291 ; comparative study, 286–288

————, an allegory, the subject beset by difficulties, 242, 243 ; an Allegory of Justification, 259, 272, 273 ; Preventing Grace, 272 ; Free Will, 272 ; Penance, 272 ; Confession, 265, 277, 278, 279 ; Eternal Life, 259, 260, 263 ; ship of Faith, 285, 286 ; Martyrdom, 281 ; Harrowing of Hell, 266 ; phantom adventures, 267–271

Guest, Lady Charlotte, translator of the *Mabinogion*, 64 ; dedication of the volume, Note F

Guileville, Guillaume de, cleric, 25 ; synopsis of *Le Pèlerinage de l'homme*, 27, 28

Guinevere, Queen, mentioned by early bards as Gwenhwyvar, 206 ; her character in later bards, 207 ; mentioned by the chroniclers as Guanhumara of Roman descent, 207 ; by Romancers as Guenever, daughter of Leodegraunce, of Camelyard, 178 ; sees Arthur for first time, 139, 208, 305 ; marriage to Arthur, 178, 209 ; sees

Lancelot for first time, 212 ; gives him her love, 215 ; her jealousy, 216 ; meets King on his return from conquest of Italy, 145 ; entrapped by Modred, 233 ; sentenced to be burned, 234 ; rescued by Lancelot, 235 ; left in Modred's care by Arthur on breaking out of Roman War (Chroniclers), 107 ; on Arthur's siege of Lancelot's castle of Joyous Gard (Romancers), 156, 310 ; flees to Caerleon, 208 ; takes the veil at Almesbury, 236 ; last meeting with Lancelot, 237, 238 ; dies in convent, 238 ; buried at Glastonbury beside the King, 239

Gwenn, son of Llywarch Hên, death of, 93 ; mention of Arthur, 93

H

Havelok the Dane, romance of, 43

Hector Sir, Arthur's foster-father, 137 ; Sir Kay's foster-brother, 138 ; would do homage to Arthur as King, 138 ; acknowledges that he is not Arthur's own father, 138 ; tells Arthur of his lineage, 300

Helen, Lady, wife of king Ban, 212 ; mother of Lancelot, 209

Historic element in the Arthurian Epic, 48

Holy Graal, *vide* Graal

Horn, king, romance of, 43

www.ingramcontent.com/pod-product-compliance
Lightning Source LLC
Chambersburg PA
CBHW032257280326
41932CB00009B/598